Basic Child Psychiatry

Seventh Edition

Philip Barker

MB, BS, FRCP (Ed), FRCPsych, FRCP(C)
Professor Emeritus of Psychiatry
University of Calgary

Blackwell
Publishing

Editorial offices:
Blackwell Science Ltd, 9600 Garsington Road,
Oxford OX4 2DQ, UK
   Tel: +44 (0) 1865 776868
Blackwell Publishing Inc., 350 Main Street,
Malden, MA 02148-5020, USA
   Tel: +1 781 388 8250
Blackwell Science Asia Pty, 550 Swanston Street,
Carlton, Victoria 3053, Australia
   Tel: +61 (0)3 8359 1011

First edition published by Crosby Lockwood
   Staples 1971
Reprinted 1973
Second edition published by Granada
   Publishing Ltd in Crosby Lockwood Staples
   1976
Reprinted 1977
Third edition published 1979
Reprinted by Granada Publishing Ltd 1981
Fourth edition published by Granada
   Publishing Ltd 1983
Reprinted 1984
Reprinted by Collins Professional and Technical
   Books 1985
Fifth edition published by Blackwell Scientific
   Publications 1988
Reprinted 1990, 1992
Sixth edition published by Blackwell Science
   Ltd 1995
Reprinted 1996, 1997, 2000
Seventh edition published by Blackwell Science
   Ltd 2004

A catalogue record for this title is available from
the British Library

ISBN 0-632-05675-4

Library of Congress Cataloging-in-Publication
Data is available.

Set by Data Management, Inc.,
Cedar Rapids, Iowa USA
Printed and bound in the UK at
TJ International Ltd, Padstow

The publisher's policy is to use permanent
paper from mills that operate a sustainable
forestry policy, and which has been
manufactured from pulp processed using
acid-free and elementary chlorine-free
practices. Furthermore, the publisher ensures
that the text paper and cover board used have
met acceptable environmental accreditation
standards.

For further information on Blackwell
Publishing, visit our website:
www.blackwellpublishing.com

Contents

Introduction

There have been huge advances in the field of child and adolescent psychiatry since the sixth edition of this book was published in 1995. The advances in our understanding of the genetics of child psychiatric disorders, and in the field of child psychopharmacology, have been particularly striking, but all areas have been moving ahead at what seems like ever-increasing speed. Research in the field has increased in both quantity and, especially, quality. New journals have started publication, and academic institutions are paying more attention than ever before to the study of the psychiatric disorders of children and adolescents.

This edition of *Basic Child Psychiatry*—like those that have gone before it—aims to provide a concise, easily read, jargon-free summary of the basics of the subject. As more information has become available, it is tempting to allow the book to grow larger with each succeeding edition. This could mean that it would cease to serve its intended purpose. I have therefore been at pains not to allow a creeping expansion of what is intended as a concise introduction to its subject. This has meant summarizing some material more concisely than in earlier editions, resisting the ever-present temptation to go into subjects more deeply than is appropriate, and instead providing the necessary references to enable the reader who needs more detailed information to obtain it. Also, some sections have been shortened to make room for new material in other parts of the book.

It seems, from the continuing sales of this book, that it has been found useful by many seeking an introduction to this fascinating and important subject. I hope it continues to serve this purpose, and I plan to revise it more frequently in future.

Philip Barker
Calgary, 2004

Author's Notes

1. There are many references in this book to the two widely used systems of classifying psychiatric disorders—the World Health Organization's *ICD-10 Classification of Mental and Behavioural Disorders: Clinical Descriptions and Diagnostic Guidelines,* and the American Psychiatric Association's *Diagnostic and Statistical Manual of Mental Disorders, 4th Edition Text Revision.* Throughout this text the former is referred to as ICD-10, the latter as DSM-IV-TR. The classification system offered in DSM-IV-TR is exactly the same as in DSM-IV, but the text describing some of the conditions has been modified and in places expanded. This applies to several child psychiatric conditions. I have chosen to use the abbreviation DSM-IV-TR throughout the book, except when I want to refer specifically to the earlier version (DSM-IV). However, for most practical purposes, readers may read DSM-IV for DSM-IV-TR.

Because these diagnostic systems are referred to frequently, I have not added the citation (World Health Organization, 1992b) or (American Psychiatric Association, 2000) each time they appear in the text, as this would have needlessly lengthened the book. Details are however to be found in the list of references.

2. During the past few decades, many effective drugs have become available for the treatment of psychiatric disorders. More data are available concerning their safety and efficacy in adult patients than in child and adolescent patients. National regulatory bodies have not approved many of them for use in children, yet there is evidence, of varying quality, that they may be of value in treating child and adolescent patients. In discussing the use of these drugs, I have been cautious, mentioning only a few examples and adding the recommendation that newcomers to child psychiatry should prescribe these drugs only under the close supervision of specialists in the field.

Chapter 1

Developmental Considerations

Understanding children's psychiatric disorders requires a sound knowledge of normal child development. What is normal at one age may be abnormal, and may be a symptom of a psychiatric disorder, at another age. Many of the problems with which child psychiatrists deal are manifestations of disordered development, rather than clear-cut syndromes. Among the latter are autistic disorders, childhood schizophrenia, obsessive-compulsive disorders and Tourette's syndrome. But the largest group of child psychiatric disorders—*conduct* and *oppositional defiant* disorders—are essentially disorders of the development of appropriate social skills and behaviour. Mental retardation, developmental language disorders and functional encopresis are other examples of disorders that are developmentally defined. Encopresis—or fecal soiling—is normal in babies; it only becomes a disorder when a child fails to attain fecal continence at the appropriate age.

Learning about normal child development

The best way to learn about child development is by being with children as they grow up, preferably in a variety of settings. Those of us with children can learn much about child development within our own families. It is important to remember, however, that the lives of children in the relatively affluent, middle-class families of most health professionals may differ significantly from those in other sections of society—to say nothing of the many other cultures throughout the world. These differences have their implications for child development.

More formal situations in which children can be observed include day-care centres, nursery schools, schools for older children, or indeed anywhere where children of various ages may be found. Supervision of your learning by experienced child health professionals is helpful. Much can also be learned from reading about child development, though this is no substitute for the 'live' observation of children of different ages.

Among the authors whose work on child development you might consult are Erik Erikson (1965, 1968), Jean Piaget [whose theories were well summarized by John Flavell (1963)], Anna Freud (1966), and Melanie Klein (1948). Also relevant is the work of John Bowlby (1969, 1979), and of Mary Ainsworth and her colleagues (1978), on attachment and the process of *bonding* between children and those caring for them. A useful book in this area is *Encounters with Children* (Dixon & Stein, 1992).

Among the many published studies of child development, the New York Longitudinal Study (Thomas & Chess, 1977; Chess & Thomas, 1984) stands out. These authors followed a cohort of children from infancy to early adult life and the results, reported in a series of books and articles, contain much of importance to child psychiatry.

Development stages

It is only possible here to mention the main points of the complex process we call child development. It is well to remember that the division of the developmental process into different stages is artificial. In fact, the process is a continuous one, and the transition from one stage to the next is not usually abrupt but takes place over a period of time.

The first year of life

This is a period of rapid change. Its main features are:

—The development of *basic trust* (Erikson, 1965), the child coming to experience the world as a place that is nurturing, reliable and trustworthy. This is considered to be the basis for the development of the capacity for intimacy.

—Great advances in social behaviour and responsiveness. Smiling, at first a reflex act (the *endogenous smile*), becomes selective by two to three months of age (the *social smile*).

—Associated with the above, the ability to distinguish between familiar and unfamiliar people. This appears at six to eight months of age. With it, there are signs of anxiety in the presence of strangers, and *separation anxiety* when the child is parted from the mother or other significant caretaker, especially if in an unfamiliar place or with unfamiliar people.

—*Bonding* between the child and the familiar caretaking figures. Features of attachment behaviour normally evident in the first year include crying, calling and stranger anxiety and separation anxiety mentioned above.

—Rapid development of motor function. By about one year of age the child is walking.

—Rapid intellectual development. The first year is Piaget's *sensorimotor period*. Children learn that objects exist apart from themselves and continue to exist when they can no longer see them; they learn simple cause-and-effect relationships and start to understand spatial relationships; and they acquire an idea of how one thing may symbolise another.

The second year of life

This is characterised by:

—Development of a sense of *autonomy* (Erikson, 1965)—a sense of being in control of oneself, as opposed to entertaining feelings of shame and doubt.

—Further acquisition of social skills. As the ability to walk and explore is acquired, the child's behaviours begin to be restricted. This helps the child learn what is permissible and what is not. The child also learns to live as a member of the family group and may have experiences outside the family in day care, nursery school or play group. Toilet training may commence in the second year.

—Rapid further development of motor skills, including walking, climbing and manipulating objects.

—Acquisition of a limited verbal vocabulary.

—Resistance to caretakers' behavioural restrictions, expressed in temper tantrums and other resistive behaviours.

—Continuing evidence of attachment behaviour.

—Further rapid advances in cognitive functioning. The middle of the second year sees the start of Piaget's *'concrete operations of classes, relations and numbers'*. The first part is the *pre-conceptual stage* in which the child starts to become able to represent one thing by another by using language symbols and drawing. In their second year children still feel at the centre of the world and remain closely dependent on their parents.

The preschool period (roughly from two to five years)

This is a period of great change. Its main features are:

—The acquisition of Erikson's (1965) sense of *initiative*—the feeling of being able to do many exciting, even almost magical things, as opposed to feeling frightened or guilty about taking the initiative. Normally developing children emerge from this stage confident in their abilities but with their impulses under adequate control.

—The development of a rich fantasy life, perhaps with imaginary friends and, often, with the use of *transitional objects*. The latter may be almost any object—an old blanket, a teddy bear, a toy—to which the child develops a special attachment and may use as a source of security in stressful situations (Shafti, 1986).

—A further big advance in socialisation, the child acquiring many more of the skills required to live as a member of a family group.

—Identification with the parents and the resulting development of the motivation to do certain things and be a certain kind of person.

—The beginnings of conscience formation. This is closely related to the process of identification with the parents.

—Rapid progress in the development of the child's sense of his or her sexual identity, so that the child begins to have a sense of being a boy or a girl. Psychoanalysts call this the *genital stage* because of the importance that has been attributed to sexual development during this period.

—Further development of intellectual functioning and cognitive skills. This is a continuation of Piaget's *pre-conceptual stage* (see above), as the ability to represent one thing by another develops further. The child still feels at the centre of the world and considers inanimate objects to have feelings and opinions.

—A rapid increase in the complexity of language used and understood.

—The establishment of a pattern of *mental defence mechanisms.* These are discussed further in the next chapter.

—The development of patterns of behaviour towards the world outside the family.

Middle childhood

This is the period from the start of school at age 5 or 6 to about age 10. Its main features are:

—Learning what Erikson (1965) calls the *fundamentals of technology*. As this happens, children gain the satisfaction that comes from doing the things they learn—things that vary from culture to culture. This is the period during which formal schooling comes to occupy a large part of children's lives. A normally developing child comes to enjoy the resulting personal satisfaction, recognition and opportunities to relate to other people. In calling this the stage of *industry versus inferiority,* Erikson (1965) drew attention to the danger that children may fail to learn what they need to at this time of life, and thus develop feelings of inferiority and failure. The teaching of children is not confined to school but also occurs in the family and in many other situations, Boy and Girl Scouts, Sunday school, youth groups and clubs and other organised youth activities.

—Continued psychosexual development, though this may be less obvious (hence to use of the term *latency* to describe this period). While in Western society sexual interests may be concealed, sex play and masturbation (the latter more frequent in boys than in girls) are common during this period of life.

—Continued development of a pattern of *defence mechanisms*. These are discussed further in the next chapter. By this time the normally developing child has a well-developed conscience. Many of the personality attributes the child has acquired tend to persist into adult life.

—Further refinement of cognitive skills. In Piaget's *intuitive substage* children can give reasons for their actions and beliefs, though their thinking in still *pre-operational*—that is based on immediate perceptions rather than on mental representation of concepts. This gives way to the *sub-period of concrete operations*. Children become able to internalise the properties of objects, and their thinking becomes less egocentric. Objects can be put in order, or classified, by size, shape or colour, without being physically compared with each other. This period also sees a great advance in the capacity for cooperative play.

Adolescence

Adolescence begins with the onset of puberty. This is marked physically by the onset of menstruation in girls and of seminal emissions in boys. These changes usually occur between the ages of 11 and 13 in girls and between 13 and 17 in boys, though the range of normal is wider. The Group for the Advancement of Psychiatry (1968) suggested that the principal developmental tasks to be completed by the end of adolescence are:

— Changing from being nurtured and cared for to being able to nurture and care for others
— Learning to work and acquire the skills to become materially self-sufficient
— Accepting and becoming proficient in the adult sexual role, and coping with heterosexual relationships
— Moving out of the family of origin to form a new family of procreation

In other words, this is the period of moving from childhood to adulthood. Other features of normal adolescence are:

— The achievement of a firm sense of identity. Erikson (1965) contrasted this with *role confusion*. A healthy young adult knows who he or she is and is confident in making this identity known to the world. This personal identity becomes the basis of the individual's relationships. On the other hand, those who are in a state of role confusion have little sense of who they are or where they want to go in life. Identity formation starts long before adolescence, of course, but should be substantially complete by the end of the teen years.

— Acquiring a more flexible cognitive style. Piaget called adolescence the period of *formal operations*. Its main features are:

— The ability to accept assumptions for the sake of argument and to formulate hypotheses and set up propositions to test them
— The ability to look for general properties and laws in symbolic, especially verbal, material and so to invent imaginary systems and conceive things beyond what is tangible, finite and familiar
— Becoming aware of one's own thinking and using it to justify the judgements one makes
— Becoming able to deal with such complex ideas as proportionality and correlation

The above is but an outline of child and adolescent development. It does not take account of the many cultural differences that affect development. Also, the developmental pathways that lead to alternative lifestyles, for example homosexual ones, differ in certain respects from those I have briefly described.

The development of self-esteem

The acquisition of a sense of self-worth is a major developmental task of childhood. Problems in this area are common in children who are presented for psychiatric assessment and treatment.

The development of self-esteem is a continuing process that starts in infancy and continues throughout childhood and adolescence. It can also continue to develop during adult life. Since there is no absolute standard by which a person's self-worth can be judged, for practical purposes we are what we believe we are. This depends very much on our childhood experiences.

Self-esteem develops initially in the context of empathic relationships with parents (Erikson, 1965). Ideally the parents' and the child's temperaments should be well matched. Parental attitudes, opinions and behaviour, and the child's experience of mastery of the environment largely shape the child's view of his or her self-worth. Parents need to be affirming and supportive, even when they have to set limits to their child's behaviour. They should also set realistic expectations for their children. If their expectations are unrealistically high, their children are likely to experience feelings of failure and, perhaps, guilt.

As childhood proceeds, the attitudes and expressed opinions of people outside the family group—teachers, peers, extended family members—play their part in determining how children grow up feeling about themselves. Important, too, are children's successes and failures. Those with handicaps may compare themselves unfavourably with others. Thus it may be more difficult for them to achieve that sense of mastery over the environment that is a major ingredient of a sense of self-worth.

As the years pass, children's feelings about their worth and capabilities become increasingly internalised so that they are less dependent on the immediate response of their environment. By the time they reach adolescence, their self-images have become part of their personality structures, or what Erikson (1968) calls their *ego-identity*. This, however, is still subject to modification, though self-image change becomes harder as one proceeds through adult life.

The importance self-esteem is acknowledged to have is reflected in the large number of books on the subject. These include books for parents (e.g. Lindenfield, 2000), for teachers (e.g. Battle, 1994), and for children themselves (e.g. Kaufman *et al.*, 1999).

Development in adulthood

Erikson (1965) describes three more 'ages of man'. These are the stages through which children's parents and grandparents pass. The first is that of *intimacy versus isolation*. The young adult, having completed her or his search for identity, is now ready for intimacy with others. This involves close relationships including sexual union. Failure at this stage results in isolation. Instead of developing close relationships the person may become isolated from, or even attempt to destroy, forces and people that appear threatening in some way.

The next stage is that of *generativity versus stagnation*. The essence of generativity is the establishing and guiding of the next generation. This is achieved not only, nor even necessarily, by parenthood. For many, though, becoming parents is a central feature of this process. Failure to achieve generativity leads to a sense of stagnation and personal impoverishment.

The final stage is that of *ego integrity versus despair*. Ego integrity is the mature integration of one's life experiences, people and things taken care of, triumphs and disappointments accepted. It is the feeling of things accomplished and of a life well lived. If ego integrity is not achieved, the result is despair. A characteristic of despair is fear of death; the person now feels that time is too short to live another life.

It is well to bear in mind that how children develop varies. The variation is due not only to differences in how they are parented but also to inborn differences in temperament and personality. These are biologically determined and, as our knowledge of genetics advances, it is becoming clear that they have strong genetic determinants. These are referred to further in the following chapter.

Family development

Most children grow up within the family unit. In Western society this is usually quite a small unit, the *nuclear family*. Traditionally, this has consisted of the two parents and their offspring. Nowadays, however, such families are in a minority. One-parent families are common and so are *blended families*, in which there is a couple, one or both whom have been married or have had children previously—children they have brought into the family.

In many parts of the world the *extended family* plays a role as big as, or bigger than, the nuclear family. On the traditional African homestead, for example, a *collective* consisting of grandparents, aunts, uncles, older siblings and more distant relatives, or even unrelated adults, care for the children. This extended family is important in developing countries where governments usually do not have the resources to provide a child welfare service that can step in when parents are unable, for any reason, to care for their children.

Families develop while their children grow up and, in making a psychiatric assessment of a child, the developmental stage the family has reached should be considered also. Family development is discussed in *Basic Family Therapy* (Barker, 1998, Chapter 2). Fuller discussions are to be found in *Marriage and Family Development* (Duvall & Miller, 1985) and *The Changing Family Life Cycle* (Carter & McGoldrick, 1989). However families do not always develop in smooth and predictable ways, and the latter book discusses many of the circumstances that affect family development and how they may alter the course of a family's growth and functioning. The assessment of a child should take into account the state of the family, and how it is functioning.

Further reading

An excellent source of information on all aspects of children's development is *Child Development and Personality* (Mussen *et al.*, 1990). A brief summary, suitable for use by parents who want to know what to expect as their child grows up, is *Growth and Development* (Pearce, 1994).

Chapter 2

Causes of Child Psychiatric Disorders

We need to consider children's emotional and behavioural problems in their developmental context. Many of the physical and psychosocial factors that contribute to the development of psychiatric disorders operate by interfering in some way with the child's developmental course. Children and adolescents have not reached the relatively *steady state* of development of most adults.

The following factors may contribute to children's psychiatric problems:

— Genetic factors
— Physical disease or injury—which may occur before, during or after birth
— Temperamental factors
— Psychosocial, including family, factors

Genetic factors

Recent years have seen great advances in our understanding of the genetics of child psychiatric disorders. These have been due in large part to the results of the human genome project (HGP). The term *genome* is defined as 'the total ensemble of genetic material for a form of life, or as the minimal complete complement of DNA molecules and chromosomes' (Anthony, 2001).

Another new term is *envirome* (Anthony *et al.*, 1995). This refers to 'the totality of . . . environmental influences; it includes predisposing factors [such] as various types of neighbourhood, family income, intra-uterine exposure to teratogens such as maternal cocaine misuse, and exposure to radiation, and provoking environmental factors that can act as triggers of psychiatric disorders, such as crises in personal relationships and social stressors' (Anthony, 2001).

The study of genetics can be approached in several of the following ways:

Family studies

These identify individuals with a particular disorder and then assess how frequently family members show evidence of that or other psychiatric disorders. Such studies have limitations since first-degree family relatives usually share common environments. Information about more distant family members, who do not share a common environment with the identified individual, may be more significant.

Twin studies

These have provided much information of value to geneticists (Kendler, 1993). Identical and fraternal twins provide a ready-made experimental design. Identical— or *monozygotic*—twins result from the division of a fertilized ovum into two genetically identical individuals. On the other hand, fraternal—or *dizygotic*—twins are not genetically identical. Their genetic make-up is no more similar than that of siblings generally.

Adoption studies

These are concerned with the relative risk of a disorder occurring in adoptees, compared with the risk in the adoptive parents, on the one hand, and in the biological parents, on the other. If both adoptees and adoptive parents share a relatively high risk of developing a disorder, this is evidence favouring an environmental cause. If the adoptees share a relatively greater risk with the biological parents, this favours a genetic cause. If monozygotic twins are placed in different families, especially if early in life, this constitutes a potentially valuable natural experiment. This rarely happens, however. Useful information can also be obtained by studying differences between twins, especially monozygotic ones, and their siblings, though age differences are a complicating issue here.

Molecular genetic studies

With the completion of the human genome project, geneticists have become able to identify specific genes and their locations on particular chromosomes. The degree to which individuals who share a particular gene are similar in respect to their physical or psychological characteristics concerned is a measure of the relative importance of that gene, as opposed to environmental causes. In practice it is not usually as simple as that because multiple genes are involved in helping cause many psychiatric and other disorders. [See Anthony (2001) and Neiderhiser (2001) for more information on this emerging area of study.] Certain conditions however have been shown to be due to specific chromosome abnormalities, for example Down's syndrome (in which there is an extra chromosome number 21); the Prader-Willi syndrome (in which the short arm of chromosome 15 is missing); and various abnormalities of the sex chromosomes (for example Turner's syndrome, Klinefelter's syndrome and the 'fragile X' syndrome).

Intra-uterine disease and injury

Various factors may adversely affect a developing fetus:

— Infections such as rubella, toxoplasmosis, AIDS and syphilis may be transferred from the mother.

— Alcohol use by the mother may lead to the 'fetal alcohol syndrome'.
— Smoking and the use of other drugs by the mother.
— Premature birth and injury during delivery.

Brain disease and injury

Possible causes include:

— Infections
— Head injuries
— Brain tumours
— Metabolic disorders
— Degenerative disorders
— 'Non-accidental injuries'—that is the various forms of child abuse
— Severe malnutrition in early childhood
— Physical diseases not affecting the brain that may have psychological reper-
  cussions because of the physical handicap they impose or the anxiety or guilt
  they cause to child, parents or family

Temperamental factors

Children's temperaments vary, probably as much as their physical characteristics. This
variation is no doubt in part genetically determined, although the genetics of temperament are not fully understood. Chess and Thomas (1984), having studied a group
of children from infancy to early adulthood, identified nine categories of temperament:

(1) Activity level.
(2) Rhythmicity (or regularity): the predictability or unpredictability in time of bio-
    logical functions.
(3) Approach versus withdrawal: this is the nature of the initial response to new
    stimuli. These may be food, a toy, a person, a place or some other experience.
(4) Adaptability: this is how the child responds to new or altered situations. It con-
    cerns not the initial responses but the ease with which these are modified in
    desired directions.
(5) Threshold of responsiveness: the intensity of stimulation that is necessary to
    evoke a discernible response.
(6) Intensity of reaction: the energy level of response, irrespective of its quality or
    direction.
(7) Quality of mood: the amount of pleasant, joyful and friendly behaviour shown
    by the child, as opposed to unpleasant, crying and unfriendly behaviour.
(8) Distractibility: this is a matter of the effectiveness of extraneous stimuli in inter-
    fering with or changing the direction of ongoing behaviour.

(9) Attention span and distractibility: how long attention is sustained and activities are continued in the face of obstacles.

Analysis of the above data revealed certain 'temperamental constellations':

— 'Easy children': these made up about 40% of Chess and Thomas's cohort. They were characterized by:

   — Regularity of biological functions
   — Positive approach responses to new stimuli
   — High adaptability to change
   — Mild or moderate mood intensity that is predominately positive

Thus easy children fall quickly into regular sleep and feeding schedules. They take readily to new foods, strangers, new schools and the rules of new games, and accept frustration without becoming unduly upset.

— 'Difficult children'—about 10% of the group. They showed:

   — Irregularity of biological functions
   — Negative withdrawal responses to new stimuli
   — Non-adaptability or slow adaptability to change
   — Intense mood expressions that were often negative

These children sleep and demand food irregularly. They adjust with difficulty to new foods, routines, people and situations. They cry and laugh loudly, are easily frustrated and are prone to having tantrums.

— 'Slow-to-warm-up children'—about 15% of the group. These show:

   — Negative responses of mild intensity to new stimuli, with slow adaptability after repeated contact
   — Mild intensity of reactions generally
   — Less irregularity of biological functioning than the 'difficult' children

About 35% of the children in the aforementioned study did not fit into any of the three categories. They had various other combinations of temperamental traits.

The foregoing descriptions are simply of behavioural styles. They are the temperamental equivalents of the variations in body build, or eye or hair colour, seen in any population. How children with particular temperamental styles fare depends largely on environmental factors, especially on how appropriately the parents respond to each child's temperament. Thus some parents are strikingly more successful in rearing children with difficult temperaments than are others. Chess and Thomas (1984) consider that an important factor is the 'goodness of fit' between the temperaments of the child and the parents.

Environmental factors

A child's personality and adjustment in society result from the interplay of genetic inheritance and biological make-up, on the one hand, and the environment, on the other.

The principal environments we need to consider are:

— The family
— The school
— The wider social environment

The family

Families are miniature societies in which children make their first attempts at adapting to the presence of others. They learn patterns of social behaviour that tend to persist throughout life.

The family should facilitate development from totally dependent infant to independent, autonomously functioning adult. As children grow up they need progressively to assume more self-control and responsibility for their lives and actions. At each age neither too much nor too little should be done for them. If too much is done, the process of growing up and becoming independent may be impeded; if too little, the child's level may become unduly anxious and a psychiatric disorder may develop.

Poor early adjustment to family life is often followed by poor adjustment in society at large. Attitudes towards parents may become generalized and in due course be applied to a wider circle of people. A secure and stable family setting facilitates the transfer of responsibility from parents to child. 'Secure and stable' does not mean that there must never be disagreements or arguments, or that members of the family will not sometimes be angry at one another. On the contrary, children need to be exposed to a range of emotions and situations, as they will be throughout their lives. They also need to witness these emotions being expressed in appropriate ways and conflicts being resolved constructively.

Children deprived of a stable family group suffer a serious handicap. Changes of family or caretakers, as when children are moved in and out of the care of child welfare agencies, or are moved frequently from one home, or institution, to another, can be damaging and may impair healthy personality development. Marital strife, divorce and parental illness, mental or physical, may also militate against the provision of the stable, supportive environment children need. The effects vary depending on the severity of the disruption of the environment and on resilience of the child. Often, however, these children grow up feeling insecure and with low self-esteem, unresolved anger and difficulty in engaging in trusting, loving relationships with others.

Since the family environment is so important in determining how a child develops, we must examine it when we wish to understand how a child's problems have arisen and are being maintained. Information on the assessment of families is to be found in *Basic Family Therapy* (Barker, 1998).

The school

Next to the family, the school is the most important influence on a child's development, especially in the early school years. Just how important it is was shown by a
classic piece of research conducted in the 1970s (Rutter *et al.*, 1979; Rutter 1980). The
progress of a large group of children entering secondary schools was studied. The
children had been assessed before entering secondary school, and the extent to
which they were at risk of developing the problems with which the research was
concerned had been determined. Large differences in the children's academic
progress and behaviour were found in the different secondary schools. These could
not be explained by differences in the children admitted to the various schools.
Much proved to depend on the characteristics of the schools as social institutions.
Favourable factors were:

— A reasonable balance between intellectually able and less able children
— The ample use of rewards, praise and appreciation by teachers
— A pleasant, comfortable and attractive school environment
— Plenty of opportunity for children to be responsible for and participate in the
   running of the school
— An appropriate emphasis on academic matters
— Good models of behaviour provided by teachers
— The use of appropriate group-management skills in classrooms
— Firm leadership in the school, combined with a decision-making process
   involving all staff and leading to a cohesive approach in which staff members
   support each other.

Bullying probably occurs in all schools and can cause great distress to those
who are bullied. It may be that about one child in five is bullied and up to one in
ten bullies others (Whitney and Smith, 1993). Bullying can contribute to the development of psychiatric disorders, including suicidal ideation, depression and
diminished self-esteem (Salmon *et al.*, 1998; Kumpulainen *et al.*, 1999; Rigby and
Slee, 1999).

Bullying Online (www.bullying.co.uk) is a charity registered in the U.K. Its website
contains information about bullying, including advice for children, parents and
teachers about how they may tackle this problem.

The wider community

Rates of psychiatric disorder are higher in urban than in rural areas, and they also
vary between different urban areas. Living in an area in which there is a high incidence of crime and much drug abuse and violence increases the risk that a child will
get involved in such activities. Peer pressures can be strong and difficult for some
children to resist. Bullying, also, is not confined to schools.

Multifactorial causation

Few psychiatric disorders are due to a single, identifiable cause. More often factors in the child—genetic, biological and/or psychological—interacting with a variety of environmental influences, combine to produce the disorders we see in clinical practice. It is a mistake to be satisfied once one causal factor has been identified. Even when there is strong evidence of a genetic basis for a disorder we must look for contributing factors among those just discussed. Whatever an individual's genetic make-up, that person's environment will inevitably play a part in determining the outcome. We must consider all the possible aetiological factors referred to in this chapter whenever we are faced with a child with problems.

  Linear thinking—which understands one thing as leading to another—is generally to be avoided. *Circular* or *systems thinking*—which is based on the concept that many things are interacting in complex, dynamic ways—is more useful in clinical work with both children and families.

Chapter 3

Classification of Child Psychiatric Disorders

Classifying psychiatric disorders, especially those occurring in childhood, is a complex undertaking. This is partly because most psychiatric disorders have multiple causes. They are not like, for example, measles, which has characteristic symptoms and is due to a specific, identifiable virus. Laboratory tests can readily determine whether a person has measles. Most child psychiatric disorders do not have such characteristic symptoms, and there are no laboratory tests that identify them.

Since child psychiatric disorders usually result from the interaction of several factors, *multiaxial classifications* have been developed. Such classifications consider various aspects of a patient's disorder and classify the disorder according to the different parameters, or axes, that are chosen. In theory a disorder might be classified along any or all of the following axes:

- — Clinical psychiatric syndrome present
- — Intellectual level
- — Specific delay(s) in development
- — Associated medical conditions
- — Temperamental style
- — Personality characteristics
- — Abnormal psychosocial factors
- — The degree of psychosocial stress the patient faces
- — A global assessment of functioning

Most, though not all, of the above have been used in multiaxial classification schemes.

Two diagnostic schemes are currently in general use. These have been developed by, respectively, the World Health Organization (WHO) and the American Psychiatric Association (APA).

The WHO scheme is part of the larger *International Statistical Classification of Diseases and Related Health Problems*, 10th revision (World Health Organization, 1992a). *The ICD-10 Classification of Mental and Behavioural Disorders* (World Health Organization, 1992b) is Chapter V of that larger volume. Although not initially presented as a multiaxial scheme, a multiaxial version has been developed.

The American Psychiatric Association's scheme

The *Diagnostic and Statistical Manual of Mental Disorders*, 4th edition, published by the APA in 1994, is usually known as DSM-IV. Some changes to the text of DSM-IV were made in 2000, and the revised version is known as *Diagnostic and Statistical Manual of Mental Disorders, Text Revision* (DSM-IV-TR). The diagnostic categories have not been changed, but the sections of the text relating to some of them, including some disorders affecting children, have been. (The next edition of the manual, which will be known as DSM-V, is not due to be published before the year 2010.)

The Axes

DSM-IV-TR is designed as a multiaxial scheme. Its axes are as follows:

  I: Clinical disorders and other conditions that may be a focus of clinical attention
 II: Personality disorders
       Mental retardation
III: General medical conditions
IV: Psychosocial and environmental problems
 V: Global assessment of functioning

Axis I: Clinical disorders
       Other conditions that may be a focus of clinical attention
This axis covers the great majority of psychiatric disorders. There are several 'disorders usually first diagnosed in infancy, childhood or adolescence'. The main ones are:

— Learning disorders
— Motor skills disorders
— Communication disorders
— Pervasive developmental disorders
— Attention-deficit and disruptive behaviour disorders
— Feeding and eating disorders of infancy and early childhood
— Tic disorders
— Elimination disorders
— Other disorders of infancy, childhood or adolescence

Axis I includes many other disorders that are considered primarily disorders of adults, but sometimes have their onset in childhood or adolescence:

— Substance-related disorders
— Schizophrenia and other psychotic disorders
— Mood disorders
— Anxiety disorders
— Somatoform disorders
— Dissociative disorders

— Sexual and gender identity disorders
— Eating disorders
— Sleep disorders
— Impulse-control disorders not elsewhere classified
— Adjustment disorders

There are also categories for delirium, dementia, other cognitive disorders, and mental disorders that are 'due to a general medical condition not elsewhere classified'.

Axis II: Personality disorders
    Mental retardation
Personality disorders are discussed in Chapter 16 and mental retardation in Chapter 20.

Axis III: General medical conditions
These are to be classified using a modification of the 9th edition of the *International Classification of Diseases* known as ICD-9-CM.

Axis IV: Psychosocial and environmental problems
This axis deals with 'psychosocial and environmental problems that may affect diagnosis, treatment and prognosis of mental disorders'. Such problems are grouped as follows:

— Problems with primary support group
— Problems related to the social environment
— Educational problems
— Occupational problems
— Housing problems
— Economic problems
— Problems with access to health care services
— Problems with relation to the legal system/crime
— Other psychosocial and environmental problems

This list can serve as a reminder of the variety of factors that may affect a child's (or an adult's) mental health or psychiatric condition.

Axis V: Global assessment of functioning
This is abbreviated as the 'GAF scale'. Functioning is rated on a scale from 1 to 100. Details of how to do this are to be found in the DSM-IV and DSM-IV-TR manuals. These also provide operational definitions for all the diagnostic categories listed.

The World Health Organization's diagnostic scheme

The 10th edition of the *International Classification of Diseases* (World Health Organization, 1992b) covers all diseases and medical conditions. Chapter V(F) is concerned with 'mental and behavioural disorders'. It is divided into 'blocks'. Blocks F70–F79 cover mental retardation. Blocks F80–F89 deal with 'disorders of psychological development'. Blocks F90–F98 cover 'behavioural and emotional disorders with onset usually occurring in childhood and adolescence'. These three blocks cover most child psychiatric disorders, but, as with DSM-IV-TR, categories that are primarily adult disorders may be used for children and adolescents.

Block F70–F79

This comprises four categories of mental retardation: mild, moderate, severe and profound. There are also 'other' and 'unspecified' categories.

Block F80–F89

Developmental disorders are classified as follows:

— Specific developmental disorders of speech and language
— Specific developmental disorders of scholastic skills
— Specific developmental disorders of motor function
— Mixed specific developmental disorders
— Pervasive developmental disorders
— Other disorders of psychological development
— Unspecified disorders of psychological development

Block F90–F98

The 'behavioural and emotional disorders' usually appearing in childhood and adolescence are classified thus:

— Hyperkinetic disorders
— Conduct disorders; mixed disorders of conduct and emotions
— Emotional disorders with onset specific to childhood
— Disorders of social functioning with onset specific to childhood and adolescence
— Tic disorders
— Other behavioural and emotional disorders with onset usually occurring in childhood and adolescence

The multiaxial version of ICD-10 is as follows:

Axis 1: Psychiatric disorders (block F90–F98)
Axis 2: Delays in psychological development (block F80–F89)
Axis 3: Intellectual level (block F70–F79)
Axis 4: Medical conditions—these are covered in the other chapters of ICD-10
Axis 5: Psychosocial adversity
Axis 6: Adaptive functioning

Summary

A single diagnostic label seldom captures all aspects of a psychiatric disorder. This is especially true of child psychiatric disorders for at least two reasons. The first is that one is dealing with a developing individual; in addition to any clinical syndrome that may be present, there may also be delays in general cognitive development (that is, mental retardation) or in specific areas of development (for example reading or motor development problems).

The second reason is that children are particularly susceptible to environmental influences. That is not to say that environmental factors do not affect adults, but children are almost totally dependent on their parents or other caregivers. The stability—or lack of stability—of their home, and also of the wider environment in which they are growing up, must be considered in the assessment of their psychiatric condition.

Because of the aforementioned considerations, and also the complexity of psychiatric diagnosis, multiaxial approaches are nowadays generally considered mandatory in child psychiatry.

Chapter 4

Epidemiology

Epidemiology is the study of the prevalence of disorders in populations. A well-designed and implemented study will tell us how many cases of a particular disorder or disorders there are in a defined population.

In child psychiatry the prevalence of specific disorders varies with the ages of the children being studied and with the characteristics of the society in which the children are living. Rural populations, for example, tend to have prevalences of some disorders that are lower than those in urban areas. The extent of drug abuse is also to some extent context dependent. Other factors that can affect the prevalence of disorders include the social cohesion of the population being studied and the quality of the schooling available. We must therefore be cautious in seeking to generalize the results of any one study to other populations.

A classic study

In the late 1960s Michael Rutter and his colleagues carried out a major study of children's disorders in the Isle of Wight—an island off the south coast of England (Rutter *et al.*, 1970). The study was a cross-sectional one, taking as its subjects all the 10- and 11-year-old children in the island. This was a pioneering study that set the standard for many studies that have since been carried out in various parts of the world.

Parents and teachers first completed screening questionnaires of known reliability and validity. These gave a preliminary indication of how many of the children had symptoms of the disorders that were being studied. These included psychiatric disorders. Randomly selected samples both of those tentatively identified as having disorders, and also of those who appeared, from the questionnaire results, to be free of disorders were then individually assessed by psychiatrists. These assessments involved both the children and their parents, and enabled corrected prevalence to be calculated. Psychiatric disorder was considered to be present if 'abnormalities of behaviour or relationships were sufficiently marked and sufficiently prolonged to be causing persistent suffering or handicap in the child . . . or distress or disturbance in the family or community'.

Rutter and his colleagues (1970) found a prevalence of psychiatric disorders, defined as above, of 6.8%. Boys outnumbered girls by about two to one. The Isle of Wight is mainly rural with a few small towns, and the prevalence of psychiatric disorders has generally been found to be higher in urban areas than in rural ones.

More than half the Isle of Wight children who were identified as having a psychiatric disorder—4% of the 6.8%—were diagnosed as having either conduct disorders or mixed conduct and emotional disorders, with the conduct problem predominating (see Chapter 6). The second commonest group consisted of children with 'emotional' disorders. They made up 2.5% of the psychiatric group, with all other conditions comprising only 0.3%. So behaviour problems might be said to be the 'bread and butter' of child psychiatric practice, with emotional problems next on the menu. However 'monosymptomatic' disorders were not included in the above totals.

Subsequent studies

Many other studies have followed that done in the Isle of Wight. A later study, using similar methods, in an inner London borough (Rutter *et al.*, 1975) found a rate of psychiatric disorder about double that found in the Isle of Wight, so prevalence rates vary from one area to another. They also vary in different age ranges. Other variables include the criteria used to determine whether a child has a psychiatric disorder.

The Ontario Child Health Study (Boyle *et al.*, 1987; Offord *et al.*, 1987) surveyed a large sample of children in the Canadian province of Ontario. A representative sample of households in various parts of the province was selected using census data; 91.1% of these agreed to participate. The households of native North Americans living on Indian Reserves were not included, nor were children living in institutions. All children aged 4 to 16 in the households selected were studied—a wider age range than in the Isle of Wight study. The percentage prevalence rates found are listed in Table 4.1.

Somatization refers to the presence of somatic symptoms without evident physical cause. The Ontario prevalence rates are higher than those found in the Isle of Wight. This may be due to the different ages of the children in the two studies, the study methods and/or the definitions of disorder used. Also the studies were conducted on two different continents some 20 years apart. Another point is that there are no

Table 4.1   Prevalence of disorders by age and sex (percentages): Ontario Child Health Study (Offord *et al.*, 1987)

Age	Sex	One or more disorders	Type of disorder			
			Conduct disorder	Hyperactivity	Emotional disorder	Somatization
4–1	Boys	19.5	6.5	10.1	10.2	—
4–11	Girls	13.5	1.8	3.3	10.7	—
12–16	Boys	18.8	10.4	7.3	4.9	4.5
16–16	Girls	21.8	4.1	3.4	13.6	10.7
4–16	Boys	19.2	8.1	8.9	7.9	—
4–16	Girls	16.9	2.7	3.3	11.9	—

large urban areas in the Isle of Wight, whereas the Ontario study covered the whole province, which contains several large urban areas.

The Ontario study also found that only a minority of the children with psychiatric disorders had received or were receiving treatment.

Differences in prevalence rates such as the above illustrate the point that there are no precise, universally applicable rates. Much depends on the context and the definitions and methods used.

Brandenburg and colleagues (1990) surveyed eight prevalence studies reported from five countries during the 1980s: Australia, the Netherlands, New Zealand, Canada and the United States. Some of these distinguished between *severe* cases and those considered to be of only *moderate* severity. Overall prevalence rates ranged from 5.0% to 26.0%. This article summarized a number of research findings. It also discussed issues that need to be considered in conducting epidemiological studies and in interpreting the results.

Cohen and colleagues (1993a, b) reported a study of subjects in the age range 10 to 20 living in two counties in New York State. They were assessed twice at intervals of $2^{1}/_{2}$ years. Full diagnostic information for 734 children/adolescents was available for both of the assessments. This study bridged the period between childhood, in which behaviour problems in boys tend to make the greatest demands on mental services, and adulthood, when depression and anxiety in women predominate. It provides valuable information about the changing patterns of disorders over the age range studied. For most disorders, one-third or more of those diagnosed at ages 9 to 18 received the same diagnosis $2^{1}/_{2}$ years later. The main exception was depressive disorders, which tend to follow an episodic course. It appears that many of the psychiatric disorders encountered in this age range are not just transient disruptions of development but have more serious implications.

Summary

The prevalence of child psychiatric disorders varies widely, depending on the nature of the communities studied, the ages of the children studied, the ascertainment criteria used. It is clear, however, that child and adolescent psychiatric disorders present a major public health challenge. In many, perhaps most, communities however only a minority of children with psychiatric disorders receive treatment.

Chapter 5

Assessing Children and Their Families

A proper psychiatric assessment of a child involves more than interviewing the child. The parents or guardians must be part of the process. It can also be helpful to meet the whole family group. Depending on the nature of the problem it may be desirable to meet with, or obtain information from, the child's teachers. What is the best approach will depend on the age of the child, the nature of the reported problems, the context in which the assessment is being done and whether the assessment is being carried out by an individual or a team.

A flexible approach is necessary in interviewing and assessing children. Some psychiatrists like to meet with the child and the parents separately. Others like to start by seeing the whole family. If the parents are seen first the child may feel, perhaps with some justification, that the parents have been reporting unfavourably on him or her. This may make it more difficult than it otherwise would have been to gain the child's confidence. If the child is seen first, the interviewer may lack important information about the presenting problems. With younger children the merits of the two approaches are generally evenly balanced; adolescents are usually best seen on their own first, unless they are seen in company with their parents.

The problem of deciding whom to interview first is avoided if all the family members are seen together. Each family member can hear what the others say and is free to disagree. It is common to hear differing views of the problem that has led to the referral or of other aspects of the family situation. A family interview also provides the interviewer with an opportunity to learn something of how the family functions and how members interact with each other. Although some needed information may not emerge during a family interview, this can be obtained later when members are seen individually or as a parental couple.

The option of interviewing the whole family is not always available, for example in hospital emergency departments and residential institutions. One must then work with whoever is available. It is usually wise, however, to obtain as much relevant collateral information as possible, in addition to speaking with the child being assessed.

Family interviews

There are many possible approaches to interviewing and assessing families. Several of these are discussed in *Basic Family Therapy* (Barker, 1998). I have found the following scheme useful. It has five phases, though they may overlap:

(1) The initial contact
(2) Joining the family and establishing rapport
(3) Defining the desired outcome
(4) Reviewing the family's history, determining its present developmental stage and constructing a genogram
(5) Assessing the current functioning of the family

The initial contact

When the first meeting is set up the family members should be told what will happen. The professional who will meet the family need not do this. A trained and informed receptionist or secretary may do it.

I like to see all family members who are living in the child's household. Some families question the necessity of having all members attend. They can be told that knowing the family in which the child is living often makes it easier to understand and help the child. Other points are that the behaviour of every family member affects that of every other; and that other family members can often be a part of the solution to the presenting problems. (It is not a good idea to suggest that they may be part of the problem.)

It is usually easy to persuade parents that they are important in their children's lives, but some are reluctant to bring siblings they consider to be well adjusted and free of problems. In that case the parents can often be helped to understand how their healthy children's strengths can be a valuable resource for the child about whom they are concerned.

Rapport

Establishing rapport is essential if an interview is to be productive. This applies both to interviews with individuals and to those with families. Establishing rapport is a requirement for the successful practice of other areas of medicine and also for people in other walks of life—salespersons, teachers, even 'con artists'—perhaps especially for them. Hypnotists and hypnotherapists have long known that rapport is an essential prerequisite for the induction of trance. Precipitate attempts to obtain information before adequate rapport is established are unwise and tend to have limited success.

But what is rapport? The *Merriam Webster's Deluxe Dictionary* (Reader's Digest Association, 1998) defines it as a 'relation marked by harmony, conformity, accord, or affinity'. That's not bad, but it doesn't capture the full meaning of the term as it used by therapists. Milton Erickson and his colleagues (1961, page 66) described it as:

'. . . that peculiar relationship, existing between subject and operator, wherein, since it [hypnosis] is a cooperative endeavour, the subject's attention is directed to the operator, and the operator's attention is directed to the subject. Hence, the subject tends to pay no attention to externals or the environmental situation.'

Once rapport is well established the therapist can say almost anything without the subject becoming upset. Remarks that could have a negative connotation will probably be taken as meant jokingly or at least not seriously.

Rapport may be fostered by both verbal and non-verbal means. The non-verbal ones are the more important, but both should be employed from the first contact with the subject or subjects even if this is a telephone conversation. Your tone of voice and manner of speaking, whether on the telephone or face to face, convey powerful messages. Your voice tone should be warm and friendly, and your approach respectful, interested and accepting.

I like to greet each family that comes to see me personally in the waiting room. I address each family member by name, if I know their names. I shake hands with all family members except for small children.

Comfortable surroundings help, but rapport can be established in prison cells, school classrooms, public parks or hospital emergency rooms. When you are seeing families with young children some toys appropriate to their ages should be available. Your dress should conform to cultural norms, but clothes that are too formal can lead some children to feel ill at ease; the same applies to the white 'lab coats' so beloved by doctors and other hospital staff.

Most important of all is the interviewer's behaviour. Rapport is promoted by matching or *pacing* the behaviour of those you are interviewing. You can do this by matching your patients' body postures and movements, respiratory rhythm, speed of talking, and voice tone and volume. You can also 'mirror' their movements, for example moving your arm or leg in response to similar movements of the person being interviewed. Movements that may be matched include crossing or uncrossing the legs, tilting the head to one side or the other, and leaning forward or settling back.

Pacing should be done sensitively and unobtrusively. It is not necessary to match all aspects of your client's behaviour. If you follow these guidelines, those you are interviewing will not become consciously aware of what you are doing. During family interviews it is best to match the behaviours of each family member in turn as you address them or they speak to you.

The developers of *neuro-linguistic programming* (NLP) paid much attention to rapport building. They describe it as leading to:

> 'a kind of synchrony [that] can serve to reduce greatly resistance between you and the people with whom you are communicating. The strongest form of synchrony is the continuous presentation of your communication in sequences which perfectly parallel the unconscious processes of the person you are communicating with—such communication approaches the . . . goal of irresistibility.' (Dilts *et al.*, 1980, pages 115–116)

Verbal communication is also important. Rapport is promoted when your *predicates*—words that say something descriptive about the subject of a sentence—match those of the person you are interviewing. These may be visual ('I see what you mean'); auditory ('That sounds terrible'), kinaesthetic ('That's a big weight off my mind'), olfactory ('This business smells fishy to me'), or gustatory ('It leaves a bad taste in my mouth'). Most people have a preference for using one sensory channel for processing information, though they may not be aware of this (Bandler and Grinder, 1979). Noting which sensory channel a person prefers to use, and matching that person's predicates, can greatly enhance rapport. It does not help, for instance, to respond to 'That sounds good', with 'I see what you mean'. A better response would be 'I hear what you're saying'.

You should also listen carefully to the vocabularies of those you are interviewing, noting the words and expressions they use. Few things impede the development of rapport as much as repeatedly using words with which those you are interviewing are unfamiliar. Some of those you interview will have less education than you, or your first language may be their second language. The words you use are especially important when you are speaking with children—since their vocabularies are inevitably limited.

Rapport may also be promoted by:

— Accepting the views of those you are interviewing without initially challenging them
— Adopting a 'one-down' position
— Talking of experiences and interests you have in common

Taking the one-down position might be something as simple as asking a girl how to spell her name or getting a boy to tell you about something of which he knows more than you do—perhaps skateboarding or videogames. With parents, it might involve acknowledging that they are the experts on their children since they know them far better than you do. You might also express interest in their understanding of the nature or causes of their child's problems. Posing as the great expert who knows all is seldom helpful, and anyway none of us knows everything.

Common experiences might be having lived in the same city, country, province or state as the family has in the past. Talking of hobbies, sports and pastimes you have in common with those you are interviewing can also be helpful. Self-disclosure should be used sparingly but can be valuable. I was once meeting with an adolescent girl who was not willing to talk freely to me and answered most questions with monosyllables, if she answered at all. She did however mention an interest in Egyptology, so I told her that I had been to Giza and had seen the pyramids. At this, her whole manner changed. For the first time she looked at me and her eyes lit up. 'Have you?' she said, 'What were they like?' Thereafter we got on much better.

Defining the desired outcome

Children are usually brought to see a psychiatrist or other professional because one or more people—be it parents, school staff, a court, a social worker or the child himself or herself—is seeking some sort of change. This may be in the child's behaviour, emotional state, school performance, relationships with others, or mental or psychological development. Defining, and if necessary clarifying, the changes sought is important for several reasons:

— It formally acknowledges the family's concerns.

— It defines your involvement as therapeutic and oriented towards promoting change.

— It helps avoid misunderstandings about the purpose of the child's or the family's attendance.

— It provides an opportunity for the family members to clarify their thoughts, and if necessary to consider the outcome they are seeking, rather than simply complaining about the current situation.

— It may inspire hope by having the family look forward to a better future, rather than dwelling on the past.

— If all, or even several, members of the family are present it offers an opportunity for them to discover whether they all have the same objectives.

— Only by starting with clear objectives is it possible to determine whether any help you provide has been successful.

The goals of a consultation should be defined in positive rather than negative terms. It is not enough for parents to say that they want their child's temper tantrums to cease. They should also be asked to explain the behaviour they wish the child to display in situations in which tantrums have been occurring. Other points that may be considered are:

— What consequences will follow when the goals have been achieved?

— Are there any drawbacks that may be associated with these consequences?

— Under what circumstances are the changes desired? Most behaviours have value in some situations.

— What has stood in the way of change in the past?

— How quickly should the desired changes come about?

Too rapid change can be stressful to those involved and adjusting to new situations can take time. (Embedded in this question is the assumption that change *will* occur. Attention is switched from whether change *will* happen to *when*.)

Reviewing the family's history, determining its developmental stage and constructing a genogram

These tasks can conveniently be tackled together with all the family members present. The parents can first be asked where they were born and raised, what kinds of families they had as children, how they progressed at school and what they have done since leaving school. As they answer these questions they will provide information about their parents and siblings. They can be asked how they met and courted, and invited to outline the course of their married life.

You may next ask about the births of the children and their development to date. It should by now be clear what stage in its development the family has reached. [Family development and its stages are discussed in Chapter 2 of *Basic Family Therapy* (Barker, 1998)]. There may emerge information about any difficulties the family has experienced in moving from one developmental stage to the next.

I like to construct a *genogram* (sometimes called a geneogram). In speaking with the family it is usually better to call it by the less technical and more familiar term *family tree*. It provides a concise, graphic summary of the family's composition and of how the family members are related. It should also show the extended family network, the ages of the family members, the dates of the parents' marriage, and of any previous marriages, divorces or separations. It can also indicate who is the 'identified patient', though I prefer to omit this while working with the family in the construction of the genogram. Brief summaries of the salient points concerning each family member—occupation, school grade, health, past illnesses, accidents, losses, incarcerations and so forth—may also be noted.

Some therapists prepare the genogram later, using the information obtained from the family members during the meetings they have had with them. I prefer, however, to do it with the active participation of the family. Thus family history is obtained and the genogram is constructed. Sometimes unexpected but significant information is revealed during this process. For example a late-adopted boy waited patiently while his adoptive family's genogram was assembled. Then, when it was all over, he said, 'And what about *my* family?'—referring, of course, to his natural family. On another occasion when her Uncle George was mentioned, a 10-year-old girl exclaimed, 'He's always drunk!' Until that moment the family history of alcoholism had not been revealed.

An example of a genogram is presented in Figure 5.1. The parents of the 'identified patient', Brad (distinguished by a double boundary), cohabited in a 'common law' relationship from 1965 to 1969, when they got married. They separated in 1973 and were legally divorced in 1980. Carmen, Brad's mother, lived with Eric from 1973 to 1976, and they had two daughters, Jane and Holly. In 1978 Carmen went to live with Ken; they were married in 1982. Carmen's two children by Eric, and one by Ken, make up the present family unit. Brad and his father, Dave, live with Katrina and her 10-year-old daughter by her former husband, Len. Katrina had a previous pregnancy that ended in a miscarriage in 1974. Carmen is an only child and both her parents have died. Dave is the fourth in a family of one girl and four boys.

Further information about genograms is to be found in Chapter 6 of *Basic Family Therapy* (Barker, 1998).

Assessing the current functioning of the family

This can be achieved in three ways:

— By the experience of interacting with the family
— By observing the interactions between family members
— By asking questions of the family
— By the use of standardized family-assessment measures

Asking the members how they believe the family functions has limitations. It usually provides more information about the family's instrumental functioning (whether family members are employed and in what fields, what the family's finan-

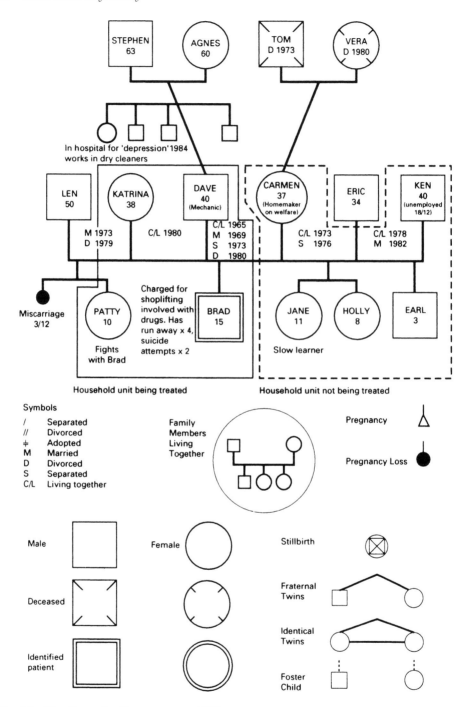

Fig. 5.1   The Green family genogram, 1985.

cial situation is, in what kind of housing they live and so forth), than about the emotional atmosphere and how the family members interact.

Interview techniques and procedures for assessing families are described and discussed in *Basic Family Therapy* (Barker, 1998) and in many other texts on family therapy.

Taking the history

At some point in the assessment a history of the child's problems and development should be obtained. If possible, both parents should be interviewed, even if they are separated. It is sometimes appropriate to interview step-parents, foster parents, grandparents (especially if they are actively involved in the child's life), other relatives, teachers, social workers and other professionals who have relevant knowledge.

I like to start by letting the parents talk freely about the child's problems, covering each problem area in turn and in their own words. Then, in follow-up questions, I rephrase their complaints in positive terms, changing the emphasis from the problem behaviours to the desired outcomes—as mentioned above.

The development of symptoms, their duration and frequency, whether they are getting better or worse or are static, and how the parents and others have attempted to deal with them—and with what success—all need to be explored.

The following is a list of areas that may need to be explored. Just how detailed the questioning needs to be will vary from case to case:

(1) *The digestive system:* eating habits, nausea, vomiting, abdominal pain, constipation, diarrhoea, faecal soiling, pica
(2) *The urinary system:* bedwetting, wetting by day, over-frequent or painful micturition
(3) *Sleep:* problems with going to bed, problems in sleeping, nightmares, sleepwalking, night terrors, excessive sleepiness
(4) *The circulatory and respiratory systems:* breathing difficulties, cough, palpitations
(5) *The motor system:* restlessness, overactivity, clumsiness, tics, abnormal gait, motor weakness, whether right-handed or left-handed
(6) *Habitual manipulations of the body:* nail biting, thumb sucking, head banging, rocking or other repetitive movement
(7) *Speech and language problems:* over-talkativeness, mutism, faulty speech of any type, late development of speech, stuttering, problems with reception and use of language
(8) *Thought processes:* disordered thinking, poor concentration, distractibility, daydreaming, delusional ideas
(9) *Vision and hearing:* problems in either area, evidence suggesting hallucinations
(10) *Temperamental traits:* see the section on *temperamental factors* in Chapter 2
(11) *Behaviour:* follower or leader, relationships with siblings, teachers and friends; fearfulness, sensitivity, tearfulness, sulking, irritability, temper tantrums;

obedience/disobedience, cooperativeness/negativism, constructiveness/ destructiveness, truthfulness/untruthfulness, stealing, wandering away from home, staying out late, group or gang membership, smoking, drinking or drug use; involvement with police, court appearances, probation, placement away from home; involvement of social agencies

(12) *Affective state (mood):* is the child's mood appropriate? Evidence of depression, elation, anxiety, fearfulness or other mood disturbance; variability of mood, relation of mood to environmental situation, evidence of suicidal ideation, past attempts at suicide

(13) *Fantasy life and play:* the types of games the child plays, whether age appropriate; content of play, whether much or little imagination; fantasy friends, transitional objects, fantasy life as expressed in drawing, painting, conversation or dreams

(14) *Sexual issues:* sex instruction given, child's reaction to it, sexual attitudes, masturbation, heterosexual or homosexual experiences, onset of menstruation, dysmenorrhoea, history of sexual abuse

(15) *Attack disorders:* epilepsy, fainting spells, other alterations of consciousness, breath-holding attacks

(16) *School:* attitudes to school, school class or grade, progress in school, social adjustment in school

(17) *Physical abuse or neglect:* evidence or history of past maltreatment

How detailed the questioning needs to be will depend on the circumstances of each case. Sometimes a general enquiry as to whether the child has had any physical health problems, rather than detailed questioning about each bodily system, is sufficient. In other cases more detail is desirable. You should enquire about the duration, frequency and degree of both problems and strengths.

It is important to ask about strengths and areas of healthy functioning. A child's good social skills, success at school, musical talent or easy temperament should be noted, as well as areas of difficulty.

The developmental history

The developmental history should start at conception and continue to the present. It should cover:

— The course of the pregnancy, any complications, and drug and alcohol use with details of how much and during which period of the pregnancy
— The child's birth and neonatal condition
— The subsequent progress of the child's development—motor, speech, feeding, toilet training, social behaviour and adjustment, including peer relationships and progress in school
— Any previous illnesses, injuries or emotional problems

I ask for a description of the child as a baby, as a toddler, in the preschool period, over the period of starting school, and so on up to the present time.

Examining the child

Flexibility, empathy and rapport are the key words here. The establishment of rapport is the first priority. Generally, the younger the child the greater is the role that non-verbal communication must play. Play is a natural activity for children, especially those in the preschool age period, so it plays a big part in the assessment process. What part verbal communication will play as you assess a child's psychiatric state emerges only as the interview proceeds. Sometimes very young children reveal a lot about themselves by what they say; with others it is through their play, their behaviour in general and their reactions to the person interviewing them that we learn most. Much depends on each child's language skills, willingness to talk and personality.

Children presenting for psychiatric assessment are seldom themselves complaining of symptoms. It is usually others—parents, teachers or both—who are concerned. To approach children with questions like 'What's troubling you?' or 'What have you come to see me about?' are therefore generally to be avoided. On the contrary, it is best to start the session by talking about subjects well removed from the reported problem area.

Rapport is basic to a successful interview. This applies at least as much to children as to adults. All the techniques for establishing rapport may be used with children. Like adults, children need to feel that their viewpoints and opinions are understood, respected and valued. There are also some special points you should bear in mind when working with children. The environment in which you see them should be child centred. Toys, play materials, and painting and drawing materials, appropriate to the child's age, should be available and in view. (This applies also to any waiting room or area the child spends time in before he or she comes in to see you. Your receptionist or secretary—indeed everyone the child comes in contact with before seeing you—plays a role in determining how successful your interview will be.)

Some children like to talk. Others are reluctant to do so, at least initially. Some will go promptly and enthusiastically to the toys or play materials. Others will approach them cautiously or not at all. I make it clear to the children I see that what they do, and whether they choose to talk with me, is their choice. I do not hurry to get a conversation going if a child seems not to be interested in talking. It often becomes possible to get a conversation going later, while the child plays.

Once I get round to talking with the child, I prefer to introduce initially topics well removed from the problem areas. I may discuss how they travelled to the clinic or office, their interests or hobbies, games and sports they like to play, toys they have at home—or wish they had—any recent birthday, their school (unless this is an area in which they are having problems), friends, siblings, and their ambitions for the future. If Christmas, Easter, Thanksgiving or some other celebration has occurred recently, I may ask what they did, what presents they received and so on.

The problems that have led to the child being brought to see me may come up as the interview proceeds. If they do not, I broach them cautiously once a good level of rapport has been achieved. It is vital to be non-judgemental. Do not put the child on the spot. Questions such as 'Did you steal such-and-such?' are not usually helpful. If the question is answered at all, the child may say yes or no. If yes, I am probably no wiser, since I probably would not have asked the question if I had not previously been made aware that the child has a problem with stealing. If no, I have placed the child in a position of withholding information from me. This may well affect adversely the relationship developing between us.

Even less helpful—indeed positively unhelpful in most cases—are 'why' questions. Here are the sorts of questions I believe are best avoided:

Why did you steal . . . ?
Why are you fighting with your little brother so much?
Why don't you want to go to school?
Why do you smoke pot?

It's not that we don't want to know the answers to such questions, but it is naïve to suppose that we can discover the true answers by enquiring in this way. If an answer other than 'I don't know' is given, the child's reply is likely to consist of a rationalisation or an excuse. And, anyway, how many of us know our true motivation in doing anything? On the whole, I think that *why* is one of the more unhelpful words in the English language. The use of 'why' questions also has the danger of placing the interviewer, in the child's mind, in the same category as other critical, punitive, lecturing authority figures.

If you want to discover why Billy is beating up on his little brother, there are many better ways of approaching the task. Invite Billy to tell you about his brother. What kind of a kid is he? What does Billy like about his brother? What doesn't he like about him? Do they sometimes play together? How do their fights start? And so on. You might like to invite Billy to draw a picture of his brother or of them doing something together.

Once rapport is well established, particular areas of the child's life may be explored. This is best done gently and sensitively. Remember that the child is under no obligation to tell you anything. Tailor your approach to suit the child's age and personality—about which you will have gained at least an initial impression.

Asking direct questions is not usually the best approach to obtaining information. It is more a matter of saying, for example, 'Lots of people have dreams when they are asleep at night . . . I wonder if you do?' If the child admits to dreaming, you may then ask for a description of a recent dream.

A time-honoured question is that of the 'three wishes': 'If you could have any three magic wishes, I wonder what they would be?' The wording, for example whether the word *magic* should be included, may be modified. With adolescents it is often not appropriate, but many teenagers are willing to state their wishes if the enquiry is made more along the lines of an adult-to-adult communication. I have found that many children take their wishes very seriously. It is important, though, to make it clear that they are only wishes and that you cannot guarantee that they will come true.

There are other ways of exploring a child's fantasy life. They can be invited to make up a story, perhaps in the context of their play. Here is another approach: 'Now I'd like you to pretend you are all alone on a desert island (or in a boat). If you could choose just one person—anyone in the whole world—I wonder who you would choose?' You may then invite the child to select a second and then a third person.

I like to enquire in similar ways for fears, worries and somatic and other symptoms. Conversation about family, friends—whom the child can be asked to name and describe—and about school should be encouraged.

Throughout the interview, you should respond appropriately and empathically to what the child says, sharing the child's sorrow over the loss of a pet, or pleasure at being a member of a winning sports team. Above all, you should convey interest in, and respect for, the child's opinions and viewpoint. This does not, of course, necessarily imply approval of, or agreement with, what you are being told.

I invite children who have not reached adolescence to draw or paint. I encourage them to draw a picture of their families. If they haven't done so spontaneously, I invite them to play with some of the toys that are available. These activities give you an opportunity to observe their powers of concentration, attention span, distractibility, and motor dexterity. The content of their play and their artistic productions may also provide useful information.

Much can be learned from children's drawings and paintings. Some pictures bristle with aggression. Guns are firing, people are being hurled over cliffs or otherwise killed, and other types of violence are depicted. Others portray sadness, with their subjects looking unhappy or crying; or subjects may be shown as being ill—even being about to die. Yet other pictures show happy scenes or illustrate fulfilment of the artist's ambitions or hopes ('This is me in a spaceship').

It is a good plan to keep children's artistic productions as part of their clinical record. Later productions can then be compared with earlier ones, providing one way of assessing progress—or the lack of it.

Helpful sources of information about children's drawings include *Interpreting Children's Drawings* (DiLeo, 1983) and *Understanding Children's Drawings* (Malchiodi, 1998).

In *Clinical Interviews with Children and Adolescents* (Barker, 1990) I offer further ideas, based partly on my own experience, on interviewing young people.

To obtain a comprehensive picture of the child, more than one meeting may be necessary. When I have finished this assessment I summarize the interview(s) under the following headings:

(1) *General appearance and behaviour:* Physical abnormalities? Bruises, cut or abrasions? Mode of dress and whether appropriate for the season and weather? Does the child look happy or unhappy, tearful or worried? Attitude to the examiner and the assessment procedure?

(2) *Motor function:* Overactive, normal or underactive? Dexterous or clumsy? Abnormal movement such as tics? Right-handed or left-handed? Able to dis-

tinguish left from right? Abnormalities of gait? Can the child write, draw and paint and, if so, how well?

(3) *Speech and language:* Articulation, vocabulary and use of language? Are non-verbal communications congruent with verbal ones? How much does the child talk? Ability to read and write?

(4) *Content of talk and thought:* What does the child talk about? How easy is it to steer the conversation towards another subject? Does the stream of thought flow logically from one topic to the next? Abnormal use of words or expressions? Evidence of hallucinations or delusions?

(5) *Intellectual functioning:* Make a rough estimate of the child's level of cognitive functioning, based on general knowledge, content of talk, level of play, and knowledge of time, date, year, place, and people's identity, taking into account the child's age.

(6) *Emotional state (additional to what has been recorded in item 1):* Happy, unhappy, frankly depressed, anxious, hostile, resentful, suspicious, or upset by separation from parents? Level of rapport established? Has the child ever wished to run away or hide from people? Suicidal ideation? Specific fears reported? Appropriateness of mood to subjects under discussion?

(7) *Attitudes towards family:* Indications during conversation or play?

(8) *Attitudes towards school:* Does the child like school? Attitudes towards school-work, teachers and other school staff, other pupils, play and games?

(9) *Fantasy life:* The 'three magic wishes'? Most desired companions on an uninhabited island? Dreams reported or made up? The worst thing—and the best thing—that could happen to the child? Ambitions in life? Fantasy material expressed in play, drawing, painting, modelling or conversation?

(10) *Sleep:* Any reported difficulty in sleeping? Fear of going to bed or to sleep? Fear of the dark, nightmares, night terrors (see Chapter 17) or pleasant dreams?

(11) *Behaviour problems:* Does the child reveal anything about behaviour problems, delinquent activities, illicit drug use, running away, deviant sexual activities, trouble with the police or school authorities, or appearance in court?

(12) *Placement away from home:* Has the child spoken of being placed or living away from home? If so, where, when, for how long and what is the child's understanding of the reason for this? Reaction to the experience?

(13) *Attitude towards the referral?* How does the child view the referral? Is the child aware of a problem and, if so, what does the child know?

(14) *Indications of social adjustment:* Number of reported friends, hobbies, interests, games played, youth organizations belonged to, leisure time activities? Does the child feel a follower or a leader, or bullied, teased or picked on? If so, by whom?

(15) *Other reported problems:* Worries, pains, headaches, other somatic symptoms, or relationship difficulties?

(16) *Play:* What is played with and how? Content of play? Are toys used for their symbolic purpose? Concentration, distractibility and constructiveness?

(17) *Self-image:* This usually has to be inferred from the sum total of what the child has said and done, the ambitions and fantasy ideas expressed, and the child's

estimate of what others think of him or her. However I always make a point of asking children what they are good at, and what they think are their good points and strengths.

In many instances it is not possible to obtain all the information one needs in a first interview. You should regard assessment as an ongoing process. It is unrealistic to expect to discover everything you need to know about a child at the first interview. Remember also that children's emotional states and behaviour are very much context dependent. They are also liable to change over short periods.

The psychiatric state of non-speaking children is assessed by making all the observations that do not require spoken replies from the child. In these situations the collateral information that must always be obtained from the adults in the lives of those being assessed is of particular importance. The fact that a child does not speak, whether because of inability or unwillingness to do so, is itself highly significant.

The physical examination

A physical examination should accompany the psychiatric assessment of the child. This may have been done by the referring family practitioner or paediatrician. If it has not been done, the psychiatrist may choose to carry out the examination, but many prefer to have a medical colleague do it, believing that if they carry out the procedure themselves it may impede the development of a sound psychotherapeutic relationship.

Other sources of information

It is good practice to obtain information about the child being assessed from as many sources as possible. Any, or even all, of the following may supply valuable information:

— The staff of the child's current school and any schools the child has attended previously
— Physicians and other health professionals who have assessed or treated the child in the past
— Other professionals who are currently involved with child or family
— Social agencies that have been or are involved with the child or the family; these may include child welfare or child protection services and probation services
— Hospitals and other institutions in which the child has been treated or has received care
— Foster parents and others who have cared for the child

Permission to contact any of the above must always be obtained from parents or guardians. It is best to have this in writing.

Psychological tests

The clinical psychiatric assessment may be supplemented by the use of psychological tests. These can be used at any stage in the assessment and treatment process, as well as in measuring outcome and in follow-up. They can be especially useful when clinical assessment has failed to produce an adequate understanding of a child's problems, in resolving conflicting and confusing data, and when decisions that may have especially serious consequences have to be made—such as whether criminal prosecution is appropriate. These tests are normally administered and the results interpreted by trained and certified psychologists.

The main groups of tests available for use with children are:

— Intelligence tests
— Tests of academic attainment
— Personality tests
— Behaviour checklists
— Tests designed to assess specific conditions, for example anxiety, depression, self-esteem and the ability to sustain attention

Detailed descriptions of these tests are beyond the scope of this book. Full descriptions are to be found in texts on clinical and educational psychology. The following is a brief outline only.

Intelligence tests

These are designed to assess children's abilities in performing various cognitive tasks, compared with those of other children of the same age. They usually consist of a number of subtests, each measuring a different skill. These can be combined to give an overall *intelligence quotient* (IQ).

Many intelligence tests exist, but the ones most used in child psychiatry are the Wechsler Preschool and Primary Scales of Intelligence—Revised (WPPSI-R)—for younger children; and the Wechsler Intelligence Scale for Children, 3rd edition revised (WISC-III-R).

These two scales provide both a global, or 'full scale' IQ and separate 'verbal' and 'performance' IQs. The former measures the subject's ability to understand and use language. The performance IQ is a measure of the child's abilities in subtests that require visual analysis and a motor response. The tests are standardized on large populations, and different norms exist for different populations. They are constructed so that each IQ scale has a mean of 100 and a standard deviation of 15. This means that 66% of all children of any specific age in a population will have IQ scores between 85 and 115. Two standard deviations (IQ 70–130) will cover about 95% of the population and three (IQ 55–145) will cover over 99%.

Tests are available for specific populations:

— The Bayley Infant Scales of Mental and Motor Development
— The Merrill-Palmer Scales

— The Gesell Developmental Schedule
— The Leiter Scales—for language and hearing impaired children, an entirely non-verbal test
— The Peabody Picture Vocabulary Test—an easily administered test of verbal skills

Intelligence tests have their limitations. Factors that may affect the result include the child's willingness to cooperate and ability to concentrate. Cultural factors may also affect the result. A statement of the psychologist's confidence in the result should be included in the report. Remember that these tests do not assess several important skills, for example creativity, musical talent, relationship skills and the special skills that are needed to excel in sports.

These tests were originally developed to be predictors of academic school performance and to identify those children who are underfunctioning and those requiring special educational services. They still perform these functions but are at times overvalued. They have sometimes been attached like labels to children. It's like saying 'James has red hair and his IQ is 90'. It's fair to say that James has red hair. That is unlikely to change unless he dyes it. But all one can say is that on a particular day, using a specified test, James obtained a score in a certain range. (Many psychologists prefer to quote a range of ability—average, low average, superior etc.—rather than quoting a figure. This is because saying, for example, that James's IQ is 90 suggests a precision which is unrealistic.)

In addition to more general tests such as those mentioned above, there are more specialized neuropsychological tests that can pinpoint particular difficulties children have and even uncover previously unrecognized neurological problems.

Tests of educational attainment

In addition to the assessment of children's cognitive skills by intelligence testing, it can be helpful to discover how they are performing academically. For this purpose, attainment tests of reading, mathematics and spelling have been developed. Like intelligence tests, these have been standardized on large populations so that the attainments of a child can be compared to the average for that child's age or school grade.

Attainment testing may be done on a one-on-one basis by a psychologist or teacher, but *group tests* are often used. Groups of children write answers to questions, or carry out instructions on forms that are often constructed using a multiple-choice format. These tests are less expensive to administer than individual tests. They can have practical value, especially in assessing group performance. Individual children's scores should be interpreted with caution, however, since it is harder to detect a child who is not cooperating, perhaps because of sickness, fatigue or hostility. These tests also have the limitation that they are predominantly verbal.

Children's educational attainments and problems are of interest to psychiatrists for several reasons. Difficulties in school can lead to both behavioural and emotional difficulties. Some children experience stress because they are struggling to perform in areas in which they have specific weaknesses. There is a strong association between behaviour problems and poor reading skills. Intellectually gifted children can run into difficulties because they are not being sufficiently challenged and stimulated in regular school programs.

Personality tests and checklists

These can assist in clinical assessment and diagnosis, but assessing personality is more difficult than measuring IQ. It is easier to define average intelligence or average reading level than to define average personality. Nevertheless personality tests can provide useful information about how people think and feel and about their attitudes towards a variety of things. They can add to information and impressions obtained during the less structured and more free-flowing interviews described earlier.

Projective tests are widely used to assess personality. They involve the presentation of ambiguous material to the subject being tested, with the aim of eliciting responses that may reflect the person's personality and mental state. The oldest and best known is the Rorschach test. The subject is presented with a series of printed shapes, originally derived from ink blots, and is asked to say what they resemble. The shapes themselves have no designed meaning, so any response must be a projection. Interpretation is difficult and requires special training.

The Children's Apperception Test (CAT) is designed specifically for children. The Roberts Test for Children is considered to have some advantages over the CAT. The Thematic Apperception Test (TAT) was designed for adults and has more realistic pictures than the CAT.

Other widely used tests are the Kinetic Family Drawing, the Draw-a-Person Test and the House-Tree-Person Test. In each of these the child is asked to draw the items mentioned. The results are examined and scored to give information about the child's personality and emotional state.

Many other personality tests and questionnaires are available that address various aspects of children's functioning, social adjustment and social maturity. Widely used is the Child Behaviour Checklist (Achenbach & Edelbrock, 1983), which consists of a list of questions to which the child's parents or other caregivers are asked to check off the appropriate answers. It has been extensively tested on clinical and non-clinical populations. It yields a variety of scores that provides information that can be helpful in assessing children's behavioural, emotional and mental states.

Symptom inventories can be helpful in diagnosis and especially in following the progress of treatment of, for example, depression.

Other tests and investigations

If there are no symptoms suggesting physical disease and physical examination reveals no relevant abnormality, further investigations of the child's physical state are not usually necessary. If there is evidence to suggest the possibility of a physical disorder it may be advisable to seek the opinion of a paediatrician or paediatric neurologist.

The electroencephalogram (EEG) is a useful aid in the diagnosis and management of epilepsy. It can also assist in the diagnosis of other brain disorders. Abnormalities in the EEG have been reported in various groups of disturbed children, including autistic children and some with severe behaviour disorders.

Various brain-imaging procedures have become available in recent years. These include computerized axial tomography (the CT scan procedure), magnetic resonance imaging (MRI) and positron-emission tomography (PET scan). In child psychiatry, these methods have so far been used mainly for research. They are not usually part of the routine psychiatric assessment of children.

Chromosome studies are playing an increasing role in child psychiatry. As we will see in Chapter 20, chromosome abnormalities are associated with various disorders, mainly forms of mental retardation.

Laboratory tests such as blood counts and biochemical tests have little role to play in the routine study of child psychiatric patients, unless there is reason to suspect an associated physical disorder. A study of laboratory tests carried out on a series of 100 adolescent inpatients by Gabel and Hsu (1986) showed that the results contributed little or nothing to the management of these patients.

The formulation

When the assessment of child and family is complete, a formulation of the case should be developed. The formulation is a concise summary of the case, setting out the main findings and the understanding of the child's problems that have emerged. Its importance can scarcely be overemphasized because it is the basis for the plan of management and treatment that is needed next. It is more important than assigning a diagnostic label to the child's disorder. It is best developed by considering the following factors:

(1) *Predisposing:* What pre-existing factors contributed to the development of the disorder? Constitutional, temperamental, physical and environmental factors should all be taken into account.
(2) *Precipitating:* What possible precipitating factors have come to light? Why did the problem(s) appear at the particular time reported? Here again it is helpful to consider constitutional, temperamental, physical and environmental factors.
(3) *Perpetuating:* What is maintaining the condition? The above four sets of factors should again be considered.
(4) *Protective:* What are the child's and the family's strengths? What factors are limiting the severity of the disorder and promoting healthy functioning?

I find the grid in Figure 5.2 to be a useful aid in the development of the formulation. It is important to remember, though, that a formulation is not just a list of factors that are thought to be relevant. It should also mention the relative importance

	Constitutional	Temperamental	Physical	Environmental
Predisposing				
Precipitating				
Perpetuating				
Protective				

Fig. 5.2   Formulation grid of contributing factors.

the different factors are thought to have, and how they may be interacting to produce the problems for which help is being sought. It should lead logically to a plan of management, treatment and, if necessary, further investigation. It should be committed to writing and, if it is followed by a period of treatment, it should be updated as new information comes to light—as it invariably does.

Chapter 6

Conduct and Oppositional Disorders

The behaviour problems of children and adolescents, with which this chapter deals, are among the most common child psychiatric disorders. Conduct disorders are also, as Costello and Angold (2001, page 1) point out,

'. . . by many centuries the oldest of the diagnostic categories used in contemporary child psychiatry. Long before psychiatry and psychology were born, people agonized over what to do about out-of-control children. We are still agonizing.'

Before child psychiatry arrived on the scene, other systems, including the educational system, the legal system and religious organizations, tried to deal with these children, mainly with a notable lack of success. These disorders now seem to have landed squarely in the lap of the psychiatry services—not that the legal and educational systems don't try and help also.

These disorders are best seen as disorders of development—that is of the development of behaviour that is deemed socially acceptable in the community. The factors that lead to this failure of development are many and complex.

Definition and classification

ICD-10 (World Health Organization, 1992b) offers us six subgroups of 'conduct disorders' (CD):

(1) Conduct disorder confined to the family
(2) Unsocialized conduct disorder
(3) Socialized conduct disorder
(4) Oppositional defiant disorder (ODD)
(5) Other conduct disorders
(6) Conduct disorders, unspecified

Dividing these disorders into groups is an arbitrary process. They are not distinct conditions as, for example, measles and whooping cough are. It is not surprising, therefore, that the American Psychiatric Association (2000), in its DSM-IV-TR, offers us a different classification. It places conduct disorders, oppositional defiant disorders and 'attention-deficit/hyperactivity' disorders in a section entitled 'Attention deficit and disruptive behaviour disorders'. In ICD-10, 'hyperkinetic disorders' are a separate category

To complicate matters further, DSM-IV-TR also divides conduct disorders into two groups, according to whether onset is during childhood or adolescence. It also requires 'severity specifiers', indicating whether the disorders are mild, moderate or severe.

Regardless of the details of how they are defined, these are children who, as they grow up, fail to adapt to certain behavioural norms—that is they do not accept, or they actively defy, some—often many—of the rules of the society in which they are living. However some defiance, and some breaking of the rules, is so common as to be within the range of normal children's behaviour. Deciding how severe and how prolonged such behaviour must be for it to be considered a 'disorder', and be given a psychiatric label, is arbitrary. What does seem clear is that 'attention-deficit' or 'hyperkinetic' disorders are a different group, though with substantial overlap with conduct and oppositional defiant disorders. They are discussed in the next chapter.

Prevalence

Angold and Costello (2001) have provided a detailed review of the epidemiology of these disorders. They point out (page 141) that, because of the many imponderables regarding definition and other factors, asking what is the 'true' prevalence of conduct disorder is a 'meaningless question'. They go on, however, to say that:

> '... across the industrialized Western world at any one time, probably between 5% and 10% of 8 to 16-year-olds have notable behavioural problems of the type commonly considered part of the spectrum of CD/ODD. In other words, CD/ODD presents a gigantic public health problem.'

Further information on both epidemiology and comorbidity in this area of child psychiatry is to be found in Angold and Costello (2001).

Causes

Like most child psychiatric conditions, conduct and oppositional defiant disorders are of biopsychosocial origin. It is seldom possible to pinpoint a specific cause for a child's antisocial behaviour. Causes in each of the following categories need to be considered.

Genetic factors and chromosome abnormalities

Antisocial behaviour tends to run in families, but this is not due entirely to genetic factors. Family and other environmental factors play a big part also. But how much is genetic and how do genetic factors operate when they do play a part? What is clear is that there is no simple genetic explanation, such as there is for physical disorders such as tuberous sclerosis, a neurological disorder characterized by seizures, mental retardation, and skin and eye lesions. It is unlikely that conduct disorders themselves are heritable; it is more probable that a subject's genetic make-up may result in certain personality and temperamental attributes that make the development of antisocial behaviour more likely.

Twin and adoption studies suggest various ways in which genetic factors may operate. For example, conduct disorders are frequently the precursors of adult antisocial personality disorder, a diagnosis that is often associated with criminality. Brennan and colleagues (1995), in an adoption study, found an increased risk of criminality in the adopted-out offspring of criminal fathers. But Simonoff's (2001) review of the literature on genetic influences in these disorders, and of how these may operate, illustrates how complex the study of these influences in antisocial behaviour is.

What are the implications of genetic studies for the day-to-day practice of child psychiatry? While we cannot at present alter the genetic make-up of our child patients, it is well consider to what extent genetic factors may be playing a part in the aetiology of the disorders with which we are faced. This may prevent us from putting too much emphasis on environmental factors and thus expecting too much from changes in the environment. It may also help adoptive parents to know that genetic factors may be playing a part in contributing to their adopted children's problems. Knowledge that particular children may be genetically predisposed to the development of antisocial behaviour may alert those caring for them to the need to take pre-emptive or preventive measures.

Chromosome abnormalities have been thought to play a role in the genesis of aggressive behaviour. Males as a group are more aggressive than females, and this has been attributed to their possession of the Y chromosome. Males with Klinefelter's syndrome, who have an XXY chromosome complement, have been reported to be more aggressive, but there may be other factors than their chromosome complement that explain this. There is evidence that, while they may have increased difficulties in behavioural adjustment, these are not necessarily aggressive in nature (Robinson and de la Chapelle, 1977).

Physical injury and disease

Children may suffer brain injury before birth, during labour and delivery, or at any time thereafter. All behaviour, including aggressive behaviour, emanates from the brain. The area of the brain believed to be specially associated with aggression is the limbic system. Situated deep inside the brain, this is one of its phylogenetically older parts. It is made up of structures known as the amygdala, hypothalamus, septum, ventral striatum, hippocampus, and the orbital frontal and cingulate cerebral cortex; also parts of the brain stem. Disease, damage or dysfunction of these structures may therefore be expected to affect a person's propensity for aggressive behaviour, for better or for worse. There is indeed evidence that problems with these structures can lead to aggressive behaviour. But the brain works as a whole. Its responses depend on incoming sensory stimuli as well as upon the integrity of the processes that deal with such stimuli and determine how the individual will react. The neurological causes are more than simple cause-and-effect processes.

It has long been known that psychiatric disorders generally are more common in children with neurological disorders (Rutter *et al.,* 1970). Indeed Lynam and Henry (2001) point out that, as long ago as 1812, Benjamin Rush considered that there was a link between the physical health of an individual's brain and antisocial behaviour. While we are still a long way from fully understanding this link, progress is being made. Herbert and Martinez (2001) have reviewed our current knowledge in this area.

It has long been known that there is a link between developmental language disorders (see Chapter 12) and antisocial behaviour. Strong support for this has come from a longitudinal study by Moffat and Silva (1988) in New Zealand. Over 1000 children were studied from birth to age 21. Lynam and Henry (2001) refer to the many publications that have reported on this project. This study showed that boys with severe conduct problems, and especially those with comorbid symptoms of hyperactivity, impulsivity and attentional problems, were the most neurologically impaired. Also, deficits in neuropsychological function at age 13 were reliable predictors of problems in later childhood.

Lynam and Henry (2001, page 256) suggest that neuropsychological deficits may exert their effects both directly and 'by disrupting socialization, impairing attachments, narrowing opportunities for change, and accruing to the individual harmful labels'. It is certain that acceptable social behaviour has to be taught and modelled by parents and others, and learned by the children. It is not difficult to see how this process may be impaired by neurological deficits.

Temperament

We have seen, in Chapter 1, that children's temperaments vary, and that about 10% of children have 'difficult' temperaments. One's temperamental style is no doubt initially determined by biological/genetic factors, though the environment can alter it. However, temperament merits mention as an aetiological factor. Parents who have more than one child often wonder why one of their children proves easy to rear whereas another presents a major challenge. 'What have I done wrong with . . . ?' they ask, referring to the difficult child. They believe, probably rightly, that they have used similar methods with each of their children but not always with the same results. Teachers and others dealing with children sometimes have similar experiences.

The answer to such questions often lies in the different temperaments of the children concerned. This knowledge can assist in management. Parents of 'difficult' children are often relieved to learn that the problems they face with their children are not of their making. Once they are apprised of the facts, they may rise to the challenge the child presents, with or without professional help.

Environmental factors

The family
The influence of the family environment on a developing child can hardly be over-stated. The family is a microcosm of the wider society in which the child learns to live as a member of a group and acquires knowledge of society's norms and standards of behaviour. In industrialized Western societies the nuclear family has the main responsibility for child rearing. In other societies, for example those in many parts of Africa and Asia, the extended family performs this function. Although single parents can certainly rear children successfully, their task is a more challenging one than that facing a stable parental couple.

Children who lack a permanent, stable family in which to grow up suffer a grave disadvantage. Fortunately the days of large impersonal orphanages are past, at least in most Western societies. But in many of the poorer parts of the world children are often abandoned to 'the streets' by parents who do not have the basic physical resources to care for them; some are even sold into prostitution or to what is virtually slavery, as they become child labourers in factories or the fields. Others have been recruited as child soldiers in the various wars that have marred the African continent. In parts of that continent 'AIDS orphans' are becoming common and, with the high rate of HIV infections in many countries, they are likely to become even more numerous. Of course the primary need of such children is not child psychiatry but fundamental social and economic change and basic public health services and education.

Even in the richer countries of the world, children do not all experience the stable, loving care they need. Some experience repeated moves from one home or parent to another. Some are abused, physically or emotionally. The emotional attachment to caregivers that is so important as a basis for learning the skills needed for successful adjustment in society is likely to be impaired when consistent parent figures are not available. The same problem can arise with institutional care, even when it is in a small group home.

Living in a permanent family group does not guarantee a childhood free of anti-social behaviour or other problems. Temperamental and biological factors may make a child more difficult to rear, but what actually happens in the family is crucial. Although probably no family is perfect, children develop best in a stable, consistent environment in which there is acceptance and affirmation of their worth as individuals, and proper social training. The latter is provided by parental precept and example, and through the consistent provision of rules and expectations, rewards and consequences being used as needed. In the setting of a happy home characterized by warm, loving relationships, the responses may need to be no more than a smile or a word of encouragement, or a frown or minor reproof. Such environments promote children's sense of emotional security and self-worth, and facilitate the process of socialization.

What should parents avoid in rearing their children? According to Patterson (1982) antisocial behaviour is associated with:

— Lack of 'house' rules—that is, no set routines for meals and other activities, and a lack of clarity about what the children may or may not do or how they are expected to behave
— Failure by the parents to monitor children's behaviour, and what they have been doing and how they feel
— Lack of effective contingencies—that is, inconsistent responses to undesired behaviour, with failure to follow through with threatened consequences or with rewards for desired behaviour
— Lack of techniques with which to deal with crises or problems in the family, so that tensions and disputes arise but are not necessarily satisfactorily resolved

Patterson has made a lifelong study of family factors that influence children's social development and, in particular, lead to antisocial behaviour (see Patterson, 1996; and Patterson & Yoerger, 1997).

Family therapists have sometimes commented on the 'idiosyncratic' roles children may play in families. One such observed role is that of *family scapegoat*. The family system may be such that a child has to be the 'bad' family member. Role problems in families are discussed further in *Basic Family Therapy* (Barker, 1998, pages 141–144).

Extrafamilial factors
These include the child's school setting, the wider social setting of the family and school, and the child's peer group. Both children's academic performance and, as we saw in Chapter 2, the characteristics of their schools as social institutions can be important factors in helping determine whether antisocial behaviour develops.

Adolescents tend to be much influenced by their peer groups. This applies to their mode of dress, their hairstyles, whether they have their body parts pierced, what music they listen to, which mobile phone model they own and many other things. Antisocial activities, including illicit drug use, also tend to be group activities. To what extent group pressures *cause* adolescents to engage in antisocial activities is not clear, however. It may be that young people with a propensity to antisocial activities prefer to associate with others with similar inclinations. What seems clear is that, once a young person is actively involved with a group of antisocial peers, the latter can act as a perpetuating factor promoting further antisocial acts.

The interaction of factors
The aforementioned causative factors do not operate independently. The greater the number of risk factors, the greater is the likelihood of a disorder appearing. Nevertheless, some children are remarkably resilient and may remain free of serious problems despite the existence of a variety of risk factors.

Description

The essence of conduct disorders is 'a repetitive pattern of dissocial, aggressive, or defiant conduct' (the ICD-10 definition). There are major violations of age-appropriate social expectations. DSM-IV-TR's definition is similar: 'A repetitive and persistent pattern of behaviour in which the basic rights of others or major age-appropriate societal norms or rules are violated . . .' It goes on to list 15 behaviours of which three or more must have been manifested in the past 12 months, with at least one in the last 6 months, for a diagnosis of CD:

(1) Bullying, threatening or intimidating others
(2) Initiating physical fights
(3) Using a weapon that can cause serious physical harm to others (e.g. brick, knife, gun, or broken bottle)
(4) Physical cruelty to people
(5) Physical cruelty to animals
(6) Stealing while confronting a victim (as in mugging, purse snatching, extortion or armed robbery)
(7) Forcing a person into sexual activity
(8) Deliberate fire setting with the intention of causing serious damage
(9) Deliberately destroying other people's property by means other than fire setting
(10) Breaking into a house, other building or car
(11) Lying to obtain goods or favours or to avoid obligations
(12) Theft of 'items of nontrivial value' without confrontation of a victim (e.g. shoplifting, breaking and entering or forgery)
(13) Often staying out late at night despite parental prohibition, beginning before age 13
(14) Running away from home overnight at least twice, or once without returning for a 'lengthy period'
(15) Often truanting from school, beginning before age 13

These criteria are in some degree arbitrary. Some are also imprecise, as for example numbers 1, 2 and 11, which must have occurred 'often'. Exactly how often, though, is not defined. Nevertheless, they give a flavour of the kind of behaviours that may justify a diagnosis of conduct disorder.

ICD-10 suggests the following categories of conduct disorder:

(a) Conduct disorder confined to the family context

This diagnostic category is for cases in which abnormal behaviour such as that listed above is entirely, or almost entirely, confined to the home and/or interactions with members of the nuclear family or immediate household. Such clinical pictures do not emerge suddenly in their complete form. Many such children have long had 'difficult' temperaments, and it has proved hard to teach them 'prosocial' behaviour. Oppositional behaviour, disobedience or aggressive behaviour, lying or stealing may have been problems long before criteria for a conduct disorder diagnosis are met.

(b) Unsocialized conduct disorder

This category appears in ICD-10, and it appeared in earlier versions of the DSM, though DSM-IV-TR does not distinguish between socialized and unsocialized conduct disorders. According to ICD-10, a diagnosis of unsocialized conduct disorder is appropriate when there is 'persistent dissocial or aggressive behaviour . . . with a pervasive abnormality in the individual's relationship with other children'. The general criteria for conduct disorder have to be met. The antisocial activities are usually, but not invariably, carried out by the young person alone.

(c) Socialized conduct disorder

This involves behaviours similar to those displayed by individuals with unsocialized disorders, the main distinction being that these children are generally well integrated in their peer groups. They have adequate, lasting friendships with other children, usually of about the same age. This does not preclude bullying or being aggressive to others. Relationships with adult authority figures tend to be poor. As their disorders progress, their antisocial behaviours may be manifest in an increasingly wide range of situations. Truancy from school, staying out late, running away from home and acts of vandalism may progress to such criminal activities as shoplifting, stealing from cars, and breaking into, and stealing from, houses.

Sometimes the behaviour problems first appear in school. They may coincide with deterioration in the child's schoolwork. This may be due to hostile attitudes expressed as refusal to do as instructed by teachers. In yet other cases, especially when conduct disorders first appear in adolescence, the problem behaviours may be first manifest in the wider community. Careful enquiry may however reveal evidence of co-existing problems at home or in school.

(d) Oppositional defiant disorders

ICD-10 classifies these as a subgroup of conduct disorders, stating that they are 'characteristically seen in children below the age of 9 or 10 years'. Oppositional defiant disorder (ODD) is defined 'by the *presence* of markedly defiant, disobedient, provocative behaviour and by the *absence* of more severe dissocial or aggressive acts that violate the law or the rights of others'. These children do not violate the rights of others by such behaviours as theft, cruelty, bullying, assault and destructiveness.

DSM-IV-TR treats these disorders as distinct from conduct disorders, although they are grouped together with conduct disorders under the heading 'Attention-deficit and Disruptive Behaviour Disorders'. Although it describes ODD in terms similar to those used in ICD-10, it makes a clearer distinction between ODD and CD. Indeed the authors of DSM-IV-TR, in developing the criteria for these two 'disorders', were careful to avoid any overlap. Their criteria for ODD are:

(1) Often loses temper
(2) Often argues with adults

(3) Often actively defies or refuses to comply with adults' requests or rules
(4) Often deliberately annoys people
(5) Often blames others for his or her mistakes or misbehaviour
(6) Is often touchy or easily annoyed
(7) Is often angry and resentful
(8) Is often spiteful or vindictive

In DSM-IV-TR, a diagnosis of ODD requires that four or more of the above have been present for at least six months. A diagnosis of CD requires that three or more of the criteria listed earlier have been present for at least 12 months. As Angold and Costello (2001, page 137) point out, a child who previously met the DSM criteria for ODD, and who later will meet those for CD, might at an intermediate stage meet the criteria for neither—for example having three ODD symptoms and two CD symptoms. Yet clinical experience tells us that ODD often—though not invariably—leads to CD. So ICD-10, in listing ODD as a subcategory of CD, is probably the more rational of the diagnostic systems in this area.

(e) Mixed disorders of conduct and emotions

ICD-10 lists only three disorders under this heading, two of them being 'residual' diagnoses:

— Depressive conduct disorder
— Other mixed disorders of conduct and emotions
— Mixed disorder of conduct and emotions, unspecified

'Depressive conduct disorder' does not appear in DSM-IV-TR, in which children who satisfy the criteria for both a depressive disorder and CD are given the appropriate two diagnoses. It is a controversial category, and some believe the term is best avoided (e.g. Zoccolillo, 1992).

There are many other problems in the classification and categorization of these various combinations of antisocial behaviours (see Angold and Costello, 2001, pages 136–145). We need to be aware that these 'disorders' are not clear-cut, distinct clinical entities, but rather commonly occurring combinations of behaviours grouped together for clinical convenience and research purposes.

Specific symptoms

Stealing

There can be few children who have never stolen anything. Stealing should be regarded as abnormal only when it is severe and persistent and fails to respond to commonsense measures instituted by parents or others. But persistent failure to respect the property of others is a sign of deviant development.

Aggressive behaviour

This common cause of referral may present as severe temper tantrums that have persisted long after the toddler period during which they normally disappear; verbal threats; or physical attacks on others, often occurring with little or no provocation.

Truancy

This is the wilful and unjustified avoidance of attendance at school by a child who is supposed to be there. It differs from *school refusal*—sometimes known as 'school phobia'—a condition in which the child stays away from school because of overwhelming anxiety associated with the idea of going to school (see Chapter 7). The truant, by contrast, fails to attend because of a greater desire to do something else, be it playing in the park, watching television or playing video games. Some of these children leave home on time and return at the appropriate time, but without having been at school. The parents may think their child has been at school, while the school staff may assume that there is a legitimate reason, such as illness, for the child's absence. It is surprising how long this sometimes continues. If no parent is home during the day, the child may sit at home, failing to answer the telephone or doorbell and destroying any letters that come from the school. Some forge notes to the school, ostensibly from their parents, excusing them from attendance. Others get friends to impersonate their parents in phone calls to the school.

Truancy may not be only the child's problem. These are often poorly supervised children whose parents may have problems of their own that make it difficult for them to supervise their children properly. Some do not rate education highly. Others may actively encourage or excuse truancy so as to have a child at home to act as babysitter for younger children or to help with housework.

Truancy, unlike school refusal, tends to be associated with poor academic progress. Many truants come from materially and culturally deprived homes, although some are rebellious children from affluent families.

Vandalism

This, 'the wanton damaging, defacing or destruction of property', is sometimes a group activity of adolescents. Whether carried out as a member of a group or as a solitary activity, it seems often to be a means of expressing hostile, aggressive feelings. Such feelings may arise from disturbed relationships with parents, but the frequent selection of schools and churches as targets for vandalism suggests that other factors can be play a part.

Fire setting

This is a relatively uncommon—compared to other CD symptoms—but serious behaviour. Many children pass through a stage of playing with matches and lighting fires, but this usually clears up in response to parental training and precept. Children who go on to set fires deliberately are often expressing severe, deep-seated aggressive feelings. Such feelings may arise from seriously disturbed family relationships. A study by Kolko and Kasdin (1991) suggests that anger and curiosity are the main motives behind fire setting in children. Further information on fire setting is to be found in Epps and Hollin (2000).

Drug abuse

This is commonly present along with other conduct disorder symptoms especially among adolescents, though younger children are not immune. The latter may sniff glue, solvents or petrol (gasoline), often in the context of severe emotional deprivation. Children addicted to inhalants are commonly found among the deprived urban populations of developing countries, and in deprived areas of more affluent societies.

Deviant sexual behaviour

Some children with conduct disorders engage in deviant sexual behaviour. This may take the form of sexual intercourse at an unacceptably early age. Some behaviourally disturbed children and adolescents sexually victimize other, often younger, children. While rape and other sexual offences may be part of a general pattern of antisocial behaviour, they may also occur as isolated acts in young people who are otherwise socially conforming. The psychopathology in such cases is largely in the area of psychosexual development. Some of these children have themselves been sexually abused.

Juvenile delinquency

This is a legal, rather than a clinical, term. It is usually applied to the commission of offences that are in conflict with the law. Whether a young person comes to be defined as a juvenile delinquent depends on various factors, including:

  — The age of criminal responsibility in the jurisdiction in which the act occurs
  — Luck—whether the act is observed by the police or someone else
  — Whether the young person has a lawyer and how skilled that lawyer is
  — What witnesses the police are able to produce
  — Local policy regarding the charging of young people for particular offences

Thus it is partly fortuitous whether a young person becomes a legally defined delinquent. Those who are tend to be those who are more frequent offenders and commit the more serious crimes.

Associated disorders

Attentional and hyperkinetic disorders

There is much overlap between CDs and *attention/deficit hyperactivity disorder* (ADHD) (DSM-IV-TR) and *hyperkinetic disorder* (HD) (ICD-10). DSM-IV-TR permits the making of both diagnoses in the same child, and it acknowledges their close relationship by including them under the same heading ('disruptive behaviour disorders'). In the ICD-10 scheme, hyperkinetic disorder is 'diagnosed with priority over conduct disorder' when its criteria are met. But ICD-10 also has a category of 'hyperkinetic conduct disorder' for use when both the overall criteria for hyperkinetic disorder and those for conduct disorder are met. ADHD and hyperkinetic disorders are discussed in Chapter 7.

Verbal and reading difficulties

It has long been known that impaired verbal ability and reading problems are found more often in children with conduct disorders than in the general population. Such problems are also common in adult criminals. Boys with the most severe conduct problems, and particularly those who also have symptoms of *hyperactivity-impulsivity-attention* (HIA), are the most neuropsychologically impaired (Moffat & Silva, 1988).

The cause-and-effect relationships of verbal/reading problems and CD are complex. It is not just that either one causes the other, though the presence of one may exacerbate the other. Common factors may be involved in the aetiology of each.

Depression

Depression, and dysthymia (a milder form of depressed mood—see Chapter 10), are often associated with CD. This relationship led to the emergence of the 'depressive conduct disorder' (DCD) diagnosis. It has been found that the psychosocial and genetic factors associated with DCD are more like those of CD than of depression. Thus some prefer to consider DCD as essentially a form of CD.

For clinical purposes it is important to be aware of the frequent association of depression and CD.

Treatment

Most conduct disorders have multiple and complex causes that must be carefully assessed before a rational treatment plan can be developed. It is often helpful to take a developmental perspective. These are children who have failed to learn and/or apply some of the rules and customs of the society of which they are part. Treatment should therefore help them learn more suitable ways of living in society.

Some of the factors that may contribute to the development of CDs are less amenable to treatment than others. A child's genetic make-up cannot be changed, but it is important always to remember that genetics and the environment interact to produce the results we see.

In the treatment plan the other conditions that may accompany CD—problems of attention and hyperactivity, delayed verbal and reading skills, and emotional problems such as depression—must be taken into account. Tackling these, even if this does not directly deal with the CD symptoms, often yields dividends. As a child's reading skills improve self-confidence may increase and the child may become less sensitive to the slights of others. A comprehensive treatment plan is therefore seldom simple or straightforward.

Parent-management training (PMT)

This is probably the most studied approach to the treatment of children with CD. It has also been extensively evaluated and has been shown to be effective. Its essence is the training of parents so that they interact with their children in ways that tend to lessen the children's deviant behaviours. The principles of *operant conditioning* underlie this approach. Operant conditioning is the planned modification of behaviours through manipulation of the consequences perceived as controlling them. It is discussed further in Chapter 22.

Family therapy

There are often problems in the families of children with CD. A certain level of stability and order is necessary if parents are to respond to PMT. Sometimes a child's 'acting out' behaviour appears to serve a function in the family system. For example, in families in which there is severe conflict between the parents it may serve to distract the parents from their disagreements and cause them to focus on their child's problem behaviours. The child's problems may be one of the few things upon which they can agree.

A careful review of the family system is important in working out a sound treatment program, although therapists from different schools of family therapy may vary in their understanding of how a child's behaviours are related to the functioning of the family.

Family therapy is discussed further in Chapter 22 and in *Basic Family Therapy* (Barker, 1998).

Cognitive approaches

Children, in common with the rest of us, vary in their understanding of their experiences of the world, and of how they should respond to these experiences. There is good reason to believe that the cognitions of children with CD are in various ways distorted and deficient. They may be unable to think of different ways of handling social situations or of understanding the likely consequence of various possible courses of action. They may make errors in attributing certain motives to the actions of others and in perceiving how others are feeling in particular situations.

Problem-solving skills training (PSST) aims to improve interpersonal problem-solving skills. It offers children (and adults) alternative ways of understanding social situations and of responding to them; and it promotes different thought processes to help children view situations in ways that are novel to them. The subjects are encouraged to engage in self-talk as they try to figure out the best way to respond. They are taught step-by-step approaches to solving problems and games; role playing and modelling are both used to widen their problem-solving skills. They practice their newfound skills and earn rewards as they develop new, better responses to the solving of problems.

There is empirical support for the effectiveness of PSST in the treatment of children with CD, particularly those with impulsive and aggressive behaviours. Kazdin (2001, pages 420–422) reviews the literature on PSST and the evidence for its effectiveness.

Medication

Drugs have at best a limited role in treating CD, except when it is associated with problems of attention and hyperactivity, as in ADHD. Stimulant medication using methylphenidate or dexamphetamine may improve attention span and reduce hyperactivity, and sometimes this leads to a reduction in the CD symptoms. Associated depression may respond to antidepressant medication, and this may or may not result in a lessening of the CD symptoms. Drugs with sedative effects are not usually effective unless they are given in doses so large as to cause drowsiness and lethargy.

Multisystemic therapy

This term is used to describe the combination of a variety of approaches, as needed by particular children with CD. Probably most treatment plans for these children need to be multisystemic. Any or all of the following approaches may be required:

— Family work to promote improved communication, effective use of rewards and punishments, better problem-solving and a generally more stable family
— Encouraging children with CD to associate with others who have more appropriate social skills and do not engage in antisocial behaviour
— Tackling learning problems and establishing effective liaison between school and family
— Individual work, which may include the promotion of cognitive change and assertiveness training that will help the child resist negative peer pressures
— Establishing working relationships with other agencies; these may include child welfare services, probation officers, other medical and mental health services, and the many nongovernmental organizations that work with children and their families

Location of treatment

It is usually best if treatment occurs while the child continues to live at home and attend school locally. The problem behaviours will usually have developed in the context of the child's family, school and neighbourhood. It is therefore appropriate to tackle them in the same context. There are sometimes available special classes and day-treatment programs for troubled children. In rare cases a time-limited placement in a residential setting—either a residential school or other treatment facility—may be helpful, especially when the CD symptoms are severe. On the whole, though, residential options have not proved particularly useful. All the treatments mentioned earlier can however be used wherever the child is.

Outcome

Many minor and some major conduct disorders (CDs) and oppositional defiant disorders (ODDs) clear up with little or no treatment. Some arise from problems children and their families are having in surmounting developmental hurdles. As these are overcome the children's behaviour problems may subside. Sometimes psychosocial stress, within or outside the family, contributes and, when this lessens or is resolved, the behaviour problems also resolve. As a rule the outcome for ODD is better than for CD, though the former may progress to become the latter.

Despite the above, the outcome in many cases of CD is not good. Children with severe conduct disorders, especially those that have appeared in court, are at risk of developing psychiatric illnesses in adult life and of continuing to engage in antisocial and criminal behaviour. Severe and persistent antisocial behaviour, especially when it has had its origins in early childhood, often persists into adult life. CD behaviour in adolescence may be the forerunner of antisocial personality disorder in adult life.

The combination of CD symptoms and educational failure, notably reading retardation, often has a particularly poor outcome, at least in boys. However Maughan and Rutter (2001, pages 507–552), in their chapter 'Antisocial children grown up', point out that while most severely antisocial adults have a long history of disruptive and deviant behaviour dating back to childhood, most CD children do not grow up to become severely antisocial adults. Their chapter reviews comprehensively what we know about how antisocial children fare in their adult lives.

Chapter 7

Hyperkinetic and Attention-Deficit Disorders

Definitions and prevalence

Some children are strikingly more active than others. When the degree of activity reaches a certain level, children are deemed *hyperactive*. Often associated with hyperactivity is a short attention span. The latter is the essential feature of *attention-deficit disorder* (ADD). When there are both hyperactivity and short attention span, as is often the case, the child's disorder is described as *attention-deficit hyperactivity disorder*. Sometimes, especially in adolescence, ADD is found with little or no hyperactivity.

The World Health Organization's treatment of these disorders in its ICD-10 differs from that of the American Psychiatric Association in DSM-IV-TR.

ICD-10 has a category of *hyperkinetic disorders*. This has two subcategories: *disturbance of activity and attention* and *hyperkinetic conduct disorder.* There are also 'residual' subgroups: namely *other hyperkinetic disorders* and *hyperkinetic disorder, unspecified* (but use of this latter diagnosis is not recommended).

The American Psychiatric Association's classification (DSM-IV-TR) divides these conditions as follows:

(1) Attention-deficit/hyperactivity disorder, combined type (ADHD-CT). This diagnosis is to be used if six or more symptoms of inattention and six or more of hyperactivity have persisted for six months or longer.
(2) Attention-deficit hyperactivity disorder, predominantly inattentive type (ADHD-I)—with six or more inattention symptoms and fewer than six hyperactivity-impulsivity symptoms.
(3) Attention-deficit/hyperactivity disorder, predominantly hyperactive-impulsive type (ADHD-HI)—with the pattern of symptoms the reverse of (2).

Hyperactivity, problems of attention, disruptive behaviour, conduct disorders and oppositional behaviour often occur together, but in various combinations. Defining specific disorders within this complex of symptoms and behaviours is difficult, and the results of attempts to do so are somewhat arbitrary. So it is that ICD-10 includes a category of hyperkinetic conduct disorder, whereas DSM-IV-TR does not. Who is right? The answer is that neither is right or perhaps that both are right. These are just two different ways of looking at something complex. For practical purposes what this means is that the diagnostic labels we use have limited value for our day-to-day work. More important is establishing precisely what problem behaviours each child displays, attempting to discover how these have arisen, and—most important of all—determining what we can do to help resolve the problems.

According to ICD-10, the cardinal features of hyperkinetic disorder (HD) are impaired attention and overactivity. These should be present in more than one situation—such as home, classroom or clinic. Children with HD have short attention spans, breaking off from tasks before they are finished, changing frequently from one activity to another, and appearing to lose interest in one task because they become involved in another. A symptom that tends to be under-emphasized in descriptions of this disorder is distractibility. Many children with HD or ADHD can concentrate well, and for long periods, if they are doing something that interests them and there are no distractions—a situation that never exists in a school class-room during lessons.

ICD-10 describes overactivity as excessive restlessness, especially in situations in which calm is required. These children fidget more than other children; they may run and jump around, get up when they should remain seated, and behave in undu-ly noisy and talkative ways. The contexts in which such behaviours occur, and the child's age and intelligence level, are factors that must be taken into account when deciding whether a diagnosis of HD is justified.

DSM-IV-TR has similar criteria for ADHD-HI but emphasizes also the impulsivi-ty of these children.

Symptoms that may be associated with those mentioned above include disinhibi-tion in social relationships, reckless behaviour in dangerous situations, and the impulsive flouting of social rules (for example talking out in class when this is not appropriate). However these behaviours are neither sufficient nor necessary for the diagnosis.

Prevalence

DSM-IV-TR (American Psychiatric Association, 2000) suggests that the prevalence of attention-deficit/hyperactivity disorders in school-age children is 3% to 7%. How-ever, Rowland and his colleagues (2001) suggest that this figure may be an under-estimate. Their study in one North Carolina county suggests a prevalence over three times that cited in DSM-IV (which was 3% to 5%). Higher prevalence rates have been reported in other studies also. The wide variation in reported prevalence studies is probably due to a variety of factors including:

— Differences in the populations studied.
— Different interpretations of the criteria stated in DSM-IV-TR and ICD-10. Some terms used in defining diagnostic criteria, for example 'clinically significant impairment' are vague. How they are interpreted can 'have a major impact on prevalence estimates' (Rowland *et al.*, 2001).
— The use of different study designs.

Rowland and colleagues (2001) discuss the problems of establishing valid preva-lence figures and also provide references to other prevalence studies.

What is clear is that this condition is more common in boys than in girls. Boy:girl ratios of between 2:1 and 3:1 have been found in most studies.

Causes

Twin studies have shown that ADHD has a strong genetic component (Thapar *et al.*, 1995, 1999; Martin *et al.*, 2002). The heritability of this disorder seems to be in the region of 70% to 80%. However there are substantial differences between teacher-rated scores on questionnaires designed to elicit symptoms of ADHD and parent-rated scores (Martin *et al.*, 2002). Although this may be because the two groups of observers are selecting different populations, it may also be simply that the children behave differently in the two settings. The latter is a strong possibility since it is well known that there are often big differences between children's behaviour at home and at school.

While the genetic component to these disorders is strong, other factors clearly contribute to the aetiology. Environment is important also, and it is commonly observed that children who display many ADHD symptoms at school may be able to sit at videogame consoles for hours without their attention lapsing. Moreover the actual behaviour children display in various situations depends to some degree on the reactions of the adults—parents or teachers—who are looking after them. Some parents and teachers are better at managing these children than are others.

Description

The main features of these disorders were set out in the opening section of this chapter. These are children who present with motor hyperactivity, restlessness, impaired attention spans and impulsivity. Although readily distractible, they usually attend only briefly to distracting stimuli.

Onset is usually before the age of 3, but many of these children do not come to professional attention until they start school. It often seems, in retrospect, that hyperactivity was manifest even in early infancy. Some mothers, principally those who have experienced more than one pregnancy, report that the child was unusually active *in utero*.

The hyperactive behaviour most often becomes apparent when the child starts to walk, though some parents, especially those who have previously had non-hyperactive children, realize that their child is different well before that. These children are typically on the go all the time, they concentrate on things poorly, and they may interfere with ornaments, the contents of drawers and other household items to an unusual extent. Sleep disturbance is common, though some seem so tired after their day of frantic activity that they sleep well.

The start of school may precipitate a crisis. Until then, some parents have been able to cope with their child's behaviour, but the special demands of school—the need to pay attention and remain seated, for example—may be too much for the child. These children may fail to respond to the disciplinary measures used by their teachers, and may disrupt the class and be noisy and over-talkative. Other children may become irritated with them, and the result may be that aggressive behaviour between the child and classmates develops.

These children's noncompliance and failure to complete tasks set them are not wilful behaviours. Nevertheless they may be blamed and even punished for their misdeeds. This may lead to secondary emotional problems. In due course they may fall behind in their schoolwork and become disheartened and even depressed. Much however depends on how early their disorder is identified, and how it—and they— are dealt with.

The early chapters of *Hyperactive Children Grown Up* (Weiss & Hechtman, 1986) are a good source of information about how these conditions affect individuals at different stages of childhood, adolescence and young adult life.

Assessment and treatment

A rational treatment plan can be developed only on the basis of a comprehensive assessment of child and family and of the child's situation in school. It is necessary to establish the type and severity of the child's motor activity and/or attention problems; the situations in which these are more or less marked, or completely absent; whether there are associated learning or perceptual problems; and whether the child is also displaying other psychiatric symptoms, such as those of conduct or emotional disorders. Also needed is an assessment of the child's social situation at home, at school and in the local community. Depending on the results of the assessment, any combination of the following measures may be indicated.

Medication

Bradley (1937) reported that some children with behaviour disorders improved when given amphetamine, a psychostimulant drug. Since that report appeared many studies have confirmed the efficacy of psychostimulant treatment for children with ADHD. Nowadays the drug most often employed is methylphenidate although dextroamphetamine is also used. These drugs usually improve concentration and classroom behaviour and decrease impulsivity. At the same time, previously purposeless activity becomes more goal directed. Spencer and colleagues (2002) provide a full account of the use and efficacy of these drugs. They are also discussed further in Chapter 22.

Although the psychostimulants are the drugs most widely used, and in most cases the most effective drugs for ADHD, others are sometimes used, mainly when the psychostimulants prove ineffective or cause unacceptable side effects. These include tricyclic antidepressants, such as imipramine; selective serotonin reuptake inhibitors (SSRIs) such as sertraline; clonidine; guanfacine; propranolol; and venlafaxine. Further information on these drugs, including dosage and side effects, is to be found in Chapter 22.

Behaviour modification

Operant conditioning programs can improve attention span and decrease impulsive behaviour. Cognitive behavioural approaches can sometimes help children with poor impulse control. The MTA Cooperative Group (1999) reported the results of a 14-month, large-scale randomized trial of treatment strategies for attention-deficit/hyperactivity disorders. This 'multimodal' study involved 579 children aged 7 to 9.9 years who were randomly assigned to one of four programs:

— 14 months of medication management
— Intensive behavioural treatment involving parent, school and child components, with therapist involvement gradually diminishing over time
— The above two treatments combined
— Standard community care, that is, treatment by community providers

Although there was improvement in all treatment groups, the greatest improvement in ADHD symptoms was in the medication and the combined groups. However the addition of behavioural treatments to medication did not result in any greater improvement in ADHD symptoms. There was a tendency for combined treatment, but not medication alone, to be superior to intensive behavioural treatment and/or community care for some non-ADHD symptoms (oppositional and aggressive symptoms; internalizing symptoms; social skills as rated by teachers; parent-child relationships; and reading achievement). Despite the large scale of this study, it left many questions unanswered. Cunningham (1999), for example, suggested that behavioural interventions might be more effective for children younger than those studied in this research project. He pointed out that various parent training programs are effective for preschool children.

Cunningham (1999) also observed that few communities have the 'financial or logistic resources' to offer the types of treatment protocols employed in this research. On the whole it is easier to prescribe medication than to set up an intensive behavioural program. But none of the aforementioned drugs is without side effects, and some parents have a philosophical problem with the idea of giving drugs to their children. Also some children dislike taking medication, especially if it causes side effects. The psychostimulants tend to reduce appetite and can cause headaches and gastrointestinal symptoms as well as sleep problems.

Further information about these drugs, including dosage and side effects, is to be found in Chapter 22.

Other measures

Parental counselling
Parents of hyperactive children often need help with managing these children. This may include advice on the arrangement of the home so that breakable items that might present dangers to their child are out of reach; suggesting how parents may best respond to their child's disruptive behaviours; and instruction in behaviour therapy techniques.

Intervention in school

School can be difficult for these children. Their short attention span and difficulty concentrating on the work they are supposed to do can be a real impediment, both to their academic learning and to their acceptance in the social milieu of the classroom. Designing a school program for them that capitalizes on their strengths, and does not demand of them feats of concentration and sustained attention of which they are incapable, can greatly facilitate their progress. Some require individual or small group teaching, especially for academic subjects. In some schools smaller classes, and aides who can work individually with children for at least part of the school day, are available.

Support for these children's teachers, especially those who have had little previous experience with hyperactive and attention-deficit children, may be an important part of the treatment plan.

Outcome

Hyperactivity tends to lessen with increasing age, but other features, notably difficulty sustaining attention, often persist into adolescence and even adult life. *Hyperactive Children Grown Up* (Weiss & Hechtman, 1986) is a mine of information about the outcome in children with ADHD. These authors consider the 'core symptoms' to be inappropriate restlessness, attentional difficulties and impulsivity. Though these symptoms may lessen in adolescence, they are often still present; the presenting symptoms are now more likely to be poor school performance, relationship difficulties and antisocial behaviour. About a quarter of these adolescents engage in antisocial behaviour. As a group, hyperactive adolescents have lower self-esteem and poorer social skills, and they are more impulsive than normal controls.

By the time they reach adult life, one-third to one-half of these individuals are indistinguishable from normal adults. Others, however, have persistent problems with attention and impulsivity. 'Adult ADD' is now well recognized (Gadow & Weiss, 2001), but in addition there is evidence that these individuals are at increased risk of developing other psychiatric disorders, especially personality and mood disorders. The risk of developing a psychiatric disorder in adult life may be even greater in girls who have had ADHD. When this diagnosis is combined with conduct problems in childhood, the risk of developing a psychiatric disorder in adult life has been reported to be high (Daalsgard *et al.*, 2002).

Chapter 8

Anxiety Disorders

Definition and classification

The essential feature of anxiety disorders is a persisting high level of anxiety, out of proportion to any stress the subject is facing. The anxiety may be expressed either directly or indirectly. Many terms have been used to describe these conditions: *neuroses, emotional disorders, anxiety disorders, somatoform disorders* and *stress-related disorders.*

There are some differences in the ways DSM-IV-TR and ICD-10 classify these conditions. All anxiety and emotional disorders are listed in the general section of DSM-IV-TR except for *separation anxiety disorder,* which appears as one of the *other disorders of infancy, children and adolescence.* On the other hand, ICD-10 has six categories of *emotional disorders with onset specific to childhood.*

DSM-IV-TR divides anxiety disorders into three groups:

(1) Anxiety disorders:

— Panic disorders, with or without agoraphobia
— Agoraphobia without a history of panic disorder
— Specific phobia
— Social phobia
— Obsessive-compulsive disorder
— Post-traumatic stress disorder
— Acute stress disorder
— Generalized anxiety disorder
— Anxiety disorder due to a (specified) general medical condition
— Anxiety disorder not otherwise specified

(2) Somatoform disorders:

— Undifferentiated somatoform disorder
— Conversion disorder (associated with psychological factors or with both psychological factors and a general medical condition)
— Body dysmorphic disorder (or dysmorphophobia)
— Hypochondriasis (or hypochondriacal neurosis)
— Somatoform disorder not otherwise specified

(3) Dissociative disorders:

— Dissociative fugue
— Dissociative amnesia
— Dissociative identity disorder
— Depersonalization disorder
— Dissociative disorder not otherwise specified

ICD-10 has six categories of *emotional disorders with onset specific to childhood:*

— Separation anxiety disorder of childhood
— Phobic anxiety disorder of childhood
— Social anxiety disorder of childhood
— Sibling rivalry disorder
— Other childhood emotional disorders
— Childhood emotional disorder, unspecified

ICD-10 also lists anxiety disorders in its general section, though under the general heading *neurotic, stress-related and somatoform disorders:*

— Phobic anxiety disorders
— Other anxiety disorders
— Obsessive-compulsive disorders
— Reaction to severe stress, and adjustment disorders
— Dissociative (conversion) disorders
— Somatoform disorders
— Other neurotic disorders

The above seven categories of disorder are divided into up to 14 subcategories. The clinical usefulness of these subcategories in child psychiatry is limited. More important than assigning children's anxiety disorders to one or other of these subcategories is achieving an understanding of the meaning of the child's symptoms and how they have arisen.

Prevalence

Many different prevalence rates for anxiety disorders have been reported. This is partly due to the use of different study methods, different diagnostic criteria and the study of different populations. Prevalence rates also vary in different age groups and between boys and girls. The Ontario Child Health Study (Offord *et al.*, 1987) found prevalence rates for 'emotional disorder' in the age range 4 to 11 of 10.2% in boys and 10.7% in girls. However in the age bracket 12 to 16 the prevalence in girls (13.6%) was much greater than that in boys (4.9%).

Verhulst (2001, pages 274–278) reviewed nine 'relatively large scale community surveys'. Again differing prevalence studies, both for anxiety disorders generally and for specific types of anxiety disorders, were reported. Prevalences of up to about 10% for all types of anxiety disorder have been found, with girls tending to outnumber boys. However the severity, and even the clinical significance, seems to vary among the children identified as having these disorders. Thus in a study in the Netherlands 10.5% of the children suffered from some form of anxiety as defined in DSM-III-R, but this figure dropped to 3.8% when only those with 'probable general malfunctioning' were included, and to 2.2% when only those showing 'definite malfunctioning' were included (Verhulst, 2001).

The prevalence of anxiety disorders in children is probably similar to that of conduct disorders, though much depends on the population concerned, the age range being studied, and the ascertainment methods and criteria used.

Causes

Successive chapters in *Anxiety Disorders in Children and Adolescents* (Silverman & Treffers, 2001) consider the causative roles of, respectively, peer influences, conditioning processes, traumatic events, family and genetic influences, and child-parent relations in anxiety disorders:

Peer influences

La Greca (2001) points out that relationships with peers are important in children's emotional development. Positive relations contribute to emotional well-being and adjustment. Many children gain much support from their friends. On the other hand, children who are disliked, criticized, made fun of, bullied or otherwise victimized by their peers tend to develop such internalizing difficulties as depression, and anxiety and loneliness (Asher *et al.*, 1990).

Conditioning processes

Fears are common in children. Those in the age range 4 to 8 fear many things—spiders, thunder, dogs or snakes—to name a few. Many of these fears are transient and may be simply part of the process of learning about the world and what is to be feared and how to defend against threats. *Phobias* are fears that are out of proportion to what is to be expected in the situation in which the fear is experienced. Field and Davey (2001) review the evidence that conditioning processes contribute to the development of some phobias. The process is complex, but in essence it is believed that once a person has been frightened by a specific stimulus, that stimulus may later re-awaken the fear. It seems however that not all phobias arise in this way. Fears of heights and of water, for example, may appear without there being any history of traumatic memories that can explain them. Nevertheless it seems likely that conditioning processes contribute to some childhood phobias.

Traumatic events

When children experience a frightening or life-threatening event they may become acutely upset, shake with fear and cling to others for comfort. This state is accompanied by various physiological changes (see Yule *et al.*, 2001). Many of these children recover from such experiences over time. Others do not but instead develop *post-traumatic stress disorder* (PTSD), a condition in which there is persisting anxiety and a variety of other symptoms. PTSD is discussed in Chapter 15.

Genetic and family factors

Anxiety disorders tend to run in families. This is due to a combination of genetic influences and the family environment. The evidence for a genetic contribution to these disorders is reviewed by Boer and Lindhout (2001). However anxiety disorders are not a genetically homogeneous group. Different genetic mechanisms seem to be involved with the different types of anxiety disorder, for example generalized anxiety disorder, phobic disorders, panic disorder and obsessive-compulsive disorder. Moreover there is evidence that the same genes may cause vulnerability to either major depression or generalized anxiety disorder, the family environment determining which condition develops, if one or the other does (Kendler *et al.*, 1992).

Parenting behaviours and the family emotional environment

There is reason to believe that parenting behaviours and the family emotional environments play their part in determining whether children develop anxiety disorders. The process is complex and not fully understood. Moreover a family environment in which one child develops an anxiety disorder may leave another child free of any such disorder. This may be because the children are genetically different, or it may be because of subtle—or not so subtle—differences in the way the two children are reared. (How different the family environments of Harry Potter and his indulged cousin were!) Boer and Lindhout (2001, pages 243–251) provide a summary of studies of how family processes may contribute to the development of anxiety disorders in children.

Family systems theory (see Chapter 2)

This may be helpful in understanding factors that contribute to children's emotional disorders. Certain family situations may be especially stressful for children (Barker, 1984):

— The child may be called upon to be a peacemaker between parents and other family members.
— The child may be called upon to be a mediator.
— The child may attempt to detour conflict in the family.
— The child may play the role of ally, supporting one or other family member—an example is the child who feels obliged to stay up all night until a family member comes home.

Problems of attachment

Attachment theory is concerned with the quality and type of emotional attachment that develops between child and caregiver—usually the parents. Insecure or anxious attachment tends to lead to anxiety and emotional insecurity in children. Attachment and its disorders are discussed further in Chapter 18. Manassis (2001) reviews studies that have explored the relationship between attachment problems and children's anxiety disorders.

State-dependent learning

This concept can help in understanding how anxiety and other emotions sometimes arise. Information learned and experiences undergone can often be recalled only in situations similar to those in which they were first experienced—that is, they are *state bound* or *state dependent* (Rossi, 1986a, b). Rossi suggests that:

> 'So-called "psychological conflict" is a metaphor for competing patterns of state-dependent memory and learning. Reframing therapeutic concepts in terms of state-bound patterns of information and behaviour renders them immediately (1) more amenable to operational definition for experimental study in the laboratory; and (2) more available for active, therapeutic utilization than the traditional process of "analysis" and "understanding".' (Rossi, 1986b, page 233)

There is much support for the above concept. Clinical experience is that children's symptoms, especially anxiety and behavioural symptoms, are often context dependent. Children may behave in one way at home and in another at school, and in yet another with grandparents or with their peers. Epidemiological studies, going back to the classic Isle of Wight Study (Rutter *et al.*, 1970) and the Ontario Child Health Study (Offord *et al.*, 1987) have found that many of the children identified as having disorders at home are not so identified at school and *vice versa*. Thus these disorders are unlike physical diseases: if you have measles you have it whether you are at home, at school or anywhere else. Not so with many emotional and behavioural disorders.

Clinical features

Anxiety disorders of childhood (ICD-10)

Anxiety disorders are rarely diagnosed in infancy, though babies can certainly become upset, as shown by crying, sleeplessness and irritability. Whether these states are of the same nature as the anxiety disorders of later childhood is uncertain. The clinical features of the main groups of anxiety disorders are as follows:

Separation anxiety disorder
The main feature, according to ICD-10 (page 274) is 'a focussed excessive anxiety concerning separation from those individuals to whom the child is attached (usually

parents or other family members), that is not merely part of a generalized anxiety about multiple situations'. The anxiety may be manifest in various situations, for example when left alone to go to sleep, when the major attachment figure is not present, or when the child has to go to school. There may be fears about some harm befalling the attachment figure or worry that something may happen to separate the child from that person. Other symptoms may include recurring nightmares, difficulty sleeping, and physical symptoms such as nausea, abdominal pain, headache and vomiting. The symptoms are worse when separation is anticipated, when it happens and immediately following the separation.

This disorder has to be distinguished from the normal separation anxiety that occurs in early childhood and is discussed in Chapter 1. Important distinguishing characteristics are the severity and persistence of the symptoms and the extent to which they handicap the child in his or her everyday life.

Phobic anxiety disorder of childhood
Most children display some fears during their early years, especially in the pre-school period. The range of possible phobic objects is almost infinite. It includes bees, other insects, thunder and other loud noises, dogs and other animals, and doctors, among many other things. These fears are usually transient and pass as the child, supported by parents and others, learns that the objects feared do not truly represent threats. When the degree of anxiety is 'clinically abnormal' the condition may be classified here. Phobic disorders generally may occur at any age. They are discussed below.

Social anxiety disorder of childhood
ICD-10 suggests the use of this term for disorders in which there is 'a persistent or recurrent fear and/or avoidance of strangers', who may be adults, peers or both, and which is of 'a degree that is outside the normal limits for the child's age and is associated with significant problems in social functioning'. This category is only to be used for disorders that arise before age 6.

Sibling rivalry disorder
ICD-10 suggests the use of this term for disorders that have the following features:

— Evidence of sibling rivalry and/or jealousy
— Onset following the birth of a younger sibling
— Emotional disturbance that is abnormal in degree and/or persistence and associated with psychosocial problems

There may be marked competition for the parents' attention and hostility towards the new sibling. Confrontational and oppositional behaviour towards the parents, temper tantrums, anxiety, misery or social withdrawal my be features of the condition.

Other, and unspecified, childhood emotional disorders
These are 'residual' categories the use of which should be avoided if possible.

Neurotic, stress-related and somatoform disorders

These categories are not specific to childhood, but may occur during childhood.

Phobic anxiety disorders

Specific, or *simple phobias*—also referred to as *monosymptomatic phobias*—are often encountered in children. They may result from previous frightening experiences, and the state-dependent learning paradigm may be relevant here. The phobic object may be almost anything: buses, dogs, cats, heights, enclosed spaces, supermarkets, crowds, snakes, dentists or a multitude of other items. Isolated phobias may differ in their aetiology from other anxiety disorders; they are not usually accompanied by general immaturity, as other anxiety disorders often are, and they are more easily understood on the basis of learning theory. They also tend to respond better to behaviour therapy.

Agoraphobia, the fear of open spaces and/or of crowds and situations from which escape is seen as difficult, is uncommon in childhood and early adolescence but sometimes develops in late adolescence.

Social phobia may occur in late childhood or adolescence. Its essential feature is a persistent, irrational fear of situations in which the subject is exposed to possible scrutiny by others. It may be manifest when the person is asked to speak or perform in public, or when using public lavatories, eating in public, or writing in the presence of others. As with other phobic disorders, the subject recognizes that the fear is excessive or irrational, and is distressed by it.

The term *school phobia* is sometimes used to described emotionally determined reluctance to leave home to go to school. It is however a complex condition rather than a simple phobia of school and is better referred to as *school refusal*.

Obsessive-compulsive disorder (OCD)

OCD is characterized by obsessional thoughts, and by compulsive actions arising from such thoughts. The *prevalence* of obsessive-compulsive disorders in children and adolescents may be about 1.9%, although only a minority of those with the condition come to psychiatric attention (Whitaker *et al.,* 1990).

The essential *clinical feature* of OCD is the repetitive intrusion into the subject's life of thoughts and ideas that are unwelcome and of which the subject would like to be rid. These thoughts are often acted out in compulsive rituals. The thoughts and rituals are not *ego-systonic*—that is, they are not in harmony with the subject's view of the world. This distinguishes them from delusional beliefs and the actions that may arise from such beliefs. A common symptom of OCD is the urge to clean and wash things when there is no need for this. The obsessive-compulsive individual knows there is no need for the hand washing he or she feels compelled to carry out. Deluded persons however are firmly convinced to the necessity of their hand washing. Rational arguments will not persuade such people otherwise.

It is necessary to distinguish between the minor obsessions and compulsions of childhood and the more serious ones that cause distress to the subjects and/or their families. Behaviours such as avoiding the crack in concrete paths, touching lamp standards as they are passed, and various eating and bedtime rituals, are common, especially in younger children. The symptoms of OCD are more severe and persistent, there is conscious resistance to them (though this tends to be less marked in children than in adolescents and adults with this disorder), and they interfere in the child's life. They can be quite complex. One boy had to shut the dining-room door three times and then touch each corner of the table before he could start eating a meal. Even more complex dressing, eating, bedtime and other rituals occur.

OCD symptoms most commonly appear around age 6, though professional help may not be sought until later. They may be preceded by 'impulsions' (Bender & Shilder, 1940). These are similar to compulsions except that there is no conscious resistance to them. Examples are behaviours such as constantly looking at an object, drawing the object, being preoccupied with an object in fantasy or thought, hoarding things, counting repeatedly and being constantly preoccupied with numbers. Impulsions are encountered principally in the age range 4 to 10 and may give way to OCD. Both types of symptom may be present at the same time, especially around puberty.

OCD often co-exists with other psychiatric disorders. The strongest relationship is with tic disorders (see Chapter 15). It has been established that there is an increased rate of tic disorders in subjects with OCD and that the converse is also true (see Salle & March, 2001, pages 106–197).

Reactions to severe stress and adjustment disorders
These are dealt with in Chapter 16.

Hysteria, conversion disorders and dissociative states
These disorders fall into two broad groups:

Those characterized by physical symptoms that may suggest organic disease, when there is no evidence of such disease. Both DSM-IV-TR and ICD-10 call these 'somatoform disorders'.

'Dissociative disorders' are those in which there are psychogenic changes in the subject's consciousness, identity or motor behaviour.

In each of the above group of conditions, the subject is consciously unaware of the underlying problem and is not malingering—that is, the symptoms are not deliberately fabricated. To the patient, they are real.

Somatoform disorders (disorders with physical symptoms)

Somatization disorders
In the past the terms 'hysteria' and 'Briquet's syndrome' have been used for these disorders. Their main features, as set out in ICD-10, are 'multiple, recurrent, and frequently changing physical symptoms'. The physical symptoms may be referred to any bodily system, but gastrointestinal complaints and skin symptoms (such as itching, burning sensations, tingling and numbness) are the most common. The subject does

not accept assurances that there is no physical basis for the symptoms. ICD-10 requires a duration of at least two years for the diagnosis to be considered, whereas DSM-IV-TR requires 'several years'. The diagnosis is seldom appropriate during childhood.

Undifferentiated somatoform disorder
This term refers to disorders in which the full picture of somatization is not present, but there are some milder features. It has little application in childhood.

Body dysmorphic disorder
The main symptom of this condition is preoccupations with a defect in the subject's appearance. The defect may be imagined, but if it does exist, the subject's concern about it is excessive. Its onset is usually during adolescence, but it is occasionally encountered in children. For further information see Albertini & Phillips (1999) and Horowitz et al. (2002).

Hypochondriacal disorder
ICD-10 requires the following to be present for this diagnosis to be appropriate:

— Persistent belief in the presence of at least one serious physical illness responsible for any one or more of a variety of symptoms, despite reassurance and, usually, extensive examination and investigations that have yielded no evidence of a physical disorder.
— Persistent refusal to accept the advice and reassurance of several doctors that no physical illness underlies the patient's symptoms. Established hypochondriasis is rare before early adult life but may be seen in older adolescents.

Other somatoform disorders
ICD-10 also lists 'somatoform autonomic dysfunction'; 'persistent somatoform pain disorder'; 'other somatoform disorders'; and 'somatoform disorder, unspecified'. These terms have limited application in child psychiatry.

Dissociative disorders

Most children have the capacity to dissociate, that is to leave the real world to exist for a while in another one of their own construction. Fantasy play is a common example. They may do this when experiencing abuse, especially sexual abuse. Fully developed dissociative disorders are however relatively rare in childhood. The following dissociative disorders are described:

Psychogenic (or dissociative) amnesia
In this disorder there is loss of memory for some past period of time or for particular events or persons.

Hysterical (or dissociative) fugue
Subjects with this disorder suddenly leave their current lives, often to travel elsewhere with a new identity. Typically they have no memory of the previous lives or identities.

Depersonalization disorder

In this condition the subject has feelings of altered perception or experience of the self, with a loss of the sense of reality. There may also be a similar alteration in the perception of the subject's surroundings ('derealization').

Multiple personality disorder (dissociative identity disorder in DSM-IV-TR)

In this condition the person displays two or more distinctive personalities and identities at different times. The transition from one state to another is usually sudden.

None of these dissociative disorders is common in children, but severe abuse, especially sexual abuse, during childhood is common in the histories of adults with multiple personality disorder. Indeed it is considered by some to be a *sine qua non* for the making of the diagnosis. It seems that many of those who have suffered such abuse have learned to avoid pain by dissociation and that this sometimes becomes a pattern of behaviour that persists into adult life.

A word of warning

Caution should be exercised in attributing physical symptoms to psychogenic causes, because there is a real danger of misdiagnosing organic disease. Moreover the two may co-exist. A frequently encountered combination is that of 'pseudo-seizures'—psychogenic attacks that resemble epileptic seizures—and true epileptic seizures. The former most often occur in subjects who also have, or in the past have had, epilepsy.

When considering whether physical symptoms are psychogenic, it is important not only to exclude, as far as possible, organic disease, but also to establish that there are adequate psychological causes for the symptoms. If the symptoms cannot be understood on either basis, it is wise to leave the diagnosis open until further information is available and progress of the symptoms has been observed for a longer period.

School refusal ('school phobia')

The main feature of this condition is reluctance to attend school associated with anxiety about going and, in some cases, depressed mood. There is usually an element of separation anxiety, at least in younger children. These children often appear frightened to go to school, hence the term 'school phobia', but this disorder is usually more than a phobia of school. There is usually quite complex psychopathology in both the child and the family.

Prevalence

This depends on the ages of the children being considered and probably also on some of the characteristics of the population studied. School refusal may appear at first entry to school, and on changing schools. It is relatively common in early adolescence and, when onset is in the teen years, there is often associated depression; there may also be social or learning difficulties in school.

Clinical picture

School refusal must be distinguished from *truancy*, the wilful avoidance of school (see Chapter 6). Truancy is often associated with other oppositional or conduct problems, and there is not the high level of anxiety seen in children with school refusal. It is this anxiety that makes it hard for children with school refusal to go to school, but the anxiety is often more about leaving home and the support of parents and perhaps others than primarily a fear of school. The associated depressed mood is another factor that may compound the problem.

When attempts are made to force the school-refusing child to attend school, increased distress is often the result. Physical symptoms such as poor appetite, nausea, vomiting, abdominal and other pains, and diarrhoea are common. They may disappear once the time for going to school has passed, which may lead parents and teachers to think that the child is malingering. In more severe cases the symptoms may persist and continue throughout the day. There may also be sleep disturbance.

School-refusing children tend to be emotionally immature, and so have difficulty coping with the everyday stresses of life at school. They may find relationships with other children difficult, and they become acutely anxious away from the safety and protection of home and family.

School attendance may finally cease, perhaps after a period of increasing reluctance to attend, in response to what may be a minor additional stress, such as a change of teachers, bullying by other children or transfer from one school to another.

The emotional immaturity of these children is often manifest also in their, often covert, aggressiveness. They have often been raised in anxious and indulgent environments, so that they have not learned to accept frustration and to channel their aggressive feelings into socially useful and constructive activities. Their anger may seldom have been aroused, since they have always been given their way. When this situation changes, they may become both panic-stricken and angry. Their anger is often expressed verbally, but some of these children become physically violent with their parents, for example if the latter try to force them, by physical means, to go to school. Their anger may also be expressed silently through refusal to speak or cooperate, both with parents and with therapists and others trying to help.

Either anxiety or depression may dominate the clinical picture. These children may also feel resentful because they are aware, unconsciously if not at a conscious level, of their inability to fulfil age-appropriate roles. Depression is seen more often in adolescent school refusers than in those in younger age groups. Bernstein and Garfinkel (1986) reported that 69% of early adolescent, chronic school refusers met DSM-III criteria for either major depression or adjustment disorder with depression.

A family constellation that has been reported to be frequent in these cases is that of the combination of an anxious and overprotective mother and a weak, passive, ineffectual or absent father (Skynner, 1975). This situation is by no means uniformly present in these families, however.

Other neurotic disorders: Neurasthenia

This is an ill-defined disorder characterized by complaint of chronic fatigue, bodily weakness and physical exhaustion after minimal effort. It is often accompanied by such symptoms as aches and pains, headaches, dizziness, sleep disturbance, inability to relax, irritability and dyspepsia. It bears similarities to *chronic fatigue syndrome* and *myalgic encephalomyelitis* (ME). These disorders often do not appear until early adult life but may occur in adolescence.

Treatment

The treatment for anxiety disorders varies according to the nature of the symptoms and the causes that have been identified in the formulation of the case.

Psychotherapy

This may involve individual work with the child, counselling sessions with the parents or therapy involving the entire family group.

Family Therapy
When the child's symptoms are seen as related to, or embedded in, the functioning of the family system as a whole, family therapy is often of value. In the treatment of school refusal, especially in adolescence when the family psychopathology is often chronic and complex, it may be especially useful. When family systems problems are a prominent feature—which is often the case—I prefer to address these first. This may lead to reduction or resolution of the child's symptoms. If it does not, individual work with the child may be needed, perhaps combined with further work with the parents.

Individual therapy
This with the child may be conducted along psychodynamic lines, or a cognitive behavioural approach (see below) may be used.

Counselling the parents
This may be necessary when there is evidence of overanxious, overprotective or otherwise unhelpful attitudes to or handling of the child. The aim may be to help the parents to an understanding of how they need to 'let go' and allow their child to develop his or her own ways of dealing with the world's challenges, while always being ready to provide support when it is really needed.

Behaviour therapy

Behavioural approaches are often effective in the treatment of phobias, especially monosymptomatic ones, for which *systematic desensitization* (Chapter 22) is an established treatment. The essence of this approach is the gradual introduction of the phobic object or situation while the subject is in a state of relaxation.

Behaviour therapy can also contribute to the treatment of obsessive-compulsive disorders. *Response prevention* (Stanley, 1980), which consists of consistently preventing the compulsive behaviours from being carried out, may be effective when compulsive behaviours are prominent. It often happens that, by the time the child is presented for treatment, family members and others who have contact with the child have got into the habit of giving in to the child's demands to carry out the rituals; they may modify the environment so that the child is allowed extra time to dress, eat meals, prepare to go to bed and so on. This usually leads to a worsening of the symptoms—even to the family getting up in the morning hours before they would need to if it were not for their child's compulsive need to carry out a succession of rituals.

Behavioural analysis may reveal that various environmental contingencies are reinforcing or promoting other anxiety symptoms. When this is so, behaviour modification interventions may yield good results.

Cognitive behaviour therapy (CBT) is often an effective treatment for anxiety disorders. CBT is a structured, directive anxiety treatment that teaches patients skills for coping with anxiety-provoking situations (Kendall, 1994). Kendall (1990) developed the *Coping Cat Workbook,* which describes a 16-week individual CBT program. A randomized trial using this program, and comparing the results with the progress of a awaiting list control group, showed it to be effective (Kendall, 1994). A subsequent trial confirmed these results (Kendall *et al.*, 1997). Follow-up at one year and three years showed continuing improvement (Kendall & Southam-Gerow, 1996). The program can be adapted successfully for group use.

Manassis and colleagues (2002) compared the results of group and individual CBT for children with anxiety disorders. They found both to be effective, but there was some evidence that children with high level of social anxiety may do better with individual treatment.

Pharmacotherapy

Benzodiazepine drugs such as lorazepam, alprazolam and diazepam may provide short-term symptomatic relief for panic disorders and generalized anxiety disorders, but their use for more than a few weeks at most is inadvisable. Tolerance, dependence and abuse may occur, and there may be adverse reactions when the drug is withdrawn after prolonged use. Poor concentration, daytime sleepiness and impaired coordination are other side effects that may occur.

Various antidepressants have been shown to be of value in the treatment of anxiety disorders. Stock and colleagues (2001) and Garland (2002) discuss them and the pros and cons of using the different categories of antidepressants. The selective serotonin uptake inhibitors (SSRIs), although regarded primarily as antidepressants, can be of real value in treating anxiety disorders, particularly OCD and panic disorders. Fluoxetine has been shown to be effective and well tolerated in the treatment of OCD, but its full effect may not be seen for eight weeks or more (Geller *et al.*, 2001; Liebowitz *et al.*, 2002). Further information is to be found in Chapter 22 and Table 22.1.

Outcome

The outlook for childhood anxieties is generally favourable. Many anxiety disorders clear up completely, with or without treatment. Much depends on the soundness of the child's personality development prior to the onset of the disorders, and on the stability of the family. Constitutional predisposition, suggested by a strong family history of anxiety or affective symptoms, and the emergence of symptoms with little apparent environmental cause, may presage a poorer outcome.

Although OCD symptoms may resolve, children with this disorder tend to do less well than those with other anxiety disorders. Sometimes the OCD symptoms are replaced by, or come to be accompanied by, tics.

Chapter 9

Mixed Disorders of Conduct and Emotions

Child psychiatric disorders do not fall neatly into categories, each with its own aetiology, symptoms, treatment and prognosis. As we saw in Chapter 2, most are complex reactions to a variety of factors within and outside the child. Many of the diagnostic categories are abstractions intended to bring some degree of order into a complex and often confusing subject.

Many children and adolescents present with symptoms of more than one of the disorders described in ICD-10 and DSM-IV. A common example is that of children who have both antisocial behaviour and emotional symptoms. They may have symptoms of conduct or oppositional defiant disorder, on the one hand, and anxiety or depression, on the other. When there is a need to make a diagnosis, there are several ways in which such situations can be addressed. The diagnostic category the symptoms of which are most prominent may be chosen; a dual diagnosis may be made; or categories for *mixed disorders* can be created.

Acknowledging that there is a large group of children who display a mixture of antisocial behaviour and emotional symptoms, the authors of ICD-10 proposed a category of *mixed disorders of conduct and emotions*. The ICD-10 manual describes these disorders as 'characterized by the combination of persistently aggressive, dissocial, or defiant behaviour with overt and marked symptoms of depression, anxiety or other emotional upsets'. However it goes on to say that 'insufficient research has been carried out to be confident that this category should indeed be separate from conduct disorders of childhood.' It does not appear in DSM-IV.

Despite being presented only tentatively in ICD-10, this proposed category merits brief discussion for three reasons.

First, these 'mixed' conditions are common. Defining them as a different disorder may draw the attention of clinicians and researchers to a group of, often, seriously troubled children who may otherwise fail to get the attention they deserve.

Secondly, providing categories of mixed disorders helps make it clear that in child psychiatry we do not, for the most part, deal with discrete, easily defined entities, but with complex, continuously variable reactions to equally complex combinations of aetiological factors in immature, incompletely developed personalities.

The third reason for having this category is that these disorders present major therapeutic challenges. Once a disorder is defined, more attention may be given to the development of methods of treatment and prevention.

Clinical features

ICD-10 proposes three types of 'mixed' disorder:

—*Depressive conduct disorder.* This requires symptoms of conduct as these are defined in the ICD-10 manual, combined with 'persistent and marked depression of mood, as evidenced by symptoms such as excessive misery, loss of interest and pleasure in usual activities, self-blame, and hopelessness'. There may also be disturbances of sleep and/or appetite.

—*Other mixed disorders of conduct and emotions.* In this subcategory there is a combination of conduct disorder symptoms and 'persistent and marked emotional symptoms such as anxiety, fearfulness, obsessions or compulsions, depersonalization or derealization, phobias or hypochondriasis.' Anger and resentment neither support nor negate the diagnosis.

—*Mixed disorder of conduct and emotions, unspecified.* This is a 'residual' subcategory for use when neither of the above two exactly fit the case.

Children whose disorders fall into these *mixed* categories may have a wide variety of symptoms—almost any combination of the symptoms described in Chapters 6 and 8, provided they meet the ICD-10 criteria for conduct disorder. In practice these are often insecurely attached children from chaotic, poorly organized families. They have lacked proper social training and have not experienced, to a sufficient degree, emotional stability and security. In older children, and especially in adolescents, there may be a serious degree of depression, along with antisocial behaviour. These children's self-esteem is usually low and they feel, unconsciously if not consciously, that they are failures, with little sense of personal accomplishment or self-worth.

Treatment

The literature on the treatment of these disorders is limited. Any of the treatment methods that may be used for conduct or oppositional defiant disorders, or for emotional or depressive disorders, may be indicated. A comprehensive assessment and an in-depth case formulation are essential before treatment can be planned. It may be best to start by tackling the most prominent symptoms, but a plan designed to tackle more than one part of the pathology may also be appropriate. These are multiply handicapped children, and there are often problems in the families, as well as in the children themselves, which need to be addressed.

Outcome

Little systematic outcome data are available regarding these children. Clinical experience suggests however that many of them do rather badly. The presence of serious conduct disorder symptoms tends to be a bad prognostic sign. When depressive or anxiety symptoms predominate, the outlook is generally better. Whatever the combination of symptoms, much depends on the stability of the family and the extent to which the parents and other family members are able to participate in a well-designed treatment program.

The quality and nature of the emotional attachment of these children to their parents are important. The more stable the family, and the more securely attached the children are to their parents, the better the outcome is likely to be. If the child has lacked proper social training and has not had good parental or other role models, the therapeutic challenge is even greater.

Chapter 10

Major Affective Disorders, Suicide and Dysthymia

Major affective disorders are characterized by a deviation of mood, in the direction of either depression or elation. States of elation are known as either *mania* or its lesser form *hypomania*. Manic and hypomanic states are relatively uncommon before puberty, but are frequently encountered more in adolescence.

Classification

Neither DSM-IV nor ICD-10 recognize any category of affective disorder occurring specifically in childhood, except for ICD-10's *depressive conduct disorder,* as discussed in the previous chapter. Otherwise mood, or affective, disorders appear in the general sections of these classifications. These categories may be used for the disorders of patients of any age. The main ICD-10 categories are:

—*Manic episode,* subdivided into hypomania; manic episode without psychotic symptoms; manic episode with psychotic symptoms; and 'other' and 'unspecified' manic episodes.

—*Bipolar affective disorder.* This has ten subcategories, plus some further subdivisions. The subcategories specify whether the current state is one of depression or mania, or is mixed, and how severe it is.

—*Depressive episode.* This may be mild, moderate or severe; the 'severe' category is divided into episodes with or without psychotic symptoms. There are also categories for 'other' and 'unspecified' depressive episodes.

—*Recurrent depressive disorder.* This category is to be used when there are repeated episodes of depression without intervening episodes of mood alteration or overactivity. There is a further division according to whether the condition is in remission or, if it is not, how severe the current episode is.

—*Persistent mood (affective) disorders.* These comprise cyclothymia, in which there is persisting instability of mood, with periods of mild depression and mild elation; dysthymia, a long-standing state of depressed mood, insufficiently severe to meet the criteria for a depressive disorder; and 'other persistent mood [affective] disorders'.

—*Other and unspecified mood (affective) disorders.*

DSM-IV-TR has broadly similar categories, and both classification schemes also have categories for adjustment disorders with depressed mood. (See Chapter 15 for more information on adjustment disorders.)

DSM-IV-TR has a category (rather than a subcategory) for *dysthymic disorder*, its main feature being a chronically depressed mood lasting most of the day, and of at least two years' duration (one year in children, in whom the mood may be irritable rather than depressed). Low self-esteem, lack of energy, poor concentration, and difficulty making decisions are common features, but the criteria for depressive disorder are not met.

Depression in children and adolescents

Only over the course of the last few decades has it become widely accepted that children can suffer 'adult-type' depressive disorders. The existence of such disorders in adolescents was accepted before it was widely agreed that they occur also in pre-pubertal children. However by 1986 Puig-Antich expressed the view that the phenomenology of major depression is 'quite similar from age 6 to senescence'. He stated that the developmental variations that do occur are 'minor compared to the steadiness of the symptomatology' (Puig-Antich, 1986, page 345). This view has become widely accepted.

Prevalence

Whitaker and colleagues (1990) suggested that in 14- to 17-year-olds the prevalence rate of major depression is about 4%, the rate in girls (4.5%) being higher than that in boys (2.9%). The rate in pre-pubertal children is almost certainly lower.

Masi *et al.* (2001) point out that the data on the prevalence of bipolar disorders 'are scarce and conflicting'. The rate of 'full-blown' bipolar disorder in adolescents may be about 0.99% (Lewinshon *et al.*, 1995), whereas mood fluctuations that do not meet the criteria for bipolar disorder or cyclothymia are more common. In adolescents, manic conditions are less common than depressive ones. Before puberty manic disorders are quite rare though they do occur.

Causes

Like most psychiatric conditions, the major affective disorders have multiple causes. The main ones are:

Genetic factors

These play a major role in predisposing individuals to depression and bipolar illnesses—conditions that often run in families. The concordance for monozygotic twins raised together may be as high as 67%, compared to that for dizygotic twins raised together (19%), whereas the figure for monozygotic twins has been found to be 67% (Akiskal & Weller, 1989). In clinical practice it is commonplace to find that there is a strong history of depression and/or bipolar disorder in the families of depressed children and adolescents.

Stressful events

These can have an important role in individuals who are predisposed genetically or in other ways (Lewinshon *et al.*, 1999).

Insecure attachment

The lack of secure attachment has long been thought to predispose individuals to depression. The emotional availability of caregivers (usually the parents) is believed to foster secure attachment bonds (Allen, 1999). The existence of such bonds may make it more likely that the individual will use that relationship for support in times of stress. Insecure attachment may therefore be a risk factor for the development of depressive symptoms (Sund & Wichstrøm, 2002).

Separation experiences, losses and bereavement

These often go together. For example, the loss of a parent by death, the separation or divorce of the parents, or the incarceration of a parent may result in the break-up of the home, geographical moves, family financial problems, the arrival of a step-parent, and emotional problems in the surviving parent.

Other psychiatric conditions

Depression may complicate conduct disorders, adjustment disorders, separation anxiety, attention-deficit hyperactivity disorders and other emotional and behavioural disorders. Sometimes it is difficult to determine which is the primary condition; this may be why the category of *depressive conduct disorder* has been proposed.

Physical illnesses and drugs

Diabetes, asthma, rheumatoid arthritis and treatment with steroid drugs may all be complicated by depression; so may the chronic abuse of cocaine and other 'street' drugs.

Depression

The central feature of depressive disorders is a mood of sadness and gloom, often with feelings of hopelessness and despair. The depressed person may have lost interest and pleasure in life and may no longer wish to live.

DSM-IV-TR lists eight symptoms of a 'major depressive episode':

(1) Depressed mood (or in children and adolescents irritable mood) most of the day, nearly every day.
(2) Markedly diminished interest or pleasure in all, or nearly all, activities most of the day, nearly every day.
(3) Significant weight loss (when not dieting), or weight gain, or a decrease or increase in appetite, nearly every day. In children failure to make the expected gain in weight, rather than weight loss, meets this criterion.
(4) Change in sleep pattern to either reduced sleep or excessive sleepiness.
(5) Psychomotor agitation or retardation nearly every day, observed by others.
(6) Tiredness or loss of energy nearly every day.
(7) Feelings of worthlessness or excessive or inappropriate guilt nearly every day. The guilt may be of delusional force.
(8) Diminished ability to think or to concentrate, or indecisiveness, nearly every day.

Some of these symptoms (especially 1, 2, 4, and 8) may either be experienced by the subject or observed by others. For the diagnosis to meet DSM-IV-TR criteria, at least five of the eight symptoms must have been present, including either item 1 or item 2, during the same two-week period.

ICD-10 lists four types of depressive episode: mild, moderate, severe without psychotic symptoms, and severe with psychotic symptoms. It lists the following symptoms as characteristic of depressive episodes:

— Depressed mood
— Loss of interest and enjoyment
— Reduced energy with increased fatigability and diminished activity
— Reduced concentration and attention
— Reduced self-esteem and self-confidence
— Ideas of guilt and unworthiness
— Bleak and pessimistic view of the future
— Ideas or acts of self-harm or suicide
— Disturbed sleep
— Diminished appetite

The lowered mood varies little from day to day and usually does not respond to changes of the subject's circumstances. An important symptom not included in DSM-IV-TR's list of eight symptoms is that of ideas of self-harm or suicide. Suicide is an ever-present danger in those who are depressed.

In addition to the categories for depressive episodes of varying degrees of severity, ICD-10 also has categories for recurrent depressive disorders of various types. These cover severity and the subject's current mood state.

The above symptom lists cover fairly well the varied clinical pictures we see in depressed children and adolescents. However to them should be added tearfulness, which is common in depressed children, and deteriorating schoolwork. Sometimes it is a falling off in the child's marks in school that first brings the child to professional attention.

The onset of depression may be acute, but it is often gradual and the parents are not always aware of what their child is experiencing.

Suicide, suicidal behaviour and deliberate self-harm

Completed suicides are rare before puberty, but the incidence increases markedly during adolescence. It is more common among adolescent boys than girls. The incidence among male adolescents has increased substantially over the last few decades, the increase, at least in Britain, being in suicides associated with substance misuse (Fombonne, 1998).

Suicide rates vary widely in different societies. For example they are much higher in native North American adolescents than in non-native adolescents (Thompson, 1987). In China, suicides are more common among young women, especially those in rural areas, than among young men (Cheng & Lee, 2000). The methods used for suicides also vary from one society to another; guns are widely used in the U.S.A., where they are more readily available than in many other countries. A study by Carlson (1990) indicated that shooting, hanging and carbon monoxide poisoning were the leading methods used by males; girls used overdoses, carbon monoxide poisoning and firearms with about equal frequency.

Types of suicidal behaviour

Parasuicide and *deliberate self-harm* are terms that cover behaviours such as taking minor overdoses of sedative or other drugs, inflicting superficial cuts on the arms or other parts of the body, or performing other minor acts of self-harm. Such behaviours are often encountered among teenage girls who are under stress. They may be accompanied by threats of suicide, or threats may be made without any actions being taken. Although these behaviours may be described as attempts at suicide, careful questioning often reveals that they are really cries for help with problems the subjects face. They should be taken seriously even though the risk of completed suicide may be small.

Serious suicidal behaviour may come 'out of the blue'. It is more common in adolescent boys than girls, but it is by no means unknown in girls. It should always be considered, and appropriate measures taken, when a clinically depressed child or adolescent is seen. The combination of depression with substance abuse is particularly serious.

Assessing suicidal young people

When a young person is seen who may be at risk of committing suicide, careful assessment is essential. I approach such situations as follows:

(1) I start by making every effort to establish the best possible rapport with the young person.
(2) I enquire for depressive symptoms, as set out above.

(3) If the subject reports depressed mood or other depressive symptoms, I ask questions such as the following:

— Have you ever felt so depressed (or sad, or unhappy, or despondent) that you have wished you were dead? (If the answer is yes, I enquire how recently the subject has felt that way, how often, when did such feelings start, and are they present now?)

— Have you ever considered harming or even killing yourself? (If the answer is yes, I ask when, how often, how recently, how seriously; and whether the young person is currently considering this and, if so, what methods of harming or killing himself or herself is the young person considering?)

— Have you ever actually tried to harm or kill yourself? If the answer is yes, I ask for full details; also what stopped the attempt(s) from being successful? I explore the history of any previous suicide attempts as fully as possible. What were the circumstances under which the attempts occurred? Was the young person alone or with others? How serious was the desire to die? Is the subject glad he or she did not succeed in the attempt at suicide? Was the attempt planned or carried out on impulse?

The most serious scenario is that in which the subject has made several determined attempts at suicide, alone and with a real desire to die.

Mania and manic states

In mania, and its lesser form, hypomania, the mood disturbance is in the direction of elation, though in adolescence irritability, rather than elation, may predominate. Manic subjects display the following symptoms:

— Elated, inappropriately happy mood
— Hyperactive behaviour, with restlessness, and being constantly on the move
— A lack of judgement and an inflated sense of self-esteem that may lead to the reckless spending of money, sometimes because the person falsely believes that he or she is a millionaire; and other wild and unwise acts
— Rapid and pressured speech, with many jokes and puns, often inappropriate to the situation
— Flight of ideas, the rapid flitting from one subject to another associated one, though the process may be so fast that others miss the association
— Delusions of grandeur, such as believing one is a king, or God, or possessed of special powers or immense wealth; such delusion may be accompanied by hallucinations

Hypomania is more common than mania. There is elation or irritability, and excess activity, often combined with some of the other symptoms mentioned above, but the full picture of mania is not present and there are no delusions or hallucinations.

Hassanyeh and Davidson (1980) described the 'bomb-in-the-room' syndrome, referring to the state of total disorder in their manic adolescent patients' rooms.

Bipolar disorders (formerly called manic depressive psychoses)

Isolated episodes of mania or hypomania may occur, but more often these states occur as part of a *bipolar affective (or mood) disorder.* Periods of depression alternate with periods of mania or hypomania. Each episode may last from a few days to several months; there may or may not be periods of normal mood between the episodes of altered mood.

DSM-IV-TR subdivides bipolar disorders into Bipolar I and Bipolar II categories. In the six types of Bipolar I conditions there must have been, or currently be, an episode of mania or a 'mixed' episode, the latter being one in which the criteria are met for both a manic episode and a major depressive episode. Bipolar II is characterized by recurrent major depressive episodes with hypomanic—but not manic—episodes. If there has ever been a manic or mixed episode, this diagnosis is ruled out.

ICD-10 does not make a distinction between Bipolar I and II disorders.

Diagnosis is sometimes difficult. Mild forms of mania or hypomania may be mistaken for conduct disorders, especially when restlessness, hostility, irritability and verbal abuse predominate. Girls may display sexually provocative behaviour. Some organic mental states may mimic manic states; so also may states of drug intoxication, especially stimulants such as cocaine and amphetamine compounds, and certain hallucinogens. Careful inquiry about possible drug abuse is therefore indicated. Although some of the symptoms of attention-deficit hyperactivity disorder (ADHD) may resemble hypomania, these conditions are readily distinguished, since ADHD has its onset in early childhood and is a long-lasting chronic condition. Manic and hypomanic conditions have their onset much later.

Dysthymia

This is a chronic condition in which the mood is less severely depressed than in major depression. The DSM-IV-TR criteria are:

—Depressed mood for more days than not, for at least two years in adults, or one year in children and adolescents. In children and adolescents the mood may be irritable rather than depressed.

—Also present, while the subject is depressed, must be at least two of the following:

(1) Poor appetite or overeating
(2) Insomnia or hypersomnia
(3) Low energy or fatigue
(4) Low self-esteem
(5) Poor concentration or difficulty making decisions
(6) Feelings of hopelessness

ICD-10 describes the essential feature of dysthymic disorders as 'a very long-standing depression of mood which is never, or only very rarely, severe enough to fulfill the criteria for recurrent depressive disorder, mild or moderate severity.'

Cyclothymia

This term is used for what ICD-10 describes as 'a persistent instability of mood, involving numerous periods of mild depression and mild elation.' There may also be long periods of normal mood. The condition may occur in the relatives of patients with bipolar affective disorder. It is rarely diagnosed in childhood or adolescence.

Treatment

Depression

Any of the following approaches may be needed:

1. *Removing or alleviating any stresses the young person faces.* These should have been identified in the initial assessment. This may involve:

— Family therapy to address problems in the family system that are causing the young person stress
— Counselling for the parents
— Intervention in the school to deal with problems the child has there, such as bullying, peer relationship difficulties and academic problems
— Treatment of depression, alcoholism and other psychiatric problems in a parent or parents
— Temporary removal of the child to a treatment centre or other placement while stresses in the home are addressed
— The provision of a, usually short-term, supportive relationship with a therapist
— Occasionally, when the family situation is seriously stressful and efforts to change it fail, long-term placement in another living situation

2. *The use of antidepressant medication.* There is good evidence that some depressed children and adolescents respond to certain antidepressant drugs. Of those currently available the selective serotonin uptake inhibitors (SSRIs) are generally considered to be the safest and most effective. The older, tricyclic drugs are of questionable efficacy in children and are more prone to cause side effects. The SSRIs are discussed in Chapter 22, dosage recommendations and the main side effects being set out in Table 22.1. These drugs are slow to act. The initial response is usually delayed for two to four weeks, and full response may take two to three months. When they prove effective, they should be continued for a long period and then discontinued slowly while the patent is monitored for signs of recurrence. It is important that patients do not stop taking these drugs as soon as they feel better, since relapse is then probable.

Other antidepressants that may prove effective when SSRIs are not include venflaxine and buproprion. These also are discussed in Chapter 22. Ryan (2002) has reviewed the pharmacological treatment of depression.

3. *Cognitive behaviour therapy (CBT)*. There is good empirical support for the effectiveness of CBT in the treatment of depression, but the relapse rate is high (at least 40% in the first year, similar to the relapse rate after discontinuation of treatment with SSRIs) (Birmaher *et al.*, 2000). It has been suggested, for example by March and Wells (2002), that better results may be obtained by combining antidepressant medication and CBT, but this remains to be conclusively demonstrated.

Bipolar disorders and manic states

For the management of acute manic states Kusumaker and colleagues (2002) recommend treatment in a low-stimulus environment, and the use of sedative medications administered orally or, if necessary, by injection. Suitable drugs include lorazepam, chlorpromazine and clopenthixol. These should be used only in the acute phase. Once the patient has settled and is no longer acutely disturbed, a 'mood stabilizer' is indicated. Lithium has long been used for this purpose and an alternative is divalproex. Carbamazepine has a reputation for being sometimes effective as a mood stabilizer in adults, but its value in adolescents is uncertain.

The treatment of acutely disturbed manic patients and of bipolar disorders in young people is a challenging and often complex undertaking; it should be carried out by, or under the supervision of, specialists in this area of practice. Weller and colleagues (2003) review both the diagnosis and the treatment of bipolar disorders in children and adolescents. They conclude that there is a dearth of well-supported evidence on how best to treat these conditions, but that lithium may be effective, though perhaps less so than in adult patients. There is 'preliminary evidence that valproate may also be effective, but the use of carbamazepine in children and adolescents is "poorly studied"'. Its use also carries the risk of aplastic anemia and agranulocytosis.

Outcome

Many episodes of depression resolve, with or without treatment, but recurrence is common. The earlier the onset of major affective disorders of any type, the greater the risk of recurrence, or continuing problems, is believed to be. Many young people who present with unipolar depression or dysthymia later develop hypomania or mania, so that a diagnosis of bipolar disorder becomes appropriate.

A poor prognosis, with increasing risk of the development of bipolar disorder, is associated with the following (Kusumaker *et al.*, 2002, page 121):

— Psychotic depression
— A history of bipolar disorder in the parental or sibling generation
— The precipitation of hypomania or mania by the administration of antidepressant drugs
— Depression with marked psychomotor retardation
— Depression with subthreshold biphasic mood symptoms

The appearance of any form of major affective disorder in adolescence is serious. Although the short-term outcome is often favourable for both depression and mania (Rajeev *et al.*, 2003), episodes early in life may foreshadow similar or related problems in adult life. This applies with even greater force if the onset is before puberty.

The Maudsley long-term follow-up of child and adolescent depression (Fombonne *et al.*, 2001a, b) found that the recurrence of adult depression in the 149 subjects studied was high for major depression (62.4%) and for any depression (75.2%). The suicide risk was 2.45%, and 44.3% had attempted suicide at least once in their lives. When there was comorbid conduct disorder, suicidal behaviour was more frequent and there were higher rates of criminal offences and 'pervasive social dysfunction'. Thus depression on its own has a poor adult prognosis, but when conduct disorder is also present the outcome is even worse.

Chapter 11

Pervasive Developmental Disorders

Pervasive developmental disorders (PDDs) are a varied group of conditions that have certain features in common, including impaired socialization, communication disorders, a lack of imagination, and repetitive and ritualistic behaviours.

DSM-IV-TR lists the following conditions under the PDD heading:

— Autistic disorder
— Rett's disorder
— Childhood disintegrative disorder
— Asperger's disorder
— Pervasive developmental disorder not otherwise specified (PDD-NOS), including 'atypical autism'

ICD-10 lists PDDs as follows:

— Childhood autism
— Atypical autism
— Rett's syndrome
— Other childhood disintegrative disorder
— Overactive disorder associated with mental retardation and stereotyped movements (This is described in ICD-10 as 'an ill-defined disorder of uncertain nosological validity'. It will not be discussed further here.)
— Asperger's syndrome
— Other pervasive developmental disorders
— Pervasive developmental disorder, unspecified

As the differences between these two lists of categories suggest, there is uncertainty about how best to approach the classification—and even the naming—of these disorders.

Recently there has been a move towards grouping several of these disorders—usually autism, Asperger's syndrome and PDD-NOS together as autistic spectrum disorders (ASDs), although some would not include PDD-NOS. While there is indeed a 'spectrum' from autism—a severe and seriously handicapping condition—through Asperger's syndrome, to PDD-NOS—the least severe and handicapping condition—the term ASD lacks diagnostic precision and, in itself, gives no indication of seriousness or prognosis.

Prevalence

The prevalence of autistic disorders is probably between 4 and 5 per 10,000 children (Fombonne, 1999), but differing prevalence figures have been found in the various studies that have been reported. Much depends on the diagnostic criteria used and the ages of the children in the populations studied and, possibly, the population studied. When the diagnostic criteria are expanded to include ASDs, higher prevalence figures are naturally found. Scott and colleagues (2002) provide a brief review of the various prevalence figures that have been reported; these range as high as 57.9 and even 67 per 100,000, for ASDs.

Asperger's disorder is more common than autistic disorder, as these conditions are defined, its prevalence probably being around 30 per 10,000. Since its symptoms are less severe, Asperger's disorder is often diagnosed at a later age than autistic disorder. Thus studies of children in younger age groups are likely to under-estimate the prevalence of this disorder. The same probably applies to ASDs generally. Another confounding factor is the vagueness of the diagnostic criteria for 'pervasive developmental disorder not otherwise specified', which leaves room for different interpretations by different clinicians and researchers.

The least common of the PDDs appears to be childhood disintegrative disorder (CDD). Four epidemiological surveys reviewed by Fombonne (2002) reported prevalence rates from 1.1 to 6.4 per 100,000; this yielded a pooled estimate of 1.7 per 100,000. This makes CDD 60 times less common than autism, assuming a prevalence of autism of 10 per 100,000.

All these conditions are more common in boys than girls by a factor of at least 3.

Causes

Genetic factors certainly play a part in the causation of many, perhaps all, cases of autism. The concordance rate for monozygotic (that is, 'identical') twins is higher than that for dizygotic (nonidentical) twins, but the precise genetic mechanisms involved are unclear. Susceptibility to autism is probably multifactorial, though it may be that as few as three genes are involved (Bailey *et al.*, 1996).

What other causal factors are involved? Many have been suggested, but none has been conclusively proved to play a part. Some of these were reviewed by Berney (2000). They range from fragile X syndrome to combined measles, mumps and rubella vaccine, but probably neither of these is a risk factor. When Leo Kanner (1943, 1944) originally described 'early infantile autism', he thought that it might be due to rearing by emotionally cold and distant parents, but that theory has long since been discarded. Nevertheless the way these children are reared is not irrelevant: autistic children tend to withdraw into their own worlds, and those caring for them may either accept this, or take active steps to counter it.

Immunological theories have been proposed, as has the idea that autism arises from the early, long-term overload of the central nervous system by opioids (see Berney, 2000, page 23).

Although environmental influences are involved it is clear that autism is an organic condition, rather than one that is psychologically caused. Abnormalities of brain function and/or structure certainly exist in these children, but we do not at present know precisely what these are. Research findings have been varied and inconsistent. Berney (2000) summarizes some of the theories that have been proposed.

Autism

Autistic children have problems with:

— Social interaction
— Communication
— Behaviour
— Cognitive function

The *onset* of autistic symptoms is within the first three years of life. Sometimes there is reported to have been a period of normal development, even with the acquisition of some spoken words, followed by regression and, often, loss of any speech that has been acquired; but in many cases the condition appears to have been present from birth.

Social interaction

There are impairments in reciprocal social interaction. Autistic subjects do not respond to socio-emotional cues as other individuals do. They fail to react as others do to people's emotions, and they do not modulate their behaviour according to the social context. The parents of a 14-year-old boy made a practice of teaching their son everything he would have to do when he was due to go to a party or other social event. All would go well as long as they didn't miss a step, or something unforeseen did not happen, but their son could never figure out what was the appropriate behaviour if he had not been rehearsed in advance.

Autistic children seem unable to 'read' their environment in the way that most of us do. They also lack the capacity for empathy with others. There is often *gaze avoidance,* the failure to make eye-to-eye contact with people.

Some parents of autistic children report that their children were unresponsive infants who did not seem to want to be cuddled or kissed. The infants may have failed to assume the posture appropriate for being picked up or nursed. The social smile may have appeared late, and these children are typically slow to distinguish between parents and strangers, approaching either without discriminating between them. These children often appear more interested in specific features of people, such as their spectacles, their facial contours or their ears, than with individuals as persons. *Indicated behaviours,* such as drawing people's attention to things by showing them or pointing to them, or alternately looking at objects and then making eye contact with another person, occur less often than in other children at similar developmental levels (Mundy *et al.,* 1986).

Communication

Both verbal and non-verbal language development is delayed. Not only do these children fail to develop normal, or sometimes any, speech, but they also fail to communicate effectively by gesture, body movement or facial expression. They differ in this respect from children with development language disorders (see Chapter 12), who often point to what they want, pull people towards things and make their wishes known in other non-verbal ways.

When autistic children do develop speech, they usually fail to use it to communicate socially in the usual way. Instead they may exhibit *echolalia*, the repeating of words or phrases spoken by others. These are used out of context and inappropriately. The echolalia may be immediate or delayed. If delayed, the words may come out of the blue much later, so that what they say seems like nonsense. Some autistic children acquire a few stock phrases that they repeat in parrot fashion, regardless of what is going on around them. Their speech tends to be stilted and monotonous, without the intonations and inflexions used by non-autistic children.

Behavioural abnormalities

The behaviour of autistic children is characterized by rigidity, stereotypies and inflexibility. The range of their behaviours is limited. As the ICD-10 manual puts it, they tend 'to impose rigidity and routine on a wide range of aspects of day to day functioning'. Some autistic children get upset by minor changes of routine, the moving of furniture in their house, having to wear different clothes, or even a change in the order in which books are placed in a bookcase. Although they can often be taught new skills, they have difficulty generalizing these to other situations or tasks.

The play of autistic children is generally stereotyped and repetitive. Typically it is neither symbolic nor imaginative; toys are rarely used as the objects they represent. Thus an autistic child may use a toy telephone to bang on the floor or to swing to and fro on the end of its cord, but will probably not imitate adults' use of a telephone by speaking into the mouthpiece.

A word of caution is in order here because non-autistic retarded children also tend to lack symbolic play, though this is usually not as marked as in autistic children, so its discriminative value is limited.

Other behaviours often displayed by autistic children include checking and touching rituals, always dressing in a particular way, rocking, twirling, head banging, and other repetitive acts. However these are not confined to autistic children and may be observed in non-autistic retarded children and in those with seriously impaired hearing or vision.

Other nonspecific abnormalities of behaviour encountered in autistic children include overactivity, disruptive behaviour and outbursts of temper, which may occur for little or no obvious reason. Overactivity may alternate with underactivity. Self-damaging behaviours such as head banging and biting the arms, wrists or other body parts may occur. Other common symptoms are sleep disturbances, apparently irrational fears and phobias, wetting and/or soiling, and impulsive acts.

Cognitive abnormalities

A majority, but not all, autistic children are mentally retarded, but in all of them, whether retarded or not, there is an abnormal pattern of cognitive functioning. Memory may be excellent—indeed in some areas it may be phenomenal—and visuospatial tasks may be well performed, but these children are poor at symbolization, understanding abstract ideas and grasping theoretical concepts. They may be pre-occupied with things like train or bus timetables, or the different models of cars or aeroplanes. One 11-year-old boy knew the numbers of all the main highway routes in the United Kingdom. Having spent many hours poring over maps, he was able, when asked, instantly to list the roads one needed to travel from any U.K. destination to any other. Abstract and creative thought, however, were beyond him.

Recent years have seen much interest in the nature of the cognitive difficulties of autistic children and those with other forms of PDD. Three theories have been proposed (Serra *et al.*, 2002):

—*Theory of mind:* This assumes that the inability to attribute mental states such as thoughts, intentions and emotions to others, so that one can use this to predict and explain the behaviours of other people, is the basic problem.

—*Central coherence theory:* This assumes that autistic subjects have 'weak central coherence', so that their cognitive style is 'biased towards local rather than global information processing'. This causes autistic individuals to focus on the constituent parts rather than on the meaning of information.

—*Executive dysfunction theory:* As Serra and colleagues (2002) put it, 'execution function covers a range of higher-level capacities necessary for the control of action, especially in novel contexts'.

The relative importance of these theories is currently the subject of discussion and research.

Atypical autism

This term, according to ICD-10, is to be used when children display many autistic features but do not exhibit the full picture as defined in ICD-10, which requires abnormal functioning in the first three areas discussed above. According to ICD-10, atypical autism is seen most often in profoundly retarded individuals whose 'very low level of functioning provides little scope for exhibition of the specific deviant behaviours required for the diagnosis of autism'. It may also occur in individuals with a severe developmental disorder of receptive language.

In DSM-IV-TR 'atypical autism' is included as a 'pervasive developmental disorder not otherwise specified'. The term is to be used for 'presentations that do not meet the criteria for autistic disorder because of late age of onset, atypical symptomatology, or subthreshold symptomatology, or all of these'.

Asperger's disorder (AD)

Asperger was a Viennese paediatrician who, in 1944, described what he called 'autistic psychopathy of childhood'. The disorder has some features in common with autism, with two notable exceptions: there is no serious delay in language development, and most children with AD are of average or higher intelligence. These children are however aloof, distant and lacking in empathy with others.

The DSM-IV-TR criteria, which are somewhat different from what Asperger described, have three main requirements for this diagnosis:

— Qualitative impairment in social interaction
— Restricted and stereotyped patterns of behaviour, interests and activities
— Clinically significant impairment in social, occupational or other important areas of functioning

To meet DSM-IV-TR criteria there must be at least two of the following four features listed in paragraph 1:

— Impaired use of eye-to-eye gaze, facial expression, body postures and gestures to regulate social interaction
— Failure to develop peer relationships such as would be appropriate at the child's developmental level
— A lack of spontaneous seeking to share enjoyment, interests and achievements with others
— Lack of social or emotional reciprocity

DSM-IV-TR also requires that at least one of the following behaviours listed in paragraph 2 must be present:

— Pre-occupation with one or more stereotyped and restricted patterns of interest that is abnormal in intensity or focus
— Apparently inflexible adherence to specific, nonfunctional routines or rituals
— Stereotyped and repetitive motor mannerisms (e.g. hand flapping, finger flapping or twisting, and complex whole-body movements
— Excessive pre-occupation with parts of objects

Although these criteria are to some extent arbitrary, they give a general idea of the behaviours seen in these children.

AD is more common in boys than in girls, male:female ratios as high as 9 or 10 often being quoted. Referral usually occurs later than with autistic disorders. It often arises from the difficulty these children often have in adjusting to school environments. Because of the stress that school presents to them as a result of their difficulty in relating to others and often inappropriate behaviour, they may develop secondary problems such as school refusal, temper tantrums and suicide threats. These children are often clumsy, another feature that distinguishes them from autistic children, who usually are not—indeed autistic children are often remarkably agile.

Is AD simply a variant of autism? Recent years have seen the term *high-functioning autism* (HFA) come into use. Is AD simply a milder form of autism? This has been the subject of discussion and debate. The issue is addressed by, among many others, Ozonoff and colleagues (2000), who conclude that 'very similar cognitive profiles and current behavioural presentations suggest that Asperger syndrome is on the same spectrum as other autistic syndromes and differs primarily in degree of impairment'. Nevertheless they caution us not to 'prematurely discard the Asperger syndrome label'. Whether or not AD and HFA are two terms for the same condition is also discussed by Blacher *et al.* (2003), who review recent literature that addresses this issue. At present there is no consensus on the subject. However HFA does not appear as a diagnostic category in either DSM-IV-TR or ICD-10.

The book *Asperger's Syndrome* (Klin *et al.,* 2000) takes a wide-ranging look at Asperger's and related disorders, and has contributions from many experts in the field. A noteworthy feature is the inclusion of four essays by parents of children with AD. These bring the syndrome to life in a way in which the dry list of symptoms in DSM-IV-TR does not.

Rett's syndrome (ICD-10) or disorder (DSM-IV-TR)

First described by Rett in 1966, this condition is now known to be due to mutations in the gene known as MECP2. It occurs almost exclusively in girls. Early development appears normal, but, starting usually between ages 7 and 24 months, there is gradual loss of manual dexterity and speech. These children often display 'autistic' features such as impairment in social interaction and language, and stereotypies such as hand wringing. Feeding difficulties increase into middle childhood but then reach a plateau. Although cognitive and language skills are limited, they do not usually deteriorate subsequently. Growth is poor, and by adulthood fixed joint deformities and scoliosis are almost invariably present. Cass and colleagues (2003) describe the development of symptoms in a group of 87 female subjects aged 2 years 1 month to 44 years 10 months. They point out that this is not a progressive degenerative condition.

The mutations in the MECP2 gene seen in females also occur in males, but unless such individual have an extra X chromosome, or the mutation arises as a somatic mosaicism (that is, it does not involve all cells), the typical syndrome is not seen. Instead there are a variety of other severe neurological symptoms (Moog *et al.,* 2003).

Although children with Rett's disorder often show some autistic features, this syndrome is quite different from other pervasive developments in its aetiology, clinical picture and progression. It should perhaps be regarded as a neurological rather than a psychiatric disorder.

Childhood disintegrative disorder

This disorder is recognized by both ICD-10 and DSM-IV-TR. Development is normal up to at least 2 years of age. There is then a loss of previously acquired skills, with regression in, or loss of, language, and regression in the level of play, social skills and adaptive behaviour. There may be loss of bowel or bladder control. There is usually a loss of interest in the environment, together with stereotyped, repetitive movements and autistic-like impairment of social interactions. A plateau state is usually eventually reached, and there may subsequently be some limited improvement. This is an ill-understood condition and, as with Rett's disorder, its classification as a pervasive development disorder is open to question (see Malhotra & Gupta, 2002).

Other pervasive developmental disorders

Both ICD-10 and DSM-IV-TR have 'residual' categories for disorders that have features in common with the various disorders discussed above but that do not fully meet the listed criteria for any of them. This reflects the wide range of disorders we are dealing with and, with their aetiology incompletely understood, uncertainty about how they should be classified. DSM-IV-TR lists *pervasive developmental disorder not otherwise specified (including atypical autism).* ICD-10 has categories for *other* and *unspecified* pervasive developmental disorders.

Non-verbal learning difficulties (NLDs)

NLD does not appear in either DSM-IV-TR or ICD-10, but it has been the subject of attention since the early 1990s (Casey *et al.,* 1991; Casey & Rourke, 1992). It has many features of Asperger's disorder, but whether these are distinct entities is unclear.

According to Rourke and Tsatsanis (2000, pages 235–236), the main characteristics of NLD are:

— Bilateral tactile-perceptual deficits, usually more marked on the left side of the body
— Bilateral psychomotor coordination deficiencies, often more marked on the left side of the body
— Outstanding deficiencies in visual-spatial-organizational abilities
— Extreme difficulty in adapting to novel and otherwise complex situations, with an overreliance on prosaic, rote (and therefore often inappropriate) behaviours
— Marked deficits in non-verbal problem solving, concept formation, hypothesis testing, and the capacity to benefit from positive and negative feedback of information in novel and other complex situations
— Distorted sense of time, reflected in poor estimation of elapsed time during common activities, and poor estimation of time of day
— Well-developed rote verbal capacities, especially excellent rote verbal memory skills
— Much verbosity of a repetitive, straightforward, rote nature
— Marked relative deficiencies in mechanical arithmetic, compared to good reading, that is, word recognition, and spelling skills

— Significant deficits in social perception, social judgement, and social interaction skills

NLD is another part of the puzzle that the conditions discussed in this chapter present. We are probably dealing with various combinations of neuropsychological deficits that may not be unique, specific disorders but rather varied, often overlapping patterns of disability.

Treatment

We have no treatments that can 'cure' these disorders. We are dealing with serious disorders of the development of a variety of functions. Ultimately we need to discover how to prevent development going awry, as it does in all the disorders discussed, but we are a long way from being able to do this. Treatment is therefore symptomatic and, to some extent, pragmatic. Educational and behavioural methods are usually the mainstays of treatment.

The management and treatment of children with all forms of PDD must be preceded by a thorough assessment of the nature of the developmental delays and problems each child has. Once this has been accomplished, any of the following measures may be required:

— For self-isolation—planned periods of interaction. Children with any of the forms of PDD will, if left on their own, become ever more isolated.
— For impaired understanding—simplified communication and individual teaching.
— For specific cognitive deficits—learning tasks that capitalize on the skills the child does possess, while helping develop those that are weak.
— For lack of initiative—a more structured and direct teaching approach than is used with normal children.
— For lack of social skills—intensive teaching, which often involves the use of behaviour modification techniques.

Learning usually has to be broken down into small steps, individualized to meet each child's needs. Teaching should take place in structured, individualized situations. Group methods are seldom appropriate.

The treatment team

A team approach is generally to be desired. Teams may be made up of behaviour therapists, teachers, speech/language therapists, psychiatrists, psychologists, occupational therapists and parents. The latter are of particular importance. Many parents of PDD children are bright, able, motivated people who, once they have been shown how to use behaviour modification and other teaching techniques, can continue to use them at home. The result is that the children receive much more therapy than what can be carried out in a clinic or special school.

In many communities there are special schools, or school classes, dedicated to the treatment and teaching of these children. Some residential facilities also exist but these should be used sparingly.

Other treatment possibilities

Medication

This may help ameliorate some of the symptoms of PDD. Fisman (2002) reviewed the various drugs that may be helpful. She recommends the treatment of target symptoms, based on the empirical evidence for the value of the drugs for specific symptoms. She provides a table listing ten drugs, and two classes of drugs (mood stabilizers and stimulants) with the target symptoms for which they are likely to be of benefit.

In summary, the drugs Fisman (2002) considered include the following, with the target symptoms for which there is evidence of definite benefit:

Selective serotonin uptake inhibitors (SSRIs)
The medications listed in Table 11.1 may also ameliorate a number of other symptoms. The most generally useful may be risperidone.

Other drugs that may be of benefit include clomipramine, buspirone, propranolol, clonidine and naltrexone. These are less generally useful but may be helpful in certain cases. [For more information, see Fisman (2002).]

All these drugs have the potential to cause side effects, some of them serious. They should be used by, or under the supervision of, a specialist in this area.

Kwok (2003) reviews the place of psychopharmacology in ASD. He suggests that, of the antipsychotic drugs currently available, risperidone and olanzapine may best combine effectiveness in producing symptomatic improvement with the fewest side effects. He also reviews the use of SSRIs, which often help in reducing repetitive behaviours, aggression and, possibly, self-injurious behaviours, while having a generally favourable side-effect profile. However he points out that medications should always be part of a comprehensive treatment plan, which should include special education, behavioural modification, occupational therapy and training in social and communication skills; and that there are no drugs that 'cure' these disorders, only some that may lead to improvement of certain target symptoms.

Table 11.1   Drugs for target symptoms

Fluoxetine	Ritualistic and other behaviours
Fluvoxamine	such as insistence on sameness
Sertraline	Sertraline may help in difficulty with transitions
Haloperidol	Aggression, hyperactivity, irritability, behaviours as above
Risperidone	Aggression, hyperactivity, irritability

Support for families

Rearing a child with PDD, and especially one with severe autistic symptoms, is usually stressful for parents and other caregivers. Regular emotional support with, when necessary, the provision of short-term respite care may enable parents to continue to provide care for their child. Without such support, this may prove impossible.

Outcome

Autism

Some autistic children show a measure of improvement at around ages 4 to 6, and active treatment along the lines set out above often helps. The higher the level of function in the early years, the better are the prospects. An average or higher non-verbal IQ and some speech at age 5 are hopeful signs. Absent speech and severely retarded development at this age usually mean that the prognosis is poor. These are chronic, lifelong conditions, and about two-thirds of all children with autism remain severely handicapped in adult life.

Some autistic children are able to remain in the care of their families into adolescence, even early adult life, but many are eventually admitted to institutions—usually when their families can no longer care for them. Fewer than one-fifth remain in the community long term, and they usually require sheltered and supported living situations. About 50% of autistic children acquire some useful speech, but few achieve normal language skills. Epilepsy develops in about one-fifth of autistic children, often during adolescence.

Rumsey and colleagues (1985) reported a detailed study of 14 men, mean age 28, with well-documented histories of autism. Half had had the diagnosis made by Leo Kanner. Social relationship difficulties, concrete thinking and stereotyped, repetitive behaviours were common. Language skills ranged 'from normal to complete mutism'. But this was not a typical group of autistic subjects, 12 having non-verbal IQs in the average range. It does show, though, that at least some of these people achieve some level of adaptive functioning in the community.

Asperger's disorder (AD)

The outlook for children with AD is generally better than it is for autistic subjects. Many complete secondary school, and some go on to further education. Large-scale, systematic follow-up data are lacking, but it seems that, in the long term, there is usually no worsening of the basic functional impairments that these individuals suffer. Tantum (2000, page 397) suggests that subjects with AD may even develop greater expressiveness over time, and that less 'extreme preservation of sameness, growing intersubjectivity and empathy' may be observed in some cases.

Further information is available in Howlin's (2000) review of what is known about the outcome in adult life for more able individuals within the autistic spectrum. She considers the findings of studies reporting long-term outcome in children with AD and *high-functioning autism.*

Some AD subjects marry and have families, but interpersonal relationships tend to be difficult. Many do lead productive lives. They do better in jobs that do not require well-developed interpersonal skills, such as telephone operators, warehouse inventory clerks, and computer programmers, operators or repairers.

Other pervasive developmental disorders

There are even fewer data on the outcome in PDD-NOS and other less well-defined clinical entities. Much seems to depend on the severity of the functional impairment, especially language and social relationship skills.

Chapter 12

Specific Disorders of Development

This chapter deals with disorders of development in specific areas of functioning, as opposed to the more general delays encountered in the disorders discussed in the preceding chapter.

ICD-10 lists specific disorders of development in four subgroups:

(1) Specific disorders of speech and language

- — Specific speech articulation disorder
- — Expressive language disorder
- — Receptive language disorder
- — Acquired aphasia with epilepsy
- — Other developmental disorders of speech and language
- — Developmental disorder of speech and language, unspecified

(2) Specific developmental disorders of scholastic skills

- — Specific reading disorder
- — Specific spelling disorder
- — Specific disorder of arithmetical skills
- — Mixed disorder of scholastic skills
- — Other developmental disorder of scholastic skills
- — Developmental disorder of scholastic skills, unspecified

(3) Specific developmental disorder of motor function
(4) Mixed specific developmental disorders

DSM-IV-TR divides these disorders up rather differently, but covers similar ground:

(1) Learning disorders

- — Reading disorder
- — Mathematics disorder
- — Disorder of written expression
- — Learning disorder not otherwise specified

(2) Motor skills disorder

— Developmental coordination disorder

(3) Communication disorders

— Expressive language disorder
— Mixed receptive-expressive language disorder
— Phonological disorder
— Stuttering
— Communication disorder not otherwise specified

These disorders become evident during infancy or childhood. The impairment or delay of the various functions listed is strongly related to the biological maturation of the central nervous system. These disorders have a steady course, without remissions or relapses. All occur more frequently in boys than in girls.

Speech and language problems (ICD-10) and communication disorders (DSM-IV-TR)

Children acquire language at different rates, and deciding when this process is so much delayed as to constitute a disorder is arbitrary. Extreme cases present no difficulty, but the line between 'normal variation' and 'delay' is vague.

In the case of expressive language disorder, DSM-IV-TR requires the child's scores on standardized measures of expressive language should be 'substantially below those obtained from standardized measures of both non-verbal and receptive language development'. As with many DSM definitions, we are left to make our own judgement as to what 'substantially below' means. ICD-10 suggests that a delay that falls 'outside the limits of two standard deviations may be considered abnormal', but we should probably take into account the child's general level of cognitive development.

For practical clinical purposes, it is important to be aware that there is a continuum ranging from rapid to slow language development, and to consider where each child we see is on that continuum. This is of more practical value than deciding whether the child is suffering from a specific disorder as arbitrarily defined in a classification manual.

ICD-10 suggests that, in assessing, the following should be assessed:

— The *severity* of the delay—'two standard deviations' being a guideline.

— The *course* of the child's language development. Has language development been pursuing its normal course, or something close to it, but is delayed? Or is development not just slow but accompanied by an abnormal language *pattern*?

— *Associated problems.* If language delay, or a history of late speech development, is accompanied by such other problems as scholastic difficulties, relationship difficulties and/or emotional or behavioural difficulties, the delay may be more than just a normal variation.

In the practice of child psychiatry, language disorders are important because of their association with other problems. The child whose language development is delayed but who is otherwise developing normally—and there are many such children—is not a psychiatric concern. Most such children will develop normal language skills in due course, with or without help from speech and language therapists. However psychiatrists also encounter children in whom language problems are part of a complex pattern of difficulties affecting school progress, relationships, self-esteem, behaviour and their emotional state. It is therefore essential to be aware that a developmental language disorder may be a contributing factor in other, often complex, problems.

Reading and spelling problems

Delay in learning to read, which is often accompanied by spelling problems, is common among boys referred for psychiatric attention. It is less common in girls. Boy:girl ratios from about 3 to 7 have been found in population studies. It is usual to take measured intelligence into account in determining who is suffering from reading delay, though there is only a moderate correlation between measured IQ and reading (Rutter & Rutter, 1993).

Causes and associations of language, reading and spelling disorders

The preponderance of boys with these disorders suggests that there is a genetic contribution to their aetiology. Low birth weight, hypoxia around the time of birth, and other insults to the developing brain may also contribute.

Reading and spelling problems often occur in children whose language development has been delayed. Environmental factors, such as lack of verbal stimulation in the home and the provision of substandard education in school, may also play their part. Lack of phonological skills—the ability to associate particular sounds with particular letters—may be important in the aetiology of spelling problems.

Reading problems have long been known to be associated with antisocial behaviour. It often seems that a circular process is occurring, children who have trouble reading becoming frustrated and angry, often developing low self-esteem, so that they act out with antisocial behaviour; on the other hand, angry and rebellious children may act out by refusing to apply themselves in school, or even by nonattendance, so that they fail to acquire reading skills. Common factors may also contribute to both the reading problems and the antisocial behaviour.

Reading and other learning problems are found with increased frequency (compared to the normal population) in other members of the families of some children with pervasive developmental disorders. These family members may possess some, but not all, of the genes responsible for the more severe disorders afflicting their families.

Clinical management

While the assessment and treatment of children with learning disorders are the province of the educational psychologist and teacher, the proper mental health assessment of children must include a careful enquiry for evidence of learning problems and academic delay. Contact with children's teachers, and sometimes visits to schools, may be necessary.

Progressive failure at school is damaging to children's self-esteem and often has adverse emotional, behavioural and social consequences. In technologically advanced societies the lack of reading skills is a major handicap. The detection and remediation of these and other learning difficulties are often an important part of the management of children with other psychiatric disorders. If such other disorders are not present when the children first come to professional attention, there is a good chance they will develop later if the children are not given the help they need when their learning difficulties first appear.

Problems with mathematics

Specific disorder of arithmetical skills (ICD-10) and *mathematics disorder* (DSM-IV-TR) are characterized by specific impairment of the skills concerned, such as cannot be explained by the child's level of general intelligence or by what ICD-10 calls 'grossly inadequate schooling'. The skills referred to are the basic ones of addition, subtraction, multiplication and division. If the difficulties are due to the direct effects of impaired vision, hearing or neurological disorders, they should not be included under these diagnostic headings. This applies also to the other learning difficulties discussed previously.

Developmental disorders of motor function

These are variously known as *specific disorders of motor function* (ICD-10), *developmental coordination disorder* (DSM-IV-TR), *the clumsy child syndrome*, and *developmental dyspraxia*. The central feature is serious impairment of the development of motor coordination, which cannot be explained as an aspect of generally retarded development. In addition, the condition should not be part of any other specific congenital or acquired neurological disorder. There is often some associated impairment of the performance of visuospatial tasks.

Features of this disorder include:

— Late development of motor skills such as dressing, feeding and walking
— Difficulty with writing, drawing and copying
— Poor performance at ball games and other activities requiring good motor coordination, such as handicrafts
— Normal performance on verbal tests and tasks

— The ability to carry out all the usual voluntary movements, while the ability to coordinate these movements to perform many tasks is deficient
— Difficulties in school arising out of the inability to write legibly and at normal speed

These children are sometimes thought to be intellectually dull because of their difficulty in writing down what they know. They may present at psychiatric clinics or offices with secondary disorders, or because their disability has not been recognized and they are thought to have an emotional/behavioural problem rather than a developmental/neurological one. The diagnosis can be confirmed by:

— Careful history taking.
— Asking the child to write and draw and comparing the results with the child's verbal productions, which will be at a much higher level.
— Psychological testing of the child's verbal and non-verbal skills. This will provide further confirmation of the diagnosis and may pinpoint the subject's abilities and disabilities more precisely.

Treatment may involve:

— Explaining the nature of the disability, with emphasis that no one is to blame, to child, family and teachers.
— Relieving these children of being required to carry out tasks that are beyond them.
— Help with the development of motor skills. This can often be provided by an occupational therapist.
— The use of computers. Many of these children can express what they know better by using a keyboard rather than by handwriting. It is nowadays often possible to arrange for these children to answer examination questions by using a computer's word-processing program.
— Capitalizing on these children's strengths in other areas of function.
— Being alert for, and dealing promptly with, secondary emotional disorders, such as anxiety, depression or low self-esteem.

The above measures are equally useful in treating other specific developmental disorders.

Mixed specific developmental disorders

Various combinations of specific developmental disorders occur, and the presence of one does not mean that there are not others. The combination of language, reading and spelling problems is frequently encountered.

Chapter 13

Schizophrenia and Other Psychoses of Childhood

The essential feature of psychotic disorders is altered contact with reality. The psychotic person is attempting to adjust to a subjectively distorted perception of the real world. By contrast, individuals with neurotic/anxiety disorders are responding in morbid ways to their real-life situations.

Establishing whether children are suffering from a psychotic disorder presents several problems because:

— Their limited verbal skills make it difficult for them to describe their subjective experiences.

— Normally developing children usually have a rich and vivid fantasy life, so that determining what is fantasy and what is psychotic delusion is a challenge.

— Related to the above, many young children have 'fantasy friends', a normal phenomenon, but one that may be hard to distinguish from hallucinatory experiences.

— The onset of psychoses in childhood is gradual, and it may be several years before a clear picture of a psychotic disorder is manifest. Schaeffer and Ross (2002) reviewed the early histories of 17 children who later received diagnoses of childhood-onset schizophrenia (COS) or schizoaffective disorder (COSAD). The initial symptoms ranged from developmental delay/learning disability, through oppositional/aggressive behaviour and 'ADHD-type symptoms' to various social and mood-related symptoms. Many other diagnoses were made before the true diagnosis emerged, and many medications had been prescribed that were probably not helpful. The mean age of appearance of psychotic symptoms was 8.6 ± 2.9 years, and the average age of first diagnosis of COS or COSAD was 10.5 ± 2.6 years.

Childhood-onset schizophrenia

Neither DSM-IV-TR nor ICD-10 has separate criteria for COS. The criteria listed for adult patients are to be used also for children, but they are more difficult to apply to child subjects for the reasons listed above. Nowadays it is generally accepted that COS and autistic disorders are distinct conditions.

Prevalence

The prevalence of schizophrenia in the general population is of the order of 2% to 3%, but in only a small minority is the onset during childhood. Remschmidt and colleagues (1994) estimated that in only 0.1% to 1% of cases is the onset before age 10, with 4% starting before age 15. Late adolescence is however a common age period for the onset of these disorders. Schaeffer and Ross (2002), in their retrospectively studied series of 17 early-onset cases of COS and COSAD, mention one child who developed psychotic symptoms at age 2, but in none of the others were psychotic symptoms reported before age 5.

Causes

The causes of COS, and indeed of schizophrenia generally, are not fully understood. Genetic factors play a part and Kumra and colleagues (2001) suggest that several genes, each having small effects, may interact to increase the risk for schizophrenia. Although environmental factors also probably play a part, their precise role is not known. Among the factors that have been suggested as favouring the development of COS are high levels of 'communication deviance' (vague, ambiguous, wandering, illogical and idiosyncratic language) (Wynne, 1981) and high levels of 'expressed emotion' in the families (Leff & Vaughn, 1985). The latter increase the risk of relapse in adult patients discharged after treatment in hospital. Whether they have a role in the causation of COS is not known.

The current consensus is that the causes of schizophrenia are basically biological. Many neurological and neurophysiological abnormalities have been found in patients with schizophrenia, but these are not consistent and vary from patient to patient. Kumra and colleagues (2001) have reviewed them.

Clinical picture

The following is a summary of the symptoms as specified in DSM-IV-TR and ICD-10:

Delusions

Delusions are false beliefs held despite evidence to the contrary, such as would be accepted by others. The delusions of schizophrenic patients may include delusions of persecution by others (paranoid delusions); delusions of reference (for example that items in newspapers, advertisements, or on television refer to oneself); the belief that thoughts are being put into, or withdrawn from or broadcast from, inside one's head ('thought insertion, withdrawal or broadcasting'); and the belief that one's thoughts are controlled by some external force. 'Delusional perceptions' arise fully fledged on the basis of a genuine perception that would be regarded as commonplace by others.

Hallucinations

These occur in clear consciousness and are most often auditory. They may consist of voices repeating the subject's thoughts out loud or anticipating them; two or more hallucinatory voices may be discussing or arguing about the patient; or voices may comment on the subject's thoughts or behaviour. They may tell the subject to do things that are out of character, even to commit violent acts.

Thought disorder

Associations are loosened so that the subject's thoughts move from one subject to another apparently unrelated or distantly related one. This process may resemble the 'knight's move' in chess. Although these patients may talk a lot, it is often hard to grasp what they are saying. Poverty of thought—the existence of little content even though many words may be spoken—is seen in later-onset patients, but is less common, or absent, in COS (Caplan *et al.*, 2000). In severe cases, talk may be completely incoherent. Caplan and colleagues (2000) report an in-depth study of thought disorder in children with COS, using the Formal Thought Disorder Rating Scale (K-FTDS) (Caplan *et al.*, 1989). They found the K-FTDS to be a useful diagnostic instrument.

Disorders of affect

The schizophrenic subject's emotional reactions are often blunted, flattened or inappropriate. Painful experiences may be described with a smile, and there may be sudden, seemingly inexplicable changes of mood.

Volitional disorders

Schizophrenic subjects may feel that their impulses, acts and emotions are under external control. They may say they feel like robots, or as if they have been hypnotized. Lack of interest and drive, with failure to initiate activities or follow them through, often leads to a falling off in school or work performance. In extreme cases catatonia—the assumption of a rigid, unmoving posture—may occur, though it is rare in childhood.

Other features

These may include:

- Reduced 'cohesion', such as the use of conjunctions to connect contiguous clauses; 'referential cohesion' (pronouns, demonstratives and articles that refer to people or objects in the preceding text); and 'lexical cohesion' (the use of word repetition, synonyms and antonyms that can link ideas across sentences (Caplan *et al.*, 1992)
- Social isolation
- Preoccupation with fantasy, delusional or illogical ideas
- Loss of a sense of identity
- Puzzlement about one's surroundings

The most common initial presenting symptoms (Russell *et al.*, 1989) are auditory hallucinations (80% in Russell's series of 35 children with COS), delusions (63%) and thought disorder (40%).

The American Academy of Child and Adolescent Psychiatry (AACAP) (2001) has published 'practice parameters' for 'early onset schizophrenia'. Appearing as a supplement to the July 2001 issue of the Academy's journal, the 'parameters' offer detailed recommendations for all aspects of the assessment and management of schizophrenia in children and adolescents.

Precursors of schizophrenia

These children have usually presented various symptoms and behavioural abnormalities well before they have met the diagnostic criteria for COS. In other words the onset is insidious, so prompt, early diagnosis is a major challenge. Other diagnoses have almost invariably been made during this prodromal period. In Schaeffer and Ross's (2002) series of 17 COS subjects, diagnoses that had been made in two or more cases were:

— Pervasive developmental delay/ learning disability
— ADHD/ADD
— Bipolar mood disorder
— Depression
— Obsessive-compulsive disorder
— Generalized anxiety disorder

Nine other diagnoses were made in one child only. Clearly the range of initial symptoms is wide.

How may the chances of diagnosis be improved? There is no substitute for a careful, detailed clinical assessment, perhaps using also the aforementioned K-FTDS. A history of schizophrenia or another major psychotic condition in a close relative should raise the index of suspicion. When it seems possible that a child may have COS, referral to a specialist child psychiatry clinic or consultant is much to be desired. This is a rare disorder and many 'front-line' child mental health professionals may never have seen a case before; indeed some may never see one in their entire professional career.

Treatment

This may be considered under the following headings:

— The use of antipsychotic drugs
— Psychosocial measures
— Educational measures
— Long-term management

Antipsychotic drugs

The various drugs that have been shown to be effective in adult schizophrenia appear also to be effective in children and adolescents, though there has been much less research into their use in the latter age groups.

The choice lies between first-generation or 'typical' antipsychotics and drugs in the newer or 'atypical' group.

First-generation or 'typical' antipsychotics include:

— Chlorpromazine
— Thioridazine
— Perphenazine
— Loxapine
— Haloperidol

Second-generation or 'atypical' antipsychotics include:

— Risperidone
— Olanzapine
— Quetiapine

These drugs are also referred to as 'neuroleptics'. The 'typical' group tend to be more effective for 'positive' symptoms such as hallucinations and delusions than for 'negative' symptoms such as flat affect and social withdrawal. They also tend to cause more side effects. The 'atypical' drugs are generally more effective for 'negative' symptoms than the 'typical' group. They are on the whole less prone to cause troublesome side effects, although clozapine, one of the most effective, can cause both epileptic seizures and agranulocytosis; it is therefore not recommended as a first-line treatment. However none of these drugs is without side effects, and any of these compounds may cause 'neuroleptic malignant syndrome'. The recommended doses and main side effects for the more widely used of these drugs are to be found in Chapter 22.

The American Academy of Child and Adolescent Psychiatry's (2001) 'practice parameters' include recommendations for the use of these drugs. Marriage (2002) provides a comprehensive review of all aspects of the drug treatment of COS. He points out that it is not, with the current state of our knowledge, possible to predict the response of particular patients to any of these drugs, partly because there is enormous individual variability in susceptibility to side effects.

The pharmacological treatment of COS should be carried out by, or under the supervision of, a specialist in this area of practice.

Psychosocial measures
A broad approach to treatment is required. Stress in the family, other environmental or psychological stress factors, substance abuse problems and other challenges that the child and/or family may face must be addressed. Traditional psychotherapy is not effective, but cognitive behavioural methods and social skills training can be (Heinssen *et al.*, 2000). The provision of a calm family environment, with suitable control of expressed emotion (Leff & Vaughn, 1985), is desirable, and communication problems in the family should be addressed. Family or group therapy may be helpful. Day-treatment programs are sometimes helpful, and in acute phases of the

condition inpatient admission, ideally in a unit designed to treat patients in the individual's age group, may be needed.

Educational measures
Many, if not most, children with COS require special educational provisions. Most do not do well in regular classroom settings. They are usually best taught in a small class setting by staff trained to work with emotionally disturbed young people, and using a curriculum tailored to their level of cognitive functioning.

Long-term management
COS is a long-term, usually chronic disorder. It is rarely appropriate to discharge these subjects from psychiatric care and regular review. Both long-term support and planning and close monitoring of progress, medication side effects, and social and educational progress by a multidisciplinary team are required. Each child should have an identified therapist who is responsible for coordinating the work of the team in the long term.

Outcome

COS is a serious, usually chronic disorder requiring long-term treatment. Although a few of these children can remain well without continuing medication, most require drug treatment long term. However response to well-planned and implemented treatment programs is sometimes gratifying, though in most cases there are continuing disabilities. The earlier the onset, the more likely it is that psychological and emotional development will be stunted or distorted. When the onset is acute, the outcome tends to be better. The condition often continues through adolescence into adult life, though partial or complete remission may occur.

Eggers and Bunk (1997) reported the results of a 42-year follow-up of 44 patients with COS: 25% of the patients were in full remission, 25% were in partial remission, and 50% were still severely affected. COS is often a lifelong illness.

Schizoaffective disorders

In DSM-IV-TR, this term is used for disorders in which there has been an uninterrupted period of illness during which, at some time, there is a major depressive episode, a manic episode, or a mixed episode, concurrent with symptoms that meet the criteria for schizophrenia. It is uncertain how common this condition is in childhood. In some studies these cases are included with other cases of schizophrenia.

Acute and transient psychotic disorders (ICD-10) and brief psychotic disorder (DSM-IV-TR)

These are somewhat ill-defined disorders in which there are psychotic symptoms such as hallucinations, delusions or a limited number of several abnormalities of behaviour, such as gross excitement and overactivity, marked psychomotor retardation, and catatonic behaviour. ICD-10 requires an acute onset (this being defined as a change from a state without psychotic features to a clearly abnormal psychotic state within a period of two weeks or less), and the presence of 'associated acute stress'. It lists several subcategories, defined by the nature of the psychotic symptoms. It states that complete recovery usually occurs within two to three months.

DSM-IV-TR requires the presence of one or more of the following:

— Delusions
— Hallucinations
— Disorganized speech
— Grossly disorganized or catatonic behaviour

DSM-IV-TR requires that the episode should last more than one day and less than one month. This presents clinicians with a dilemma because, if it is taken literally, the diagnosis cannot be made until the symptoms have resolved since only then can one know how long this has taken. However DSM-IV-TR acknowledges, in the text relating to this disorder, that brief psychotic conditions lasting one to six months occur in 'developing' countries.

DSM-IV-TR also has subcategories for brief psychotic disorders with and without 'marked stressors'. This contrasts with the ICD-10 requirement that there must be an associated acute stress.

Brief psychotic disorders, however defined, are rare in childhood, and less so in adolescence.

Toxic confusional and delirious states

In these conditions there is diffuse, general impairment of brain function, with a state of delirium or confusion. In delirium, consciousness is clouded and the subject's awareness of the environment is altered. Orientation for time, place and person is impaired. Attention is ill-sustained, and the stream of thought is disordered. There may also be illusions, the misinterpretation of sensory stimuli (for example perceiving an inanimate object as a monster about to attack); bizarre or frightening fantasies; and hallucinations, often visual. In severe cases the subject appears to be completely out of touch with reality.

Confusional states are characterized by milder degrees of disorientation and confusion, without the full picture of delirium.

These conditions may be acute, coming on quite suddenly, or subacute, starting gradually over the course of a few hours. The following are examples of conditions that may be responsible for these states:

— Systemic infections, especially when there is a high fever
— Metabolic disturbances, for example hypoglycaemic reactions in diabetics
— Acute brain injury

— Acute infections of the brain
— Some rare forms of epilepsy
— Accidental or intended drug overdoses
— The use of 'street' drugs (see Chapter 19)

The *treatment* of these conditions is supportive—that is to say the appropriate medical measures are applied—while the underlying cause is addressed.

Chapter 14

Enuresis and Encopresis

Both ICD-10 and DSM-IV-TR include enuresis and encopresis in their listings of child psychiatric disorders, but they are really in that borderline territory where psychiatry and paediatrics meet.

Enuresis

Non-organic enuresis, as ICD-10 calls it, is characterized by 'involuntary voiding of urine, by day and/or by night'. It must be abnormal in relation to the subject's mental age, and it is not due to poor bladder control resulting from a neurological disorder, nor to epilepsy or to a structural abnormality of the urinary tract.

Enuresis (not due to a general medical condition) is defined a little differently in DSM-IV-TR, which allows for the voiding of urine to be either involuntary or intentional, though it is usually involuntary. The chronological age should be at least 5 years or the equivalent developmental level.

Enuresis may be *nocturnal, diurnal* or *both nocturnal and diurnal.* It may also be *primary*, the child having never achieved continence; or *secondary*, the onset being after a period of continence of 3 to 12 months, depending on which of the different definitions that have been proposed is chosen.

Prevalence

DSM-IV-TR quotes a prevalence of enuresis of 5% to 10% in five-year-olds, 3% to 5% among ten-year-olds and about 1% in those aged 15 or older. This is therefore a condition that many children grow out of, usually with no specific treatment. Most studies have found the prevalence of nocturnal enuresis in boys to be greater than that in girls, the boy:girl ratio being about 2:1. Verhulst and colleagues (1985) reported on a study of 2600 children. They found that enuresis was rare in girls after age 11 and in boys after 13.

Diurnal enuresis is less common than night-time wetting and is more common in girls than in boys. It is uncommon after age 8 (DSM-IV-TR).

Causes

The main factor responsible for 'non-organic' enuresis is probably delayed neurological maturation. Genetic factors play a part. DSM-IV-TR states that 75% of enuretic children have a first-degree biological relative who has had the disorder, and the risk of having enuresis is five- to seven-fold greater in the offspring of a parent who has a history of enuresis. The concordance for enuresis is greater in monozygotic twins than in dizygotic twins.

Emotional factors may play a part, especially in daytime wetting. Anxiety about using school or public toilets, or about passing urine in public, leads some children to try to avoid passing urine until they are able to do so in a place where they feel safe. They may then find themselves unable to restrain themselves before they find a 'safe' place. In some children with severe disruptive behaviour disorders, urinating in inappropriate places may be one aspect of generally rebellious behaviour.

Assessment and treatment

The first step is to establish whether there is any neurological, anatomical or endocrinological cause for the enuresis. It is best to start with a thorough assessment by a paediatrician. If no organic condition comes to light, and the case is one of uncomplicated primary nocturnal enuresis, psychiatric involvement is unlikely to be needed. In such cases the wetting is likely to resolve in time, but before it does so it may cause the child distress or at least inconvenience. It may prevent overnight camping events or 'sleepovers' at the homes of friends. It may also become a source of embarrassment or shame. If it is handled inappropriately, secondary emotional problems may arise. Treatment of uncomplicated cases may therefore be indicated. The options are as follows:

(a) Support and reassurance for child and family
The symptom is usually best referred to as a 'delay in learning to control the bladder when asleep' (or 'when excited'), rather than as a serious disease. It is a common problem and is nobody's fault—neither the child's nor the parents'.

(b) Conditioning
This is often a good choice. It involves the use of an *enuresis alarm*. This is a device that wakes the child when he or she starts to pass urine. Many models, marketed by commercial companies, are available. A battery-operated bell or buzzer apparatus is connected by wires to electrodes similar to press fasteners. The child wears underpants or pyjamas, and the two electrodes are pressed together with the material separating them, when the child goes to bed. They are so placed that they will get wet when the child passes urine. The device is switched on and as soon as the child begins to pass urine, the circuit is completed, the bell or buzzer sounds, and the child gets up and passes urine in the toilet. The child is thus conditioned to wake up as soon as the bladder is full. With a well-motivated and cooperative subject, a success rate of 80% or so may be achieved. Commercial alarms all come with detailed instructions for their use.

(c) Medication

This may be helpful. Desmopressin is an analogue of the antidiuretic hormone vasopressin and is probably the drug of first choice for nocturnal enuresis (Schulman *et al.*, 2001; Glazener & Evans, 2002). It is best administered at bedtime by intranasal spray. For children aged 7 or older, the initial dose should be 20 micrograms, increasing to 40 micrograms if the lower dose is not effective. Desmopressin may also be administered by mouth in tablet form. In that case the initial dose should be 200 micrograms, increasing if necessary to 400 micrograms.

Tricyclic antidepressants such as imipramine and amitriptyline, given at bedtime, may be effective. Imipramine should be given in a starting dose of 25 milligrams (mg), increasing if necessary to 50 mg, in children up to age 11; or to 75 mg for children over age 11. If amitriptyline is used, the starting dose for children up to age 10 should be 10 mg, increasing if necessary to 20 mg. For children aged 11 or older, a starting dose of 25 mg and a maximum dose 50 mg are recommended.

Although medication is often effective in the short term, the relapse rate is high. It is advisable to discontinue treatment for at least a week, after three months free of enuresis, but if the enuresis recurs treatment may then be re-instituted. Butler and colleagues (2001) suggest a 'structured withdrawal program' and present evidence that this may reduce relapse rates.

(d) Hypnotherapy

This may be effective (Edwards and van der Spuy, 1985) and may lead to results comparable to the enuresis alarm. Formal trance induction may not be necessary.

Outcome

When enuresis is associated with other psychiatric disorders, such as anxiety or disruptive behaviour disorders, the latter should be tackled first. Improvement in the associated condition is often accompanied by resolution of the enuresis.

Encopresis

Encopresis, or fecal soiling, is the passing of feces in inappropriate places, for example the clothes, in bed or on the floor. In extreme cases, patients may smear feces around the house or in other locations.

DSM-IV-TR requires the behaviour to have occurred at least once a month for at least three months; and the child should be aged at least 4 or, if general development is delayed, at an equivalent level of development. It defines two subtypes:

— With constipation and overflow
— Without constipation and overflow

ICD-10 has less specific criteria and states that this may be a monosymptomatic disorder, or part of a wider disorder, especially an emotional/anxiety disorder or a conduct disorder.

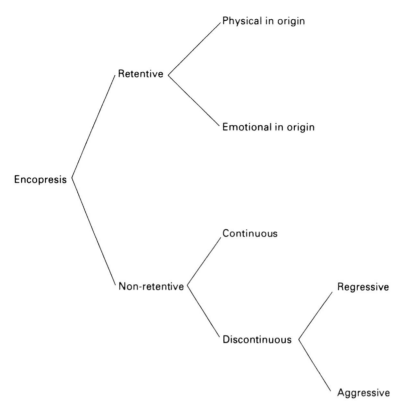

Fig. 14.1   Types of encopresis.

Causes

Figure 14.1 summarizes the various ways in which encopresis may arise.

Encopresis may be retentive or non-retentive, the distinction depending on whether feces have accumulated in the colon and rectum in abnormal amounts.

Retentive encopresis may have physical or emotional causes. Physical causes include anal fissure (a longitudinal fissure in the wall of the anus that can make defecation painful); and Hirschprung's disease, a rare disorder in which the nerve ganglia are congenitally absent from a section of the colon, so that the smooth muscle of this section does not contract properly and feces are not moved on as they should be.

The emotional factors contributing to encopresis are often less clear-cut than the physical ones. In the days when psychodynamic theories were more in vogue than they are nowadays, and when parents tended to start toilet training at an earlier age and to be more coercive than they now usually are, a disturbed parent-child relationship was postulated as a common cause (Anthony, 1957; Pinkerton, 1958). The theory was that early and coercive toilet training by obsessive parents with a high regard for order and cleanliness, for whom achieving toilet training at an early age was a matter of pride, led to rebellion on the part of the children. The children were presumed to have deliberately held back from defecating, leading to accumulation of feces in the large intestine, with fecal impaction and dilation of the bowel wall. The muscles in the bowel wall thus became stretched and therefore ineffective. It was then impossible for the child to defecate normally and eventually feces start leaking out of the anus, the child being unable to control this.

We do indeed see children with impacted feces who present the above picture, and in whom there is no history of anal fissure, nor any other indication that a physical cause may have started the process. In some of these cases, however, constipation may have developed because of a physiological predisposition. DSM-IV-TR (page 117) suggests that 'ineffectual straining or paradoxical defecation dynamics, with contraction rather than relaxation of the external sphincter or pelvic floor during straining for defecation', may start the process.

By the time impaction is established, there may be secondary emotional problems as a result of the embarrassment, shame and—sometimes—attitudes of other children who may shun the subject or engage in unflattering name calling. By this time determining how the fecal retention started may be impossible.

Non-retentive soiling may be 'continuous'—that is, present from birth, or discontinuous—when the child had been continent of feces at some time, the soiling having later recurred.

Continuous soiling may occur in children who have been poorly toilet trained. They have often been poorly cared for in other respects; they may present as dirty and badly dressed; and they may show other evidence of poor social training. They may have a history of playing truant from school and of below-average academic progress. The families of such children may have other problems such as unemployment, low income, debt, poor housing, and drug and/or alcohol abuse.

Discontinuous non-retentive soiling may be either *regressive* or *aggressive*. Regressive soiling is usually a reaction to some stressful event, such as the birth of a sibling, or the loss of a loved one by death or departure; it is often but one feature of a more general emotional regression that may feature regressed speech, clinging behaviour and anxious insecurity. It is more likely to occur when continence has only recently been achieved. (Some short-lived episodes of regressive soiling may be more appropriately classified as adjustment disorders—see Chapter 15).

Aggressive non-retentive soiling may have a psychopathology similar to that of some cases of retentive soiling. Instead of refusing to defecate at all, some of these children may be expressing anger by refusing to do so at the time and place they are expected to. The disorders of children who smear feces over toilet and bathroom walls, and elsewhere, may belong in this category.

Clinical features

As we have seen, the essential feature of encopresis is the passing of feces in inappropriate places. Most often this is in the clothes. It may consist of anything from the staining of underwear to the passing of complete motions. In severe cases of retentive soiling the rectum is found, on digital examination, to be greatly dilated and packed with feces. Around these, liquid or semi-liquid fecal material is leaking from the anus, the child having no control over this, indeed sometimes not even being aware of it. Occasionally the soiling is confined to certain situations such as home or school. When this is the case it suggests that the child may have emotional issues related to the situation concerned.

In assessing encopretic children a detailed history must be obtained, not just of the soiling itself, but also of the bowel-training methods that have been used. Was the training coercive, lackadaisical, inconsistent or even absent? At what age did it start? How did the child respond at the time? Relaxed, laid-back training may be effective in stable families in which the children feel secure and wish to please their parents. In chaotic, disorganized families toilet training is often inconsistent. It may vary unpredictably between punitive and *laisser-faire*.

Aggressive soilers, whether retentive or non-retentive, often present as clean, well-dressed but inhibited children. They are often doing well at school. They may present as ashamed of their disorder and may try to conceal it by hiding or destroying underclothes. They are often reluctant to talk about anything relating to bowel function, though they may allude to it in their play or drawings. In about half of these subjects the parents also report associated food refusal, though these are usually well-nourished children. They may be reluctant to engage in rough play, and they may be less self-assertive than is usual in their age group. It seems they give vent to their aggressive feelings through their soiling rather than in more usual ways. Typically, aggressive soilers are bright, successful pupils at school, in contrast to the 'never properly trained' continuous soilers who usually are not.

Regressive soiling is distinguished by the presence of other regressive behaviours, such as clinging to mother, 'baby talk', infantile feeding behaviour, reluctance to sleep or go to bed alone, or a return to immature patterns of play.

Mixed forms of encopresis occur, and the distinction between the various types is not always as clear-cut as the above descriptions might suggest. For example, aggressive soiling can occur in socially disorganized and deprived families as well as in the rigid, obsessive, materially successful ones.

Other associations of encopresis
Soiling may be associated with such other child psychiatric disorders as pervasive developmental disorders, conduct disorders and adjustment disorders. In such cases the primary focus of attention is likely to be the other condition, though if there is chronic constipation or fecal impaction, that must be dealt with.

Treatment

Detailed history taking, physical examination and the necessary medical investigations, including radiological examination of the large intestine, should precede any psychiatric measures. This is best done in a paediatric setting.

It is essential to determine whether there is fecal retention, with or without impaction. If this is present, dealing with it is the first priority. It may involve administration of laxatives, enemas, or even manual removal of feces. When the bowel has been seriously dilated for a long time, it may take many months or years of treatment with laxatives and, when needed, enemas, before normal bowel function is restored.

Whether or not there is fecal retention, behaviour modification is usually the mainstay of treatment. Other psychosocial measures may be needed. A prerequisite is the establishment of rapport and a trusting relationship with the family. This is the context in which behaviour modification can proceed.

If bowel training has been inappropriate, inconsistent or absent, the parents must be taught suitable bowel-training methods and then supported in employing them. In all cases bowel function, and how it may go wrong, should be explained to the parents, in terms appropriate to their educational level and understanding. If the soiling is believed to be a means of self-expression in a child who has felt unable to express angry feelings in other ways, the appearance of more open and normal ways of expressing anger may be interpreted as an indication of progress. The treatment team's understanding of the child's problems and of how the parents can help—and their role in treatment is usually vital—may need to be discussed and explained repeatedly. If there are issues of family functioning, as is often the case, family therapy may be helpful.

Loening-Baucke (2002) provides a review of current approaches to the assessment and treatment of encopresis, with references and recommended reading.

Outcome

Given appropriate treatment and a cooperative family, the outcome is usually favourable. Active measures to deal with fecal retention are however essential if recovery is to occur. Regressive soiling usually resolves once the stress to which it is a response no longer exists. When encopresis, of whatever type, is associated with a seriously disorganized and dysfunctional family system, the outcome depends on the skill of the therapist or treatment team in engaging these sometimes very challenging families.

Encopresis usually improves with treatment but sometimes persists into adulthood. Co-existing behaviour problems may be associated with poorer outcomes (Loening-Baucke, 2002). Benninga and Taminiau (2001) report that non-retentive soiling may persist into adult life in up to 22% of cases.

Chapter 15

Reactions to Stress

Adjustment disorders

Adjustment disorders are short-term reactions to stress. Most diagnostic entities are defined according to their clinical features, but the diagnosis of adjustment disorder depends on identifying its presumed cause. According to ICD-10 there has to be 'strong, but not presumptive' evidence that the disorder would not have arisen if the subject had not experienced the stressful circumstance(s) to which it is being attributed.

DSM-IV-TR defines 'adjustment disorder' as the development of 'clinically significant emotional or behavioural symptoms in response to an identifiable psychosocial stressor or stressors'. ICD-10 states that the symptoms 'usually [interfere] with social functioning and performance. According to ICD-10, onset is 'usually within one month' of the occurrence of the stressful event or life change; DSM-IV-TR allows for a period of up to three months. Each diagnostic scheme lists subtypes of adjustment disorder, according to the main symptoms. The ICD-10 list is:

— Brief depressive reaction
— Prolonged depressive reaction
— Mixed anxiety and depressive reaction
— With predominant disturbance of other emotions (This subcategory is to be used when several types of emotional reactions are reported, for example anxiety, depression, worry, tension, or anger, but none predominates. It is also to be used for childhood regressive reactions such as may be characterized by bedwetting or thumb sucking.)
— With predominant disturbance of conduct
— With mixed disturbance of emotions and conduct
— With other specified predominant symptoms

DSM-IV-TR lists six subtypes. These are characterized by, respectively, 'depressed mood', 'anxiety', 'mixed anxiety and depressed mood,' 'disturbance of conduct', 'mixed disturbance of emotions and conduct', and 'unspecified'.

Casey and colleagues (2001) point out that the line between 'the varied manifestations of adjustment disorder and normal adaptive reactions' is indistinct. Neither of the diagnostic schemes defines this clearly. Casey *et al.* (2001) also point out that both ICD-10 and DSM-IV-TR specify that if the criteria are met for another disorder, that disorder's diagnosis should prevail. DSM-IV-TR states that if five or more depressive symptoms have been present for longer than two weeks, the correct diagnosis is major depressive episode—even if the symptoms have been present only a little longer than two weeks and there is a close temporal relationship between an identifiable stressor and the symptoms. But if only four depressive symptoms are present the diagnosis is adjustment disorder. This should warn us against the too rigid application of operational definitions appearing in the manuals of diagnostic schemes.

The above authors quote Clarke and McKenzie (1994) who cautioned that:

'The subtle balancing of consideration of quantity and quality of symptoms has occurred intuitively in clinical practice but is at risk of being lost as we "operationalise" criteria.'

Prevalence

Reported prevalence rates of adjustment disorders in clinical populations range from 2.3% to 20%, depending on the populations studied (Casey *et al.*, 2001). Prevalence rates are higher in primary-care settings and in medical settings, suggesting that these patients are rarely referred for psychiatric assessment or treatment. No reports are available for the prevalence in entire populations, nor are figures relating specifically to child populations available. These are however common disorders. Casey and colleagues (2001) point out that this diagnosis presents a number of problems, including its loose definition and the 'validity debate'—that is discussion of whether it is a real entity. This is probably true of more than adjustment disorders.

Clinical features

It will be clear from the variety of subtypes of adjustment disorder listed above that there is no one clinical picture that characterizes these conditions. The child may be anxious, depressed, angry, oppositional, distracted or otherwise upset. There may be sleep or appetite disturbances, difficulty in concentrating on things and a falling off in schoolwork.

In determining whether a child or adolescent is suffering from an adjustment disorder it is necessary to ask:

— Are the symptoms severe enough to support the diagnosis?
— Is it clear that these are new symptoms that were not present previously or, if they were, did they markedly worsen following the postulated cause?
— Is the stressful event or situation severe enough for it to be the likely cause of the symptoms?
— Is there a temporal relationship between the stress(es) and the symptoms?

Establishing the diagnosis requires thorough history taking, careful mental-state assessment, and mature clinical judgement. The diagnostic criteria set out in DSM-IV-TR and ICD-10 should be taken into account, but they should not be interpreted too rigidly.

Treatment

This involves:

— Identifying the source(s) of stress and, if they are still present, taking steps to ameliorate or remove them
— Providing emotional and, where appropriate, practical support to child and family
— Symptomatic, and usually short-term, treatment of symptoms such as anxiety and sleep problems

Outcome

Provided the stresses that are responsible do not continue, most adjustment disorder symptoms resolve within weeks or a few months, with or without treatment. DSM-IV-TR distinguishes *acute* cases, in which the disturbance lasts less that six months; and *chronic* cases, in which the disturbance lasts longer than six months.

Post-traumatic Stress Disorder (PTSD)

This is described in ICD-10 as 'a delayed and/or protracted response to a stressful event or situation—brief or long-lasting—of an exceptionally threatening or catastrophic nature, which is likely to cause distress in almost anyone'.

DSM-IV-TR states that the 'traumatic event' responsible for the disorder should involve both of the following:

(1) The experience of witnessing, or being confronted with, an event or events involving actual or threatened death or serious injury, or a threat to the physical integrity of the self or others
(2) A response involving intense fear, helplessness or horror, or—in children—disorganized or agitated behaviour

The events that may be responsible include, but are not confined to, natural and man-made disasters such as earthquakes, volcanic eruptions, hurricanes and explosions; serious accidents; terrorist attacks; rape; robbery; mugging; torture; and many of the experiences children may undergo in times of war. The book *No Place to Be a Child: Growing Up in a War Zone* (Garbarino *et al.*, 1991) describes the many varieties of children's reactions to severe stress.

Prevalence

DSM-IV-TR quotes a lifetime prevalence of PTSD in the adult population of the United States of about 8%. It is clear however that the prevalence is likely to be higher in populations that have experienced such events as the Rwandan genocide; the wars in Bosnia, Liberia, Iraq and other parts of the world; major earthquakes; and other disasters. Whole population figures may not therefore mean much. Children may be especially prone to develop PTSD, though their vulnerability varies.

Clinical features

The main clinical features of PTSD are:

— 'Flashbacks' in which the trauma is relived. Children may engage in repetitive play in which aspects of the trauma are expressed.
— Reliving the trauma in dreams. Children may experience frightening dreams without recognizable content.
— Feeling as if the traumatic event or situation is recurring. Children may actually re-enact the event in their play.
— Intense distress when reminded of the trauma, whether by flashbacks or dreams, or by external cues such a sights, sounds, television reports or even words associated with the traumatic event or situation.

Other features of PTSD include:

— Efforts of avoid thoughts, feelings, talk, places, activities and people that may lead to recollections of the trauma
— Inability to recall some aspects of the traumatic event or situation
— Decreased interest and participation in activities that the subject previously enjoyed
— Feelings of numbness or detachment from the real world
— Sleep disturbance—either trouble getting to sleep or waking during the night
— Irritability and/or outburst of anger
— Difficulty concentrating on things
— Hypervigilance and an exaggerated startle response

DSM-IV-TR suggests more detailed diagnostic criteria than ICD-10 and also requires that the duration of the symptoms is at least one month, and that they cause 'significant distress or impairment in social, occupational or other important areas of functioning'. The disorder is defined as *acute* if symptoms last less than three months and *chronic* if they last longer than three months.

The DSM-IV-TR and ICD-10 diagnostic criteria for PTSD are not suitable for use with very young children. PTSD does occur in children of preschool age (Terr, 1988), but the diagnostic criteria that have been developed for use in older subjects may not be helpful in this age group. Criteria for use in preschool children are discussed by Scheeringa et al. (2003).

Treatment

This may involve:

— Providing short-term emotional and, when necessary, practical support and help to child and family

— If flashbacks, panic attacks, sleep disturbances and other anxiety symptoms persist, offering short-term or long-term psychotherapy, either play therapy to enable the child to work through the trauma in the context of a safe situation, or the use of a cognitive behavioural approach
— The use of anxiolytic drugs, either the short-term (up to three weeks or so) administration of benzodiazepines or, if needed, the longer use of certain of the SSRIs (see Chapter 22)

By the time the diagnosis of PTSD is appropriate the causative event is usually past, or the traumatic situation no longer exists, but if the child is still in a dangerous, threatening or insecure situation, efforts should be made to make the environment less threatening, or the child should if possible be removed from it.

Outcome

With suitable treatment, most PTSD symptoms clear up over time, but this may take many months. The outlook is better when the subject's premorbid personality has been sound and the subject has not previously been prone to anxiety symptoms.

Acute stress reaction (ICD-10) and acute stress disorder (DSM-IV-TR)

These terms are used for short-term reactions to stresses such as those that may lead to PTSD. They are to be diagnosed only in individuals who do not have a pre-existing psychiatric disorder that is exacerbated by the stressful event.
The ICD-10 and DSM-IV-TR criteria are not quite the same, but the essential points about these disorders are:

— The symptoms appear soon after the stressful event.
— They last for a minimum of two days and a maximum of one month (DSM-IV-TR) (if they last for more than a month a diagnosis of PTSD may be appropriate).
— Symptoms may include feelings of helplessness or fear, and depression, anger, despair, overactivity or withdrawal.
— Dissociative symptoms may include a sense of numbing, detachment, lack of emotional responsiveness, derealization, depersonalization or amnesia (these symptoms being emphasized by DSM-IV-TR and not by ICD-10).

Treatment

This is supportive and may involve the very short-term (usually no more than two or three days) use of anxiolytic drugs such as benzodiazepines. Measures should be taken to deal with any continuing stress.

Outcome

This is usually favourable. It is likely that most children with these conditions do not come to the attention of psychiatrists.

Chapter 16

Other Psychiatric Syndromes

Personality disorders

A diagnosis of personality disorder is seldom appropriate in children or in adolescents before they reach their middle to late teens. This is because children's personalities are still developing. Personality development will not even approach completion until their mid-teens. DSM-IV-TR specifies that one of these diagnoses—antisocial personality disorder—should not to be made before age 18. Up till age 18, disorders with symptoms that would later meet the criteria for antisocial personality disorder should receive a conduct disorder diagnosis.

Causes

The following have been suggested as factors that may contribute to the development of personality disorders:

— Genetic factors, although the precise role of genetics is unclear
— The interaction of temperamental factors and the child's environment
— Early adverse experiences, such as attachment problems; the lack of ordered, appropriate parental care; early emotional deprivation; and institutional, as opposed to family, care
— Long-term emotional insecurity
— Emotional and/or physical abuse

The major role that used to be attributed to early experiences in the development of personality has been questioned by, among others, Rutter and Rutter (1993), who pointed out that 'provided that later experiences are really good, the ill-effects of early deprivation or adversity are surprisingly evanescent in many respects' (page 33). But early adverse experiences are often followed by further adversity in later childhood. Personality development is an ongoing process, continuing throughout childhood and even into adult life.

Table 16.1 lists the categories of personality that appear in ICD-10 and DSM-IV-TR. These are mostly only of value in adulthood. I do not use them in my work with children or with adolescents up to, at the earliest, their mid-teens. However we do, from time to time, see children and adolescents who are showing traits that suggest they may in due course develop one of the disorders listed in Table 16.1. Mention of

Table 16.1 Categories of personality disorder

ICD-10	DSM-IV	Main features
Paranoid	Paranoid	Suspicious, jealous, sensitive to slight or imagined insults, affective responses restricted
Schizoid	Schizoid	Distant, cold, aloof, detached, introspective, unresponsive, few or no close friends
Dissocial	Antisocial	Lacking feeling for others, disregarding social norms and obligations, failing to plan ahead or learn from failure, poor work and parenting record
Emotionally unstable	Borderline	Impulsive, unpredictable, with unstable but intense interpersonal relationships; identity uncertain, mood unstable, fearful of being alone, self-damaging
Histrionic	Histrionic	Overdramatic, flamboyant, labile mood, suggestible, drawing attention to self, egocentric, dependent
Anankastic	Obsessive-compulsive	Rigid, inflexible, obsessive, ritualistic, perfectionist
Anxious (avoidant)	Avoidant	Hypersensitive to rejection, avoiding relationships, socially withdrawn, desiring affection and acceptance; feelings of tension and apprehension
Dependent	Dependent	Helpless, clinging, passively compliant, lacking vigor
—	Schizotypal	Social isolation, ideas of reference, 'magical' thinking, recurrent illusions, odd speech, suspiciousness, hypersensitivity
—	Narcissistic	Grandiosely self-important, with fantasies of success, power, brilliance or ideal love; requires attention and admiration, resents criticism, lacks empathy and takes advantage of others
'Other' and 'unspecified'	Not otherwise specified	—

such traits in the diagnostic formulation may, if they are pronounced, be appropriate, but I do not recommend their inclusion when formal diagnoses are made. Indeed ICD-10 lists them under the heading 'Disorders of Adult Personality and Behaviour'. Detailed descriptions of each of them are to be found in the manuals of the two diagnostic schemes.

Psychosexual problems

Gender identity disorders

This term, which appears in both ICD-10 and DSM-IV-TR, is used for the disorders of children who experience persistent, severe distress about their assigned sex.

They either desire to be, or insist that they really are, of the opposite sex. They may repudiate the anatomical attributes that define their gender. Onset is before, often well before, puberty, and the first manifestations may appear in the preschool years.

Gender identity disorders must be distinguished from failure to conform with sex-role stereotypes, which is more common. The diagnosis requires, in the words of ICD-10, 'a profound disturbance of the normal sense of maleness or femaleness'. Nevertheless, there seems to be a continuum from those who are completely identified with their anatomical sex to those who completely reject it. Traits of effeminacy in boys and 'tomboyishness' in girls may be mild forms of this disorder, but they do not justify the diagnosis of a gender identity disorder.

Society tends to be more accepting of tomboyish behaviour in girls than of effeminacy in boys. Girls may wear masculine clothes and play boys' games without causing concern, whereas boys who wear girls' clothes and engage in 'feminine' behaviour are less readily accepted.

Causes

Biological, especially genetic, factors combine with environmental ones to produce a child's sense of gender identity. Among the biological factors, hormonal influences are important. Just how this happens, and the relative importance of the different factors, are incompletely understood.

Treatment

Psychotherapy for child and parents is the treatment usually employed. It should have the following aims:

— To increase the child's comfort in being anatomically male or female
— To reduce sex-role behaviours that peers regard as inappropriate
— To strengthen the child's relationship and contact with the same-sex parent
— To facilitate the child's involvement with a same-sex peer group that will accept him or her

These aims may be addressed by any of the following:

— Individual therapy with child and parents
— Cognitive behaviour therapy, usually with the child
— Group therapy
— Family therapy

Before any treatment is instituted the informed consent of child and parents should be obtained. A full discussion of available treatment options should lead to the preparation of a written statement of the treatment aims and proposed therapy methods.

Outcome

Systematic data on outcome, with or without treatment, are lacking, but some of these children's symptoms resolve with treatment; others learn to live with their doubts about their gender identity; a few have severe symptoms that persist into adult life and lead to their seeking sex-reassignment treatment.

Other psychosexual problems

Various other psychosexual problems may occur in young people. These include *voyeurism*, in which the subject spies on unsuspecting people who are undressing, or naked, or having sexual intercourse; and *exhibitionism*, the exposing of one's genitals to strangers to achieve sexual excitement. Some children and adolescents who have been sexually abused later victimize others.

The causes of these problems are complex and imperfectly understood. Some of these children have had unstable lives and/or periods of institutional care, or deviant rearing. Some have been exposed to pornographic material.

Treatment may involve individual psychotherapy, counselling for the parents, family therapy or behaviour therapy, or some combination of these. The treatment of severe, established cases can be very challenging.

Tics and Tourette's syndrome

Tics, sometimes known as habit spasms, are repeated, sudden movements of muscles or groups of muscles not under voluntary control and serving no obvious purpose. Motor tics occur most often in the muscles of the face and eye-blinking tics are common. Facial contortions may occur, and muscle groups in other parts of the body may be involved. The head and neck may be suddenly and briefly moved in one direction or contorted. There may be similar movements of trunk and limbs. The same movements tend to occur repeatedly, in severe cases scores or hundreds of times daily. This is in contrast to the involuntary movements seen in the various forms of chorea, which are more varied and less predictable.

Vocal tics may or may not accompany motor tics. They are sounds or words, occasionally obscene, which are emitted involuntarily.

Tics may be subdivided into 'simple' and 'complex' varieties. Examples of simple tics are:

— Eye blinking, shoulder shrugging, grimacing
— Grunts, sniffing, throat clearing

Examples of complex tics are:

— Hitting one's self, jumping

— Saying words, often socially unacceptable ones that may be obscene, repetition of one's own words (The term coprolalia is sometimes applied to the uttering of obscenities.)

Three categories of tic disorder are listed in both ICD-10 and DSM-IV-TR:

— Transient tic disorder
— Chronic motor or vocal tic disorder
— Combined motor and vocal tic disorder, also known as Tourette's disorder

ICD-10 adds:

— Other tic disorders
— Tic disorder, unspecified

Transient tic disorder is the term used for tics that last for less than a year, though they may recur. It is the most common form of this condition and is frequently seen in children in the four- to five-year-old age range. Such tics as eye blinking, facial grimacing and head jerking appear but do not continue for longer than one year, often for only a few weeks. There may be remissions and relapses during the year. Occasional, mild tics are common in normally developing young children; the borderline between such tics and transient tic disorder is not a well-defined one.

Chronic motor or *vocal tics* are characterized by either motor or vocal tics, but not both, lasting more than a year. The tics may be simple or complex, or both.

In *Tourette's syndrome*, which ICD-10 calls *combined vocal and motor tic disorder*, and DSM-IV-TR calls *Tourette's disorder*, there is a history of both motor and vocal tics, though they need not be present at the same time. In severe cases there are complex and multiple tics, sometimes with the use of obscene words and phrases (*coprolalia*). These may be accompanied by obscene gestures (*copropraxia*).

Associated symptoms include various other symptoms and disorders that may occur along with tics. These include obsessive-compulsive disorder, behaviour problems, attention-deficit symptoms, hyperactivity, learning difficulties and sleep problems (Singer & Walkup, 1991). Tics sometimes develop or intensify in children with attention-deficit hyperactivity disorder (ADHD) who are receiving methylphenidate or other stimulant drugs. It is not clear, however, whether these drugs play a part in precipitating, or even causing, the tics, or whether it is just that these conditions naturally occur together.

Prevalence

Prevalence studies have come up with widely differing figures, ranging from 2.9 to 59 per 100,000 (Leckman & Cohen, 1994). This is partly due to differences in the ages studied and partly due to the study methods used. It is clear that the prevalence in children is greater than that in adults (probably by a factor of 5 to 12) and that tics occur in males more often than in females, M:F ratios of between 3:1 and 9:1 having been reported (Leckman & Cohen, 1994).

Causes

Biological, including genetic, factors are believed to play major roles in the causation of tics. In some families there appear to be common genetic factors responsible for both tics or Tourette's disorder and for obsessive-compulsive disorder (OCD). A study of 60 OCD patients revealed that 15 had a lifetime history of tics and 45 did not (Hanna *et al.*, 2002). The findings of this study also suggested that tic-related OCD may differ from non-tic-related OCD in that certain compulsive symptoms— ordering, hording and washing compulsions—were more common in patients with no tic history. A study of the prevalence of 29 tic symptoms in 85 individuals with Tourette's disorder (TD) suggested there are several heritable components of TD (Alsobrook & Pauls, 2002).

The precise location in the brain of the dysfunction that causes tic disorders is unknown, but it seems likely that the problems reside in the general area of the basal ganglia.

Recent years have seen much interest in PANDAS (paediatric autoimmune neuropsychiatry disorders associated with streptococcal infection). Children with PANDAS have tics and OCD that are temporally related to streptococcal infections (Dale & Heyman, 2002). Sydenham's chorea is a post-infectious autoimmune disorder of the basal ganglia of the brain. Its features include choreiform movements and behaviour disturbances. It has been suggested that a similar process may be at work with PANDAS, the symptoms of which include, in addition to tics and OCD, attention deficits, anxiety, oppositional defiant disorder and depression (Leonard & Swedo, 2001). It may be that group A beta-haemolytic streptococcal infections cause the production of autoantibodies (antibodies that react with proteins occurring naturally in the body), which react with proteins associated with the basal ganglia. The review by Swedo (2001) discusses current thinking concerning post-streptococcal autoimmunity and the hypotheses under investigation.

Environmental factors are unlikely to be a primary cause of tic disorders, but stresses of various sorts may exacerbate tics or cause them to appear or re-appear in those who are biologically predisposed.

Walkup (2002) provides further information about the possible causes of tics and the neurochemical abnormalities in the brain that may be involved.

Treatment

Tics may be associated with a variety of other symptoms and disorders as described above. In many cases they are not the condition that is causing the child and/or the family most concern. Therefore tic suppression may or may not be the first priority when the treatment plan is formulated. Any of the associated symptoms may need to be addressed first. These will be tackled using the methods described in the sections of this book that deal with them. Children with transient tic disorders, unless the symptoms are unusually severe, seldom need treatment directed specifically to the tics.

Invariably needed are support and explanations for child and family. When they first present for help, most families do not know much about these disorders or their implications. They may be assured that the prognosis is generally favourable, even though in a minority of cases the symptoms continue into adult life.

When tic suppression is indicated—usually because it is particularly severe or is causing distress to the child—several pharmacological treatments are available. The substituted benzamide sulpiride is currently the drug of choice. It is usually effective in reducing the number and frequency of tics and tends to cause fewer side effects than haloperidol, which is also effective in tic suppression (Walkup, 2002). Risperidone is often effective in reducing tics and leads to relatively few side effects (Scahill *et al.*, 2003).

Outcome

Many tic disorders are mild, short-term conditions that resolve spontaneously. Tics are less common in adults than in children, so it is clear that most children grow out of them, with or without treatment. Nevertheless a minority of tic subjects continue to be troubled by this symptom well into adult life.

Stuttering

Stuttering, sometimes called stammering, is the repeated interruption of speech by repetition, prolongation or blocking of sounds. In the speech of children around the ages of 2 to 4 years there are often hesitations and irregularities of the rhythm of speech. This is known as clutter. It sometimes precedes true stuttering, but more often it gradually disappears and the child then speaks normally.

The onset of stuttering is usually before the age of 10. There may or may not have been a period of normal speech before its onset. It occurs in about 4% of boys and 2% of girls. About 1% of children continue stuttering in adolescence, more of them boys than girls.

The causes of stuttering are not fully understood, but there is often a positive family history and genetic factors may play a part. Other psychological factors seem to play a part; for example some stutterers can sing fluently or speak normally while acting on a stage but stutter in everyday conversation.

The severity of stuttering varies from occasional repetition of speech sounds to severe blocking of speech, which seriously interferes with communication. There may be associated movements of the face or other parts of the body, coinciding with the repetitions, prolongations or pauses in the flow of speech. Anticipatory anxiety may occur, leading to avoidance behaviour. At first a few letters or sounds may be avoided. Later many places and social situations may be shunned. Stuttering may cause children to become isolated and impair their ability to take part in school activities.

Stuttering is not usually part of a general psychiatric disorder. In most cases, emotional factors seem to play only a small part in its causation. It may, however, lead to the development of an anxiety disorder and to social adjustment difficulties.

Treatment is usually carried out by speech therapists, and the psychiatric contribution is minimal. Measures to help relieve anxiety and promote relaxation and self-confidence may help. Remediation may also involve:

— Discussing with parents what they can do to facilitate their child's speech fluency
— Speech-language modification, which consists of identifying those speech production strategies the child is using that are causing the fluency of speech to be disrupted
— A combination of the above two approaches

Treatment of young children in parent-child stuttering groups has been advocated by Conture (1990).

The *outcome* is generally favourable. Stuttering is most often mild and transient. Most children grow out of it by their mid-teens, though in a few cases it persists into adult life.

Elective mutism (ICD-10)/selective mutism (DSM-IV-TR)

In this condition children who are able to talk decline to do so in certain situations. The terms above refer to the same disorder and the traditionally established term *elective mutism* (EM) will be used in this section.

Prevalence

The prevalence of EM varies with the age group studied. Brown and Lloyd (1975) surveyed 6072 five-year-old children starting school in Birmingham, England. Interviews with their teachers revealed that 42 were not speaking in class after eight weeks in school, a prevalence of 7.2 per 1000. During the following four terms the number of mute children fell steadily, so that after 64 weeks only one child remained silent in school. The condition is therefore fairly common as an initial reaction to starting school but rare as a persisting problem. Immigrant children were over-represented among the children who were late starting to talk.

Kolvin and Fundudis (1981) quote a prevalence of 0.8 per 1000 in seven-year-olds. Bergman and colleagues (2002) report a prevalence of 7.1 per 1000 among kindergarten, and first-grade and second-grade children in a California school sample. DSM-IV-TR states that the prevalence is less than 1% among 'individuals seen in mental health settings'.

Unlike most child psychiatric disorders, EM occurs as frequently in girls as in boys.

Causes

The aetiology of EM is multifactorial, and it is often associated with social anxiety and language delay (Kristensen & Torgersen, 2001). Genetic factors probably play their part. Personality traits such as taciturnity have been reported as being present more often in first-, second- and third-degree relatives of children with EM than in relatives of control subjects (Steinhausen & Adamek, 1997).

Many of these children are unusually shy. Kolvin and Fundudis (1981) reported some 'subsidiary' patterns of behaviour: 'submissive', 'sensitive and weepy', and 'moody, sulky and stubborn'. The last named was the most common. These children tend to be late talking, have speech abnormalities when they do start to talk, and are enuretic and encopretic more often than controls. The increased prevalence that has been reported in immigrant groups suggests that sociocultural factors may play a part.

EM is probably a complex disorder to which genetic, personality, emotional, family and sociocultural factors all contribute.

Clinical features

The main clinical feature is the child's refusal to talk in certain, sometimes most, situations while talking freely in others—especially at home and when in the company of family members or other familiar figures. The situations in which these children do not talk are many—school, public places, clinics, doctors' offices and consulting rooms. Brown and Lloyd (1975) found that children who were mute at school showed other behaviour patterns that distinguished them from children who spoke. They were more likely to stop an activity when their teacher approached and to avoid playing with other children. They were also less likely to draw, go the toilet or approach the teacher's table.

In clinical settings, these children often behave as negativistically non-verbally as they do verbally. Some will nod or shake their head in reply to questions, and others deny the interviewer even these responses. At the same time they are usually looking around and appear to be taking in what is going on. They can be extraordinarily stubborn, remaining silent for session after session. One girl who was making good, if non-verbal, progress at school was observed on closed-circuit television to be talking freely when alone with her family, but as soon as a member of the clinic staff entered she became silent and remained so until that person left the room.

It is hard to categorize children with EM as they are seen in clinical practice. There are however some in whom anxiety seems to dominate the clinical picture and others in whom negativism does.

Kolvin and Fundudis (1981) reported a mean IQ of 85 in 24 children with EM, while the mean IQ of a speech-retarded comparison group was 95 and that of a normal control group was 101.

Dummit and colleagues (1997) systematically assessed 50 children with EM. They found that all met DSM-III-R criteria for either social phobia or avoidant disorder, while 24 (48%) had additional anxiety disorders. They concluded that EM usually presents in the context of anxiety disorders.

Treatment

Many treatments have been suggested for EM. These include suggestion, persuasion, coercion, psychodynamically oriented play therapy, speech therapy, family therapy, behaviour therapy and medication. It is not clear how effective any of these approaches are—if they are effective at all. Early diagnosis and treatment have been reported to yield good results, but since most young children start to speak without treatment, these reports may only reflect the natural history of the condition.

Since EM is often a short-term reaction to starting school, it is reasonable to wait for a few months after a child with EM starts school, unless there are other problems that justify intervention. For children in whom treatment is indicated, there is some evidence that a small group setting with speaking peers and adults who expect the child to talk and do not accept the mutism as inevitable, combined with family intervention, may help (Wright *et al.*, 1985). For older children, combinations of behavioural interventions, family therapy and, in some cases, play therapy may offer the best prospects of success.

Outcome

Follow-up studies have shown that children with EM eventually start to speak in all or most situations. However many have continuing communication problems and other personality difficulties. Remschmidt *et al.* (2001) followed up 45 children with EM, average age 8.7 ± 3.6 years. They were reassessed at an average of 12 years later. Their findings were:

— There was a high load of individual and family psychopathology.
— Of the subjects, 41 (39%) were in complete remission.
— The formerly mute subjects described themselves as less independent, less motivated to achieve in school, less self-confident and less mature and healthy than a control group.

If there was history of mutism in the 'core family' at the time of referral, this predicted a poor outcome.

The Kleine-Levin syndrome

The main feature of this disorder is excessive sleepiness, which may last for several days or a week or two or occasionally longer. Other symptoms include greatly increased appetite and, in some cases, various psychiatric symptoms such as depression, mania, anxiety, hypersexuality and delusional ideas, including erotic ones. Onset is usually in mid-adolescence, but occasionally it is before puberty (Ferguson, 1986). It occurs more often in males than females. Gadoth and colleagues (2001) reported a series of 34 cases (26 male and 8 female), with a mean age at onset of 15.8 ± 2.8 years. The mean duration of a single hypersomnolent attack was 11.5 ± 6.6 days.

This is a sporadically occurring condition of unknown aetiology, though an autoimmune process has been suggested (Dauvilliers *et al.*, 2002). One instance of the condition occurring in two sisters has been reported (Katrz & Ropper, 2002). No treatment is known to be effective, though stimulant drugs have been suggested. Spontaneous recovery is usual, and the long-term prognosis is excellent.

Episodic dyscontrol syndrome/intermittent explosive disorder

The 'episodic dyscontrol syndrome' (EDS) consists of recurrent attacks of uncontrollable rage, usually with minimal provocation and often out of character (Gordon, 1999). According to Gordon, the outbursts may be preceded by feelings of tension and fear, and also by hyperacusis, numbness of the limbs and nausea. The term does not appear in either DSM-IV-TR or ICD-10.

'Intermittent explosive disorder' (IED) may be the same condition as EDS. It appears in DSM-IV-TR in the section on 'impulse-control disorders not elsewhere classified', along with kleptomania, pyromania, pathological gambling and trichotillomania. Its 'essential feature' is the occurrence of discrete episodes of failure to resist aggressive impulses that result in serious assaultive acts or destruction of property.

Both these disorders (if they are separate conditions) occur in adults and children. The DSM-IV-TR criteria exclude aggressive outbursts due to a 'general medical condition'. Gordon (1999) comments on the possible associations and/or causes of EDS.

There has been little research into these conditions, but McElroy (1999) described 27 subjects who met DSM-IV-TR criteria for IED, and reported an association of the explosive episodes with 'manic-like' symptoms, a high rate of lifetime history of comorbid bipolar disorder and favourable response to mood-stabilizing drugs. He suggested that IED may be linked to bipolar disorder, but this remains to be confirmed.

Gordon (1999) suggested that carbamazepine may be effective in EDS. Propranolol and other drugs have been suggested as possible treatments, but evidence of their effectiveness is absent.

The aetiology of these conditions remains unclear, and their status as distinct diagnostic entities is uncertain.

Factitious illness by proxy

This condition is also known as *Munchausen's syndrome by proxy.* Its essence is the fabrication of a history and/or the physical signs of an illness in a child, usually by a parent, most often the mother (Fisher & Mitchell, 1992). It is not strictly a child psychiatric condition as it is the mother or other person responsible who has the disorder. It does not appear in ICD-10, but is listed in DSM-IV-TR in Appendix B, in a section headed 'criteria sets and axes provided for further study'. DSM-IV-TR suggests that it is 'the intentional production or feigning of physical or psychological signs or symptoms in another person who is under the individual's care' (page

781). It also suggests that the motivation of the perpetrator is to assume the sick role by proxy.

The symptoms induced or reported as occurring in the child are usually physical rather than psychological. It is the mother or other perpetrator who has the psychiatric disorder in these cases, so the condition is not discussed further here. However all who deal with children and families should be aware of this syndrome.

Chapter 17

Mind-Body Relationships

Both physical and emotional factors play a part in most, maybe even all, illnesses. The division of diseases into those that are 'organic' and those that are 'non-organic'— or into 'physical' and 'psychological' categories is, at best, an oversimplification and perhaps quite wrong. Mind and body are not separate entities.

The brain is the organ of the mind. Changes in a person's emotional state inevitably have their correlates in the activities of the brain, whether these are chemical, electrical, physical or structural. In most instances some combination of changes is involved.

We know that the levels of *neurotransmitters*—substances that facilitate the transmission of messages between brain cells—have important relationships with abnormal mood states such as depression. Modern brain-imaging procedures are teaching us much about which areas in the brain serve different functions, and how these functions may go wrong. We are still far from understanding fully the workings of the brain—an enormously complex organ—and may never do so, but we do know that what goes on in the brain is intimately related to how we behave and feel.

The influence of the body on the mind

It is common knowledge that when people are told that they have a serious or life-threatening illness, this may have major effects on their mental and emotional states. Having chronic diseases such as diabetes, cystic fibrosis, asthma, rheumatoid arthritis, congenital heart disease or eczema affect the self-images, development and emotional states of children. This applies also to congenital deformities, dwarfism, cerebral palsy and other physically obvious and handicapping conditions (Barker, 1993a).

With all the above disorders, the effect of the bodily condition on the mind is mediated by the subject's awareness of the condition, the handicap it causes and its effects on the attitudes and behaviours of others. The body can also affect the mind in other ways. Some are obvious, such as the effects of brain tumours and diseases, but many other physical diseases affect people's emotional states, thinking processes and behaviour. In diabetics, fluctuations in blood-sugar level, and the accumulation of ketones in the blood, affect the mental state. High or low levels of thyroid hormones also lead to changes in the mental state.

These relationships are not usually one-way. The effective severity of a handicap may vary according to the person's emotional reaction to it. Is it a matter for despair or a challenge to be addressed? Notable examples of people who have overcome serious handicaps include Douglas Bader, who continued flying as a Battle of Britain pilot after having both his legs amputated; and Helen Keller, who was remarkably successful in overcoming the dual handicaps of blindness and deafness.

The effects of the mind on the body

We are all familiar with some of the effects the mind can have on the body. These are subsumed in phrases such as 'scared stiff' and 'shaking with laughter'. People who are frightened or anxious often lose their appetite or feel the urge to urinate or defecate. Peptic ulcer symptoms may worsen in times of stress, and many other conditions are stress related in similar ways.

Despite everyday experiences such as those mentioned above, the power of the mind over the body is too often overlooked or underestimated. Rossi (1986a) reminds us of the significance of phenomena such as voodoo deaths and the placebo response. In some cultures people die simply because they believe a spell has been cast over them. Similar processes may promote recovery from illnesses. The culture of the Western world is that of the vitamin tablet, antibiotic or herbal remedy, rather than the witchdoctor's spell, but similar processes may be involved. We know that prescription of inert 'medication' may promote recovery in 30% to 40% of patients with certain disorders.

The phenomena of hypnosis also provide compelling evidence of the influence of the mind over the body. There have been many reports of major abdominal, dental and other surgical operations being carried out with the patient under hypnosis without the use of any conventional anaesthetic. Hypnosis has been shown to be of value in pain control, for example in severely burned subjects (Patterson *et al.*, 1992). Painless and haemorrhage-free dental extractions can be carried out with the patient under hypnosis, even in haemophiliacs, who can be taught to control the flow of blood to the dental sockets. Swirsky-Sacchetti and Margolis (1986) investigated a comprehensive self-hypnosis training program for haemophiliacs and found that, during an 18-week follow-up period, the amount of factor VIII concentrate (factor VIII being what is lacking in the blood of haemophiliacs) used to control bleeding in the research subjects was significantly less than used by control subjects. These authors claim that self-hypnosis can be both an effective and a cost-effective treatment for haemophilia.

Psychosomatic considerations in child psychiatry

What are the implications of the relationships outlined above? I believe it is that the concept, which for long held sway, that some disorders are 'physical' and others are 'psychological' disorders, with a few—the 'psychosomatic' group—falling in between, is outdated. In a sense, every disorder is psychosomatic, in that both physical and psychological factors are involved to some extent. This applies even to a condition as 'physical' as a fracture of a leg bone. Not only is there inevitably some emotional reaction to such an injury, but the attitudes of injured people, and the extent to which they cooperate in their treatment and rehabilitation, affect how quickly their injury heals and how soon they resume their normal lives. Another relevant point is that some children are more accident prone than others; and in some families the risk of their children being involved in accidents is greater than in other families, for a variety of reasons.

Graham (1985) suggested that one can construct a hierarchy of conditions on the basis of the relative importance of physical and psychological components in their aetiology and treatment. He proposed that, among disorders commonly dealt with by paediatricians, psychological factors might be ranked in the following ascending order of importance:

— Congenital malformations
— Cancers
— Metabolic disorders
— Infections
— Epilepsy
— Failures of growth
— Bronchial asthma
— Enuresis/encopresis
— Accidents
— Emotional/behavioural disorders

The above is more realistic than labelling disorders as either 'psychosomatic' or not, though not everyone would necessarily agree with the order in which Graham placed the conditions. It suggests that there is a constant relationship between physical and psychological factors in each of the conditions listed. In reality the relative importance of these factors varies from child to child, and even from time to time, and it is not simply a matter of what the diagnosis is. For example anorexia nervosa may start as a largely emotional disorder but may progress to become a physical, even a fatal, one.

A word of warning is in order here about the dangers of *linear thinking*. In many, perhaps most, conditions we are dealing with circular processes rather than linear ones. **A** may be seen to cause **B**, but **B** may then influence **A**, either directly, or through the mediation of **C**, or even **D**. Consider the example of retentive soiling (Chapter 14). Retention of feces may be a reaction to coercive toilet-training methods. The more the child resists defecating, the more coercive and even punitive the parents' efforts may become. Thus the fecal retention increases, leading to impaction of feces. We now have a situation of chronic constipation, psychogenic megacolon and overflow incontinence. A physical disorder has become established, and now the child can no longer control the process of defecation. There may also be parental despair and demoralization of the child, who may be shunned by peers because of the smell of feces.

Asthma

Sufferers from bronchial asthma experience recurrent episodes of difficulty breathing, due to constriction of the smaller air passages in the lungs. This is due to contraction of the muscles in the walls of the air passages and the accumulation of secretions in the air passages. The subject has difficulty coughing up the secretions in the lungs, which get overfilled with air. Breathing is accompanied by wheezing as the patient gasps for breath and may turn blue from lack of oxygen. Asthma attacks are sometimes fatal.

Any one or more of the following may contribute to asthma attacks:

— Allergies
— Infections of the respiratory system
— Emotional factors

Also necessary is biological susceptibility to asthma, which may run in families and may be associated with eczema.

Asthma is a paediatric rather than a psychiatric disorder, but because of the role that emotional factors may play in its aetiology, and also the emotional consequences to which it may lead, the help of child mental workers is sometimes sought in its management. The consequences may include anxiety, fear of dying, insecurity and the disruption of the child's life by repeated emergency admissions to a hospital. Parents of asthmatic children understandably worry about their children and may communicate their anxiety to their asthmatic children.

Eating disorders

In few, if any, disorders are physical and emotional factors so inextricably intertwined as in the eating disorders of childhood and adolescence. The most important of these are anorexia and bulimia nervosa, childhood obesity, pica and rumination disorder of infancy. The latter two are discussed in Chapter 18.

Anorexia nervosa (AN)

The main features of anorexia nervosa are:

— A profound aversion to food
— Severe weight loss
— Distorted body image, with denial of being underweight
— Excessive physical activity
— Depression
— Cessation of menstruation (if it has started)
— Pre-occupation with food and, often, interest in preparing it for others

In due course, if the disease process is not arrested, the effects of self-starvation set in. These include:

— Weakness and lethargy
— Slow pulse and low blood pressure
— Constipation
— Hirsutism
— Blue and cold extremities
— Low blood levels of luteinizing hormone, follicle-stimulating hormone and estrogens

Both ICD-10 and DSM-IV-TR require that the patient's weight is at least 15% below that which is expected or that the body-mass index (BMI) (weight in kilograms divided by the square of the height in metres) is 17.5 or less.

Causes
The causes of AN are not fully understood. The interaction of the following factors may be involved:

— Biological predisposition, which is at least partly genetic. The risk of getting AN is increased in first-degree relatives, and concordance is significantly higher in monozygotic than in dizygotic twins (DSM-IV-TR, page 588).

— Sociocultural influences, particularly the culture of 'thinness' that exerts pressures on adolescent girls and young women. Decreases in the percentage of average weight for height have been documented in both the centerfolds of *Playboy* magazine between 1969 and 1978 (Garfinkel & Garner, 1982) and in the Miss America contestants between 1959 and 1978 (Garner & Garfinkel, 1980). AN is also more common in prosperous countries than in the developing world.

— Sometimes AN seems to start with dieting that gets out of hand.

— A fear of growing up and adopting the adult role in society can lead to AN.

— Complex family dynamics may be involved. These may be such that the child needs to be the centre of the parents' attention or feels a need to rebel against the parents and chooses eating as the stage on which to do this.

Onset and prevalence

The onset of AN is most often between the ages of 14 and 18, but onset may be as early as age 8. Girls outnumber boys by a ratio of about 10:1, although in pre-pubertal cases the girl:boy ratio is lower. Prevalence figures vary widely, depending on the country and the age group studied. DSM-IV-TR suggests that the lifetime prevalence among females is 0.5%.

Treatment

Treatment should be 'multidimensional' (Halmi, 2002), as no one measure is likely to be sufficient. Both the young person and the family should be involved. The following principles apply:

—Rapport with all concerned must be established. While this applies to the treatment of all disorders it may be of particular importance in the management of AN.

—The approach to these young people should be firm, accepting, non-punitive but unyielding. It is quite usual for these young patients to be expert at manipulating those who are striving to get them to eat.

—The adults concerned, that is parents and professional staff, must be united and supportive of each other. Fossen and colleagues (1987) observed that 'children with anorexia seem to be particularly adept at creating conflict, not from planned behaviour or malice, but as a habitual way of relating, generalized from family interaction'. Replacing the conflict by order and cooperation is essential. All concerned must make it clear to the child that she must eat.

—In treating patients who have lost much weight, and therefore have been admitted to the hospital, close cooperation with a paediatrician is desirable. Restoring the patient's weight to a safe level is a high priority. The paediatrician may monitor the child's emotional state, electrolyte balance and diet; prescribe the necessary dietary intake; and advise on the weight gain needed before it is 'safe' for the child to be given certain privileges. At the same time the psychiatrist coordinates the psychological care of child and family.

—For patients who have been admitted to the hospital, skilled nursing is essential. In few areas of nursing practice are psychiatric nursing skills so important. Not only are excellent interpersonal skills needed in dealing with these young people, but the parents also need skilled, sensitive support. Being firm with a daughter and not yielding to her threats and guilt-provoking statements ('You hate me', 'You've never loved me', 'I hate you' or 'You just want me to die in this hospital') can be hard for parents who are used to surrendering to such emotional blackmail.

—It is a good plan to have minimum and maximum target weights. These young people usually have a fear of becoming fat, and it seems to reassure them that, while they must reach a certain minimum weight, they will not be allowed to go above the maximum weight.

—Once a safe weight has been achieved, family therapy may begin. An assessment of the family system (see Barker, 1998) should be followed by therapy sessions to address the problems that have been found. Enmeshment, overprotectiveness and a lack of strategies for conflict resolution often characterise these families. Sometimes the family's pattern of functioning is overly rigid.

—Admission to the hospital should be avoided if possible. The initiation of treatment as early as possible, in the context of care within the family, is much to be desired (Blank *et al.*, 2002).

—At some stage individual therapy with the patient should be instituted. Cognitive behaviour therapy has been reported to be helpful in some cases for both adolescent patients and their parents (Lock, 2002).

—Medication has little part to play in the treatment of AN. If there is clear evidence of clinical depression, antidepressants such as the SSRIs (see Chapter 22) may be indicated, but in the absence of a co-existing depressive disorder they are probably of little or no value, though some authors recommend their use (for example, Halmi, 2002). The drugs that have been suggested are reviewed by Kotler and colleagues (2002). Subsequently Boachie *et al.* (2003) reported an uncontrolled study of the effect of the antipsychotic olanzapine on four children with AN treated in an inpatient setting. They reported an average weight gain of 0.99 kilograms per week while the children were in hospital, together with decreased agitation and improved sleep and compliance with treatment. Further study will be needed to verify that this drug is indeed effective in the treatment of AN.

Outcome

Most patients with AN recover, a few become chronic sufferers, and a very few die. The numbers falling into each category vary from study to study. However a study of long-term outcome reported from the Mayo Clinic shows no increase in mortality 30 years after the initial diagnosis of AN (Korndorfer *et al.* 203). As Palmer (2003) has pointed out, these results are at odds with most studies. Also it is an incontrovertible fact that some people do die of AN. It might be that AN protects subjects from other causes of death, but evidence for this is lacking. It is clear, though, as Palmer says, that AN needs to be taken seriously. He points out that while for some it is 'a transient blip in their lives, for others [it is] a major blight'.

There is evidence that a significant number of young women who have recovered from adolescent eating disorders may be left with some psychosocial impairment and, in their early twenties, may report lower self-esteem, more depression, less family support and poorer health (Striegel-Moore *et al.*, 2003). However many adolescents with eating disorders have other co-existing disorders and it may be these, rather than the eating disorders themselves, that are at least in part responsible for the later problems.

Bulimia nervosa (BD)

Bulimia nervosa shares many features with anorexia nervosa. The psychopathology is similar, as is the age and sex distribution, though BN tends to present a little later. The symptoms, however, are different, even though there is the same fear of gaining weight. Some patients with AN go on to develop BN. The main symptoms are:

- —A persistent, irresistible craving for food
- —Episodes of overeating in which large quantities of food are consumed over a short period
- —Attempts to avoid gaining weight by one or more of self-induced vomiting, alternating periods of self-starvation, excessive use of laxatives, or use of appetite-suppressing drugs and/or diuretics

DSM-IV-TR subdivides BN into 'purging' and 'non-purging types'. The disorder may not readily become apparent to others, since most patients with BN are not grossly underweight as those with severe AN are. Indeed cases have been reported in which individuals have had the disorder for many years without their spouses becoming aware of it. The excessive use of laxatives and diuretics may lead to metabolic disturbances such as lowered blood-potassium levels. The blood chemistry should therefore be checked when the diagnosis is made and periodically during treatment.

Treatment
The treatment of BN follows the same general lines as for AN, except that there is better support for the efficacy of antidepressants in BN than in AN. Kotler and colleagues (2002) suggest that fluoxetine in doses up to 60 mg may be useful in adults, but little information is available about the efficacy of these drugs in adolescents.

Outcome
Bulimic symptoms tend to lessen or disappear over the long term, but little information is available about the course of adolescent-onset cases.

Chapter 18

Infant Psychiatry

Infant psychiatry, often referred to as infant mental health, has become a major sub-specialty of child psychiatry. Some special considerations apply to work with infants and young children:

(1) In this age group we are dealing, to an even greater extent than in later childhood, with development and its disorders, rather than with clearly identifiable psychiatric syndromes. The borderline between psychiatry and developmental psychology is blurred.

(2) Neither of the two psychiatric diagnostic schemes currently in general use—ICD-10 and DSM-IV-TR—has been designed to address the diagnostic issues that arise in this age group. This has led to the development of schemes designed specifically for infants and preschool children, such as *Zero to Three* (1994).

(3) Infant psychiatry involves the study of infants and how their development may go awry, but also of infant-adult relationships. Those concerned with the mental health of infants must, as Zeanah (2000, page 1) puts it, 'be concerned fundamentally with the context in which they are developing'. While this is true also of older children, it applies with even greater force the younger the children with which we are dealing. Infants are totally dependent on those caring for them, so that the latter are of equal concern to infant-health workers.

(4) The assessment of infants and young children demands special skills, and the use of techniques different from those we use with older children and adolescents. Children who have not yet developed speech, or whose verbal language skills are at an early stage of development, cannot provide us with the sort of information we can usually obtain from older subjects. Infants cannot tell us in words how they feel, or what they are thinking or subjectively experiencing. So the infant-mental-health worker must be skilled in interpreting non-verbal behaviour, the natural means whereby infants communicate. Also collateral information—from parents and others—is essential.

(5) The intimate involvement of infants and young children with their families, and their total dependence on those caring for them, means that they are very susceptible to tensions or other problems in their families or wherever else they may be living. The tragic deterioration that occurs in babies placed in impersonal institutions, documented many years ago by Spitz (1946), is testimony to this.

Assessment

The assessment of children in their first year or two requires an approach different from that used with older children. Infants do not talk. Instead they cry, smile, make cooing noises and, in various ways that the perceptive parent learns, communicate fear, anger, sadness, joy, contentment and so on. The observation of these communications by the clinician is an essential part of the assessment process.

Even more important than observing the behaviour of the child is observing the interactions, non-verbal ones especially, between parents and child. Actually what we need to assess is not the infant but the infant-in-context—in other words the infant in his or her natural environment. It is therefore important that both parents—or whoever are the people providing care for the child—are present. If one parent is reluctant to attend, every effort should be made to secure that person's attendance.

The assessment should begin with an interview with child and parents (or others who are caring for the child). If there are other children in the family, it may be helpful to have them present also, but not necessarily at the first interview. As Hirshberg (1993, page 181) puts it, 'the family interview process presents an opportunity to attend carefully to the sample of interaction between each parent and the baby'. The parents should be encouraged to do whatever they would normally do, for example if their child cries, needs changing or appears hungry. Hirshberg suggests that the following aspects of the relationship should be considered:

The attachment relationship. Does the infant use the parents as sources of security and comfort? If so, how is this achieved? When the infant seeks comfort from a parent, is this provided and how? Does the child then feel free to resume exploration?

Safety and protection. How vigilant and diligent is each parent in ensuring that the child is safe and properly protected from dangers? (Parents may be overprotective as well as neglectful in this area.) How does the child respond to the parents' protective measures?

Physiological regulation. How do the parents respond to changes in the child's physiological state—hunger, cold, sleepiness, need to become active and so on? Do the parents intervene in an effective way to meet the child's physiological needs, or respond appropriately to the child's attempts to become more or less active?

Play. If it does not happen naturally, opportunity should be provided for the parents and child to play together for a time. Are the parents relaxed and at ease with the child? Do they respond appropriately to the infant's signals, understanding what their child wants and initiating play activities when structure and organization are needed?

Teaching and learning. This is related to play and is concerned with how the parents help the infant learn things. The parents may be asked to 'help the baby learn' a task appropriate to the baby's developmental level. How willing and able are the parents to do this? How do they approach the task and how flexible are they in carrying it out?

Power and control. How do the parents present themselves to the infant? Do they appear calm, confident and in control? Or do they seem passive, disorganized or confused . . . or tense and potentially explosive?

Regulation of emotion. What is the overall affective tone as parents and infant interact? How freely is emotion expressed? Are voice tones, facial expressions, gestures and non-verbal communications generally congruent? Are there differences between the reactions of the two parents and, if so, what are they? How do the parents react emotionally to each other? Hirshberg (1993) considers that the expression and communication of emotion, and the regulation of these processes, is 'probably the most important area of relationship functioning'.

In addition to the above observations, the parents should be asked how they function in each of the above areas. It can be helpful to ask each parent to describe how the other reacts in different areas of the infant's life and in different situations, and then to find out whether each agrees with the other's perception. Differences in the parents' ways of interacting with their child should be explored.

Zeanah and colleagues (2000) offer another scheme for the assessment of infant-parent relationships; and Seligman (2000) suggests a method of interviewing the families of infants.

Disorders of infants and young children

Although a major focus of infant psychiatry is on whether development is taking a normal course, there are certain defined disorders that occur in infants and young children. These include:

- Autism (discussed in Chapter 11)
- Other pervasive development disorders (also discussed in Chapter 11)
- Mental retardation (Chapter 20)
- Disorders of motor development (Chapter 12)
- Post-traumatic stress disorder (Chapter 15)
- Sleep disorders
- Failure to thrive
- Feeding disorders
- Disorders of attachment
- Communication disorders (often evident at the toddler stage) (Chapter 12)

The *Handbook of Infant Mental Health* (Zeanah, 2000) also has chapters on *regulatory disorders, depression, aggressive behaviour disorders,* and *somatic expression of disease* (see Chapter 17).

The main features of those disorders of infancy that are not discussed elsewhere in this book will be outlined here. Further information in available in the aforementioned book.

Regulatory disorders

These are patterns of atypical behaviour associated with specific difficulties in sensory, sensori-motor or organizational processing, as described in *Zero to Three* (1994). The following subtypes have been described:

— The hypersensitive type
— The underreactive type
— The motorically disorganized/impulsive type
— A mixed type, for regulatory disorders that do not fit into one of the above three types

The *hypersensitive* type of regulatory disorder may be characterized either by a fearful and cautious pattern of behaviour or by a negative and defiant one.

Children with the *underreactive* type of regulatory disorder may be either withdrawn or difficult to engage, or self-absorbed.

Children with the *motorically disorganized/impulsive* regulatory disorder display high activity levels and reckless and impulsive behaviour.

The validity of regulatory disorders as a diagnostic entity is unclear. However the descriptions of the various categories at least serve to draw attention to various ways in which infants may respond to sensory stimuli. Defining clinical problems characterized by these ways of responding may alert those caring for such children to their special needs.

Barton and Robins (2000) discuss regulatory disorders at greater length.

Sleep disorders

Many parents express concerns about the sleep patterns of their infants and young children. Some of these arise simply from lack of knowledge of what is normal. Children's need for sleep varies, and temperamental factors may play a role in determining the ease with which they are able to settle into regular patterns of sleeping and waking. Failure to settle into a regular sleep pattern may also occur in chaotic and disorganized families in which there are no regular bedtimes and bedtime routines.

Failure to sleep, often with crying, is common in babies but normally resolves after a few months if the feeding and general care of the child are satisfactory. Persistence of such problems into the toddler period is fairly common, however, and there may be an association between waking at night and other behavioural and temperamental difficulties (Richman, 1985).

The following specific sleep problems may be encountered in infants and young children:

— Nightmares
— Night terrors

— Sleepwalking
— Sleep apnoea

Nightmares and night terrors are collectively known as *parasomnias*.

Nightmares

These are unpleasant or frightening dreams that occur during *rapid eye movement* (REM), that is, light sleep. The child does not wake up nor necessarily become overtly disturbed while having the nightmare, and if woken up reacts normally.

Night terrors

ICD-10 calls these *sleep terrors* and DSM-IV-TR *sleep terror disorder*. Night terrors occur on waking from 'stage 3' or 'stage 4', that is deep sleep, usually during the first third of nocturnal sleep. The child wakes up in a frightened, even terrified, state and is inaccessible, not responding when spoken to nor appearing to see objects or people. Instead he or she appears to be visually and/or auditorily hallucinated, talking to and looking at people and things not actually present. The child may be difficult to comfort, and the period of disturbed behaviour may last up to 15 minutes or occasionally longer. Eventually the behaviours subside, with or without comfort from an adult, and the child goes back to sleep, awakening in the morning with no recollection of the incident. Night terrors are said to occur in up to 3% of toddlers (Clore & Hibel, 1993). In a few cases they persist into the school-age years. They are not usually associated with another psychiatric disorder but may occur in the course of a febrile illness.

Sleepwalking

This also occurs in a state of deep sleep and is closely related to night terrors. It also may appear during a febrile illness. The child gets up, usually during the first third of nocturnal sleep, and walks around with a blank, staring facial expression, not responding when people try to communicate with him or her. It is usually difficult to waken the child, but once awake the subject appears normal, perhaps after a short period of disorientation and confusion. Sleepwalking episodes may last from a few minutes to half an hour.

Although the above parasomnias are listed as disorders in both ICD-10 and DSM-IV-TR, most children who experience them show no other evidence of psychiatric problems. The sleep problem is probably best regarded as a transient development disturbance. When there is no evidence of any other abnormality, the parents can be reassured.

Sleep apnoea syndrome

This is the most common organic sleep disorder in young children (Anders *et al.*, 2000). Our breathing is under involuntary control for much of the time, including during sleep, but is also subject to voluntary control in the awake state. The essential feature of sleep apnoea is the occurrence of periods of failure to breathe while asleep. These may be due to:

— Mechanical obstruction of the airway, for example by enlarged tonsils or adenoids, or as result of severe obesity; or
— Disorders of the control systems in the central nervous system, principally failure of the subcortical control system; or
— A combination of neurological dysfunction and peripheral obstruction.

When the cause of the failure to breathe is mechanical obstruction, we have what is known as 'obstructive sleep apnoea'. When it is neurological, this is known as 'central sleep apnoea'. Mixed types are labelled as such.

When breathing stops during a period of sleep apnoea, the oxygen level in the blood becomes dangerously low, whereupon the subject wakes up and voluntary control of breathing takes over. This may occur repeatedly during the night. This can cause chronic loss of sleep and consequent daytime sleepiness, chronic fatigue and, in severe cases, intellectual deterioration, depression, personality changes and outbursts of irrational behaviour. If there is repeated interruption of sleep over a long period, this may result in a reduction in the secretion of growth hormone, which occurs during stage 4 sleep. This in turn may lead to growth failure or even the failure-to-thrive syndrome.

Treatment of sleep disorders

While many sleep problems are transient developmental glitches that resolve spontaneously, these disorders sometimes persist into later childhood. Also children who won't go to sleep at bedtime can disrupt family life to an extent that may be considerable. This section therefore discusses the treatment of sleep disorders at whatever stage of childhood or adolescence they occur.

When sleep problems are reported it is a good idea to look closely at the parent-child interactions and to assess whether any other psychiatric condition, for example an anxiety disorder, is present. If it is, the appropriate treatment should be instituted. But often no other disorder is found. If that is so, behavioural approaches are often effective.

When children are not sleeping at the appropriate times—what ICD-10 calls 'nonorganic disorder of the sleep-wake cycle'—the problem may be tackled either by addressing bedtime routines and management or by dealing with the situation in the morning.

Richman and colleagues (1985) describe the results of an approach designed to help children stay in bed quietly without disturbing their parents and to settle down to sleep without parental attention. Alteration of the parents' responses to the children's night-time behaviour seemed often to lead to rapid resolution of the problem, suggesting that the parents' previous responses had contributed to the maintenance of the problem. Treatment was in each case developed following a behavioural analysis. Complete or marked improvement occurred in 27 of 35 children, but five did not complete treatment, and the improvement rate in those that did was 90%. At follow-up five months later it was 80%.

Sometimes sleep disorders are manifestations of problems with the individual's 'biological clock'. The term *circadian rhythm* is used to describe the diurnal variation of bodily activity that is normally in synchrony with a person's life. Our metabolism slows down towards bedtime, and we feel sleepy as the body prepares for a night's rest. Our metabolic rate remains low during the night, increasing towards morning as the time to awaken and get ready for the day's activities approaches.

Many of us who lead a regular life do not even need an alarm clock to wake us at the right time because our biological clock has become set to do what an alarm clock would. However some people's 'clock' is not set as it needs to be. The teenager who stays up late playing videogames or watching television, and then has difficulty waking in the morning, is an example of this, but anyone can have this problem. The solution is to reset the clock by ensuring that the individual is woken at whatever time is appropriate to the person's commitments and to expose the person immediately to light that is as bright as possible. No crawling back under the bedclothes and covering the head! It is light that tells the body that the time for the day's activities is at hand. It may take two or three months of this regime before the 'clock' is reset, but as the subject begins to wake earlier, so the 'clock' will adjust itself to bring forward the time at which the metabolic rate begins to slow down in the evening, so that the individual becomes drowsy and ready for sleep earlier.

The *parasomnias* often do not themselves need to be treated, but any associated disorders such as anxiety or depression should be. Medication has little or no place in the treatment of sleep disorders in infants and young children.

When sleep apnoea is due to airway obstruction, steps should be taken to relieve the obstruction. This may involve removal of the tonsils and/or adenoids or, less often, other surgical procedures on the upper respiratory tract. If obesity is contributing, a weight-reducing regime should be instituted. When there is no physical obstruction of the upper airways, a careful neurological appraisal is indicated, and any neurological condition that may be contributing should be treated if possible.

Anders and colleagues (2000) discuss sleep problems in more detail than is possible here, including various approaches to classifying them.

Feeding difficulties and failure to thrive

Appetite and feeding problems in infants may be symptoms of physical or of emotional and/or relationship problems within the family. Sometimes there are elements of both. Children may eat, or be thought by their parents to eat, too little, too much, or the wrong sorts of foods; or they may try to eat inedible items (*pica*).

Failure to thrive (FTT)

This term describes the condition of infants and young children who show serious failure to gain weight. FTT is a symptom, not a disorder, although ICD-10 includes a category of *feeding disorder of infancy and childhood*.

FTT may be 'organic'—when a medical problem is found to be responsible; or 'non-organic'—when no medical cause is found, although medical consequences may follow a period of inadequate nutritional intake. We are concerned here with the 'non-organic' variety of FTT.

Benoit (2000) describes FTT as a 'multifactorial problem involving biological, nutritional, and environmental factors'. While inadequate nutritional intake is a central feature of failure to thrive, the factors that lead to the nutritional intake being inadequate are complex. The following may contribute:

— *Factors in the child.* Various temperamental, behavioural and emotional abnormalities have been reported in some children with FTT, but distinguishing between cause and effect is difficult.

— *Environmental factors.* Poverty, violence, substance abuse, criminality, and dysfunctional relationships have been documented in the families of children with FTT. The mothers often have histories of mental illness and/or abuse, whether in childhood or later in life (Benoit, 2000, pages 344–345).

— *Problems in the parent-infant relationship.* Mothers of infants and toddlers with FTT, compared with mothers of those without FTT, have been found to be 'less responsive, less flexible, more controlling, more intrusive, overstimulating, less affectionate, less accepting and less sensitive'. They have also been found to use more physical punishment and to express more hostile and angry emotion during interactions with their infants (Benoit, 2000, page 345).

The consequences of FTT can be serious. The brain grows rapidly during the first two years of life. Inadequate nutritional intake during this period can stunt brain development and lead to lowered intelligence and to language, reading and other learning disorders later.

The *management and treatment* of FTT require a multidisciplinary team. A comprehensive assessment of child and family is first necessary. Particular attention should be paid to the parent-child relationship, but the stability of the family as a whole and the care given to the children are also important. If there are serious problems of family functioning, addressing these should be a high priority. Family therapy may be needed, and it may be necessary to place the FTT infant in a hospital or a special foster home for a short period.

Another high priority is ensuring that the child receives adequate nutrition. The active involvement of a dietician is helpful. In extreme cases tube feeding may be necessary.

Education of the parents, both about their child's nutritional needs and about how to handle the feeding situation, can be crucial.

Rumination disorder of infancy appears as a diagnostic category in both ICD-10 and DSM-IV-TR. Its main feature is the repeated regurgitation of food in the absence of other gastrointestinal symptoms, with failure to gain weight or with loss of weight. The usual age of onset is between 3 and 12 months. It has been reported to have a 25% mortality (Benoit, 1993). The behaviour is self-induced and usually occurs when the child is alone. So-called *psychogenic rumination* is believed to be associated with disturbed parent-child (usually mother-child) relationships, whereas *self-stimulatory rumination* is associated with mental retardation. The relationship of these disorders with FTT is unclear.

Disorders of attachment

A major focus of infant psychiatry is the study, and often the modification, of parent-child relationships and interactions. Attachment theory considers the processes whereby emotional bonds are formed between infants and young children, on the one hand, and those caring for them—usually their parents, sometimes other caregivers—on the other.

Ainsworth and colleagues (1978), on the basis of the study of the effects of brief separations and reunions of infants and their mothers, identified three groups of infants:

—*Securely attached infants* seek contact with their mothers under stress, are calmed by this and explore actively in the presence of their mothers.

—*Anxiously attached infants* seem ambivalent towards their mothers and seek contact but apparently fail to be comforted by it. The anxiously attached infant is chronically anxious in relation to the mother and is unable to use her as a secure base from which to explore unfamiliar situations. These mothers are less responsive to crying and other communications than are the mothers of the securely attached infants.

—*Anxious-avoidant infants* show avoidant behaviour when reunited with their mothers after a period of separation. They do not seek close contact with their mothers, even in high-stress situations; and they seem undisturbed when separated from their mothers. The mothers tend to be rejecting and angry, rebuffing or roughly treating their infants when the latter seek physical proximity. This appears to teach the infants to avoid seeking proximity. In other situations and with other adults, however, these infants can respond positively to close physical contact.

Main and Solomon (1990) subsequently described a fourth category:

—*Disorganized/disoriented,* in which the infant shows attachment behaviour that is interrupted, confused or incomplete.

It seems that for optimal, that is secure, attachment to develop there should be sensitive parental care in which the parent is neither too highly involved with the child nor too uninvolved. The former may lead to the emergence of avoidant infants, whereas the latter may lead to anxiously attached ones.

Since the work of Ainsworth *et al.* (1978) was published much further research on attachment and its disorders has been reported. Zeanah and Boris (2000) propose the following classification:

—*Disorders of nonattachment.* The nonattachment may be accompanied by emotional withdrawal or indiscriminate sociability.

—*Secure-base distortions.* Four subcategories are proposed here, namely attachment disorder with, respectively, self-endangerment; clinging/inhibited exploration; vigilance/hypercompliance; and role reversal.

—*Disrupted attachment disorder.* This category is for situations in which a child suddenly experiences the loss of the attachment figure, as for example when the sole attachment figure dies or there is an abrupt change of foster parent.

Disorders of attachment are widely believed to contribute to the causation of various child psychiatric conditions, including relationship problems in later childhood, anxiety disorders, behaviour problems and mood disorders. Well-supported research data are few however.

Various approaches to the *treatment* of attachment disorders have been proposed. Zeanah and Boris (2000, pages 365–366) list:

— Individual psychotherapy for child and/or caregiver
— Parent training with emphasis on developmental expectations and sensitive responsiveness
— Family therapy
— Caregiver-child dyadic therapy
— Infant-parent psychotherapy, integrating crisis intervention, developmental guidance, attention to instrumental issues such as poor housing and inadequate medical care, and psychotherapy in which the baby is present

Hard data on the effectiveness of the above are currently lacking, and the area is one in which research is much needed.

A fuller review of the disturbances and disorders of attachment in early childhood is provided by Zeanah and Boris (2000).

Depression

The last several decades have seen a progressive lowering of the age at which it is believed, at least by many working in this field, that depressive disorders may occur. It is now widely accepted that such disorders can occur in school-age children, but may they also occur in preschool children? The answer to this question is unclear, but depressive symptoms are sometimes observed in preschool children. The many issues to which this question gives rise are discussed by Luby (2000).

Aggressive behaviour disorders

While children in the age range 1 to 3 can behave aggressively, it is not clear whether it is appropriate to distinguish a diagnostic category of aggressive behaviour disorders so early in life. The ICD-10 and DSM-IV-TR diagnostic criteria for conduct disorders and oppositional defiant disorder are not designed for application at this age. However Shaw and colleagues (2000) make a case for the establishment of a diagnostic category. They argue that the roots of later aggressive behaviour patterns are often to be found in the first three years of life, and that there is often continuity between early aggressive behaviour and similar behaviour later in childhood.

Shaw *et al.* (2000) provide an in-depth discussion of this issue on which there is no current consensus.

Treatment in infant psychiatry

Treatment efforts in infant psychiatry are usually directed at the relationship between child and parents, or other caregivers, or aim to improve the functioning of the family as a whole. Preventive measures are also important. These include ensuring that pregnant women receive the best medical care and nutrition, and that they are informed of the dangers of smoking, excessive alcohol use and the use of other drugs. Some require education about child care and related matters such as household budgeting and nutrition.

Treatment approaches for some of the other specific disorders mentioned earlier are discussed in the relevant chapters of this book. The *Handbook of Infant Mental Health* (Zeanah, 2000) also includes five chapters on, respectively, 'Prevention Science and Prevention Programs', 'Parent-Child Relationships in Early Intervention with Infants and Toddlers', 'Infant-Parent Psychotherapy: Core Concepts and Current Approaches', 'Interaction Guidance: An Approach for Difficult-to-Engage Families', and 'Infant Massage Therapy'.

Chapter 19

Special Problems of Adolescence

The developmental tasks of adolescence were summarized in Chapter 1. Some special considerations apply when adolescents are interviewed. The establishment of rapport is especially important. Many adolescents attend at the behest of others rather than because they have a desire to be interviewed and assessed. Their view of their problems, if they are prepared to admit they have problems, may be different from that of their parents, teachers, probation officers, social workers or others who may have recommended that they attend. I find it is often best to start by taking a 'one-down' position, asking the young person to help me understand how it is he or she has come to see me. 'Who wanted you to come here?' is a good question to ask.

Adolescents are usually best seen initially on their own or in the company of their parents. It is usually a mistake to see the parents first, in the absence of the young person. If this is done, the latter is likely to be suspicious about what is going on, and may think, perhaps correctly, that the parents have reported unfavourably on him or her. This may lead to suspiciousness and a lack of co-operation.

It is also important to define the limits of confidentiality that apply. How much of what the young person tells the interviewer will be passed on to the parents? My practice is to tell adolescents that I will pass nothing on without the young person's permission, with certain specific exceptions:

—If I believe that the young person is likely to commit suicide or to attack or attempt to kill someone, I must tell the parents or some other responsible adult. 'I can't let people walk out of my office and kill themselves or someone else,' I say.

—If I am under a legal obligation to report something, as when the child welfare legislation in the jurisdiction in which I am working compels me to report, for example, that I suspect a young person I am seeing is being abused or neglected.

Everything else, I tell the young person, is 'strictly between you and me. I may ask for your permission to share something you have told me with your parents, but if you say *no*, I will respect that'. I normally mention that I will be sending a report to whomever has referred the young person, and I ask the patient if there is anything he or she does not want me to include. The situation is different, of course, if the subject is being interviewed at the request of a court or agency. If that is so, the young person should be told that what he or she says may be included in the report sent to that court or agency.

Prevalence of psychiatric disorders in adolescence

Studies of adolescent populations have yielded prevalence rates for psychiatric disorders ranging from 8% to 21%, depending on the diagnostic criteria used, the population studied and the study methods used. Most studies have found higher rates in adolescence than in childhood, but more striking are the differences in sex ratios. Among pre-pubertal children, boys with psychiatric disorders outnumber girls by a margin of about 2:1; then as puberty arrives and adolescence proceeds, the ratio becomes about 1:1. In adult life it is reversed, the prevalence of psychiatric disorders in women being greater than that in men. Urban rates are higher than rural ones, for adolescents as for younger children.

The pattern of psychiatric diagnoses changes as childhood gives way to adolescence. Schizophrenia, rare before puberty, becomes more common. Major affective disorders, especially depression, are encountered more frequently in adolescence, whereas encopresis, enuresis and some developmental disorders become less common. The onset of anorexia nervosa is usually during adolescence, though it can start before puberty.

Much of the change in the sex ratio is due to the increased prevalence of affective disorders, principally depression, in girls, whereas the prevalence of developmental disorders, which predominantly affect boys, decreases. Suicide and attempted suicide, rare before puberty, become more frequent. Mania and hypomania, also rare before puberty, increase in frequency though they are relatively uncommon in early and middle adolescence. Alcohol and drug abuse are other conditions that often make their appearance in adolescence, though the inhalation of solvents, petrol (gasoline) and like substances may start before puberty.

Adolescent disorders may be considered under three headings, though subdividing them in this way is somewhat artificial, especially the distinction between categories 2 and 3:

(1) Unresolved childhood disorders
(2) Disorders related to puberty and adolescence
(3) Adult-type disorders arising in adolescence

(1) Unresolved childhood disorders

(a) Conduct and oppositional defiant disorders

These disorders may become exacerbated with the onset of puberty, though this is not always the case. The tendency to rebel and reject adult standards that may be encountered in adolescence may reinforce pre-existing antisocial feelings and behaviour. Adolescents who do not have secure relationships with their parents, and lack internal controls based on identification with them, may be especially at risk of becoming involved in antisocial behaviour.

(b) Anxiety/neurotic disorders

These disorders sometimes improve around puberty, as the biological drives towards independence develop. The support of the young person's peer group, which tends to become more important in the lives of young people during this period of life, may also help. There are usually big changes in the school environment at this time. From being in a primary or elementary (terminology varies from jurisdiction to jurisdiction) school, with one main teacher and, usually, a high degree of supervision, the child may move to a larger, more impersonal secondary, or high school where more responsibility and independence of decision are expected. This may be a helpful experience if enough support over the transition is available from family, friends and, if needed, school staff. These changes may help emotionally immature children who have been overdependent on their parents to become more self-reliant.

These aids to emotional growth are not always enough. Some children prove to have insufficient emotional resources to meet successfully the challenges of adolescence. Instead of becoming increasingly independent they fall back into the security and comfort of their families. Their anxiety and feelings of insecurity continue or worsen.

School refusal in adolescence may be a continuation of a problem that existed before puberty, or it may appear for the first time. Even if its onset is in adolescence, its origins can often be traced to earlier years. The young person probably did not enter adolescence feeling secure and self-confident. The onset of school refusal in adolescence is often more gradual than it is in middle childhood, with increasing withdrawal and isolation from peers. Symptoms of separation anxiety are usually less prominent and difficulties in school more so. The problems there often concern relationships with peers or teachers.

School-refusing adolescents tend to have difficulty expressing aggressive feelings and asserting their independence in normal ways. The adolescent's desire, conscious or unconscious, to be independent, plus awareness of the parental protectiveness that is felt to be preventing this, can lead to a build-up of angry feelings. These may find expression in outbursts of rage or physical violence in a young person who at other times is passive and dependent. In such cases, treatment for the whole family may yield the best results. School refusal in adolescence is often associated with more serious pathology in child and family than tends to be the case in earlier childhood. Depressive or conduct disorder symptoms may accompany it.

(c) Affective disorders

These may be continuations of disorders that existed before puberty, but they often arise *de novo* during adolescence. This applies especially to mania and bipolar disorders, which are rare before puberty, but many individuals experience their first episode of depression during adolescence.

(d) Autism and other pervasive developmental disorders

The handicaps of children with these disorders persist into adolescence, and epilepsy is sometimes added to them. Hyperactivity may lessen, and adolescents with autism are often underactive. They lack initiative and drive, and their inappropriate social behaviour and responses, and lack of empathy for others, isolate them from their peers. Consequently they remain closely dependent on their families and other caregivers. At the same time the hormonal and physical changes of puberty, especially their increase in size and physical strength, may cause them to become more difficult to manage. Assertiveness, often in areas in which it is not appropriate, may make it difficult or impossible for their parents to manage them. This may necessitate institutional placement.

(e) Developmental disorders

By the time they reach adolescence, many children with developmental disorders have overcome their speech, language and motor-coordination problems, or have learned to accommodate to them, for example by using a keyboard instead of writing. Reading difficulties often persist, however, and are common in adolescents with conduct disorders. Poor reading skills are a serious handicap and limit employment opportunities in modern society. The resulting failure to obtain satisfying work may lead young people to drop out of mainstream society, which often has serious consequences.

(f) Attention-deficit disorders and hyperactivity

Hyperactivity often lessens or subsides completely around puberty, but other symptoms of attention-deficit hyperactivity disorder frequently do not. Distractibility, impulsivity and problems with concentration often persist, though they may gradually improve over the years. Low self-esteem, poor school performance and poor peer relationships may continue. Some of these individuals exhibit antisocial behaviour, though different studies have yielded widely varying estimates of how many (see Weiss & Hechtman, 1986, Chapter 4).

(2) Disorders related to puberty and adolescence

The emotional, social, psychological and physical changes of adolescence provide the context for some of the disorders occurring at that time of life. The following issues are relevant and may present challenges to both parents and their adolescent children:

(a) The dependence-independence conflict

Adolescents are neither dependent children not independent adults. They are somewhere in between. They feel, in varying degrees, the urge to be independent, and they are subject to social pressures that foster this. At the same time they feel unsure how far they can act independently. A desire to fall back to the security of their families may alternate with shows of independent, but sometimes ill-judged, decision making.

(b) Doubts about sexual role and sexual adequacy

The physical and emotional changes of puberty may start as early as age 10 or as late as 17 in normally developing young people. Puberty tends to come earlier and to be completed more quickly in girls than in boys, although there is much overlap. Consequently some young people feel out of step with their peers, especially if puberty comes late to them. Fears of sexual inadequacy are common during this time.

The upsurge of sexual feelings and activity, and the development of sometimes intense relationships with the opposite sex, may provoke feelings of anxiety and confusion. The young person may want to enter into relationships, while feeling shy and lacking the necessary confidence. On the other hand, some adolescents become involved in sexual relationships early, leading to unwanted pregnancies. These are usually stressful experiences, whether they are aborted or carried to term.

(c) Peer group influences

During adolescence the peer group assumes increasing importance in the lives of the young person. Adolescents tend to form groups, sometimes of one sex, sometimes of both sexes, that provide their members with support in meeting the social and emotional challenges of this period. With the support of the group, many young people are able to do things they would shy away from if on their own. Adolescent groups may be as small as two or three, but membership may run to 20 or 30, or even more. Some remain constant, but most change as members leave to join other groups, and others join. One young person may have affiliation with several groups at the same time.

The influence of adolescent groups is not always beneficial. Delinquent gangs may have seriously adverse effects on their members and indeed can become major problems in their neighbourhoods. Some young people feel different from the other group members, and some are treated differently because of their appearance, race or background. This may lead them to do rash or daring things to 'prove' themselves to the group. Adolescent groups vary widely in how they function, but most require a fair degree of conformity to their standards and unwritten rules. Inability on a member's part to meet the group's requirements may lead to anxiety or even rejection by the group.

(d) Discrepancies between individual development and the demands of society

A newspaper cartoon pictures a couple at a theatre box office over which a sign reads, 'Children under 16 must be accompanied by their parents'. The stylishly dressed couple are explaining, 'We're under 16 but we're parents'. This sums up a dilemma of many young people in contemporary society.

Puberty is occurring earlier (in Western countries the average age of the menarche is now about one year earlier than it was 50 years ago), yet many of society's institutions take no cognizance of this. For many young people formal education and financial dependency are increasingly prolonged, whereas those who choose not to remain in formal education beyond their mid-teens often find it difficult to obtain rewarding work and a satisfying place in society. At the same time society's attitudes towards sexual activity in adolescents have been changing. These seem to have become permissive and becoming pregnant before marriage is no longer frowned on.

Many single teenage girls who become pregnant opt to keep their babies and strive to provide good care for them, but this is an enormous and often stressful challenge that they cannot always meet successfully. It also puts the next generation at risk.

(e) Family development problems

For some parents, accepting and adjusting to the arrival of adolescence in their children proves difficult. Attitudes and parenting methods that have worked well before puberty may no longer be successful but are sometimes hard to modify as the need arises. The process of change should be one of gradual, sensitively monitored handing over of responsibility from parents to child. Unfortunately this sometimes becomes a battle of wills; or the opposite situation may happen, with the parents relinquishing control and handing over responsibility to the young person too soon, so that their son or daughter runs wild and gets into difficulties.

Adolescent behaviour problems

Conduct and oppositional defiant disorders are at least as prevalent in adolescence as in middle childhood, and the numbers of antisocial acts performed in the community, as opposed to in the home or school, are probably greater.

Some adolescent conduct disorders are continuations of behaviour patterns established earlier, often much earlier, in childhood. Others have their onset in adolescence. The latter group lacks the association with reading problems commonly found in cases of earlier onset, and their symptoms and the associated family problems are generally less severe and chronic. They seem sometimes to be no more than exaggerated reactions to some combination of the five challenges listed above in paragraphs (a) to (e). The soundness of the parent-child relationship before puberty, and how the parents react to their offspring's rebellious behaviour, affect the severity and persistence of these disorders.

Sometimes an insecure adolescent's rebellious behaviour seems to have the unconscious aim of provoking the parents to take charge. Some adolescents are afraid of their own aggressiveness and feel a need for someone to take over control. In other instances the behaviour seems to be a protest against over-strict demands by the parents. In yet others it is associated with feelings of rootlessness and aimlessness in young people lacking a safe and secure background for this stage of their development. These adolescents may have been deprived of love and a consistent family setting in the past, and some may have been emotionally, physically or sexually abused.

Adolescent conduct disorders may be transient blips in the course of the young person's development, or manifestations of long-standing deviant personality development—or anything in between. The severity of the behavioural disturbance is, on its own, an imperfect indication of the seriousness of the problem. Also important are adjustment before puberty, indeed as far back as the preschool years; family stability and parental attitudes; the young person's educational status, especially reading skills; and adjustment in situations in which the parents are not directly involved. The latter include school, peer group and the interview situation with the psychiatrist or other health professional.

Many adolescents emerge as mentally healthy, well-adjusted individuals after going through difficult times in their teenage years. Antisocial behaviours are less common in young adults than in adolescents, suggesting that this is often a transient phenomenon.

'Running away' from home is a common problem in adolescents, though younger children sometimes run away. The term applies to leaving or staying away from home, with the intention of staying away for a period of time, in circumstances in which those remaining at home will miss the young person. The prevalence of this behaviour varies greatly from one community to another. The homes of runaways are characterized by high rates of parent-child conflict, parental death and divorce, and physical and sexual abuse (Tyler & Caunce, 2002). A high prevalence of disabilities such as mental retardation and communication disorders has been found in runaway children (Sullivan & Knutson, 2000). It may be that such children are less well equipped to deal with abuse when they are subjected to it. While running away is often the best solution the young person can see to escape conflict and/or abuse in the family, it may also be a way of avoiding defeat in a battle for independence from the parents.

Drug and alcohol abuse

In this section the term *drug abuse* will be used to include the abuse of alcohol, except where the context implies otherwise. Alcohol is a powerful mind-altering drug, and its use can lead to abuse, dependence and, ultimately, death. It is often just one of a variety of mind-altering substances used by the drug abuser and addict. Separating it out for special consideration can have unfortunate consequences, its use consequently being regarded as less serious than that of 'real' drugs—implying that addiction to alcohol is not as serious as addiction to other mind-altering substances.

In discussing 'substance use disorders', distinctions are made, in both DSM-IV-TR and ICD-10, between such concepts as 'use', 'abuse', 'dependence', 'compulsive use' and 'harmful use'. These are discussed and explained by Mirza (2002). This section, however, will be limited to a general discussion of how adolescents may use and abuse drugs, rather than of the niceties of the subcategorization of substance use disorders.

Adolescent drug use and abuse are serious problems in many, perhaps most, parts of the world. Prevalence rates vary from place to place and from time to time, and are difficult to determine. Different drugs come in and out of fashion, and availability and cost are factors that help determine what is used.

Drug users may be subdivided into the following groups:

— Experimental
— Situational (or recreational)
— Compulsive

— *Experimental use:* Many adolescents experiment, at least with alcohol, cigarettes or cannabis, at some point. The experimentation may be brief and does not usually lead to regular use.

— *Situational (or recreational) use.* A smaller group uses drugs at parties and in particular situations, usually in the company of a group of peers, but use is confined to such situations.

— *Compulsive use.* This is use by those who are dependent on the drug or, more often, drugs—the addicts. This is an even smaller group than the situational users.

What determines who becomes dependent on drugs? This is incompletely understood. Social pressures can be important in leading to drug use but probably do not determine who becomes dependent. The following factors may contribute to the development of drug dependency:

— Genetic predisposition
— The emotional stability and personality of the individual
— The presence of serious personality problems or psychiatric conditions such as chronic depression (There may be a history of early deprivation, abuse and/or other adverse rearing experiences.)

There is some correlation between drug use and both delinquency and failure in school, though how these are causally connected—if they are—is not clear. Other factors that have been found to be associated with drug use, but not necessarily dependence, include:

— Social isolation
— Low self-esteem
— Poor relationships with parents
— Depression
— Unconventional beliefs and values concerning drugs and their use (among Rastafarians, for example)

Young people may seek to have their felt needs for affiliation, satisfaction of curiosity, altered states of consciousness, recreation, anxiety reduction and the masking of concerns and worries met by the use of drugs, especially in the company of others.

Prevalence
It is not possible to state definitively what the prevalence of substance use disorders in adolescents is because this varies with the population studied, the age of the ado-

Table 19.1   Prevalence of drug use, in percentages, of subjects aged 14 to 16 years (Ontario Child Health Study)

	Boys	Girls
Tobacco		
Occasional use	31.1	45.6
Regular use	15.8	23.4
Alcohol		
Occasional use	42.5	48.8
Regular use	10.6	15.9
Marijuana	13.3	17.6
'Hard' drugs	5.3	7.5
Inhalants	3.8	4.5

lescents investigated, the drugs that are considered and the assessment measures used. We do know, however, that alcohol, tobacco and cannabis are the most frequently used substances in most 'western' societies.

Drug use was investigated during the Ontario Child Health Study. Of a representative sample of 1302 adolescents aged 12 to 16, a total of 1265 participated (97.8% of those eligible) (Boyle & Offord, 1986). The prevalence figures, expressed as percentages, for the age group 14 to 16 are listed in Table 19.1.

'Hard' drugs included amphetamines, other stimulants, psychedelics, and heroin and other opiates. The prevalence rates for all drugs, except inhalants, were lower in the 12- to 14-year age bracket. Inhalants, however, were used by 8.3% of the boys and 9.6% of the girls in the younger age group. There was a tendency for drug use to be more common among girls than among boys, but only in the case of cigarette smoking was the difference statistically significant. There is a clear progression in drug use with age, and the mid-teen years are a common time for drug use to begin. It usually starts with drinking beer or wine, though the use of tobacco may precede this. Subsequent progression is most often to hard liquor, cannabis, and then other illegal drugs such as LSD, MDNA, cocaine and opiates.

Since 1991, the Ontario Student Drug Use Survey (Adlaf *et al.* 2000) has been estimating the use of drugs in large samples of students in grades 7, 9, 11 and 13 (roughly ages 12 to 18). Self-report surveys were carried out every two years from 1991 to 1999. The number of students that participated varied, but it was never less than 2868 and in 1991 it was 3945. The drugs about which the students were asked were:

'Tobacco; alcohol; cannabis; glue; other solvents; barbiturates; heroin; methamphetamine; stimulants; tranquilizers; lysergic acid diethylamine (LSD); other hallucinogens; cocaine; crack cocaine; phencyclidine (PCP); crystal methamphetamine; and "ecstasy" (MDMA or methylenedioxymethamphetamine).'

In the case of every one of the above drugs, reported use increased between 1993 and 1999, though not all the increases reached statistically significant levels. In the case of some drugs—alcohol, glue sniffing, other solvent use, barbiturates and 'other solvents'—there were even statistically significant increases between 1997 and 1999. These figures represent reports of any use during the 12 months prior to each survey—even smoking one cigarette or having one alcoholic drink. They do not refer to regular use and still less to addictive use. Being derived from self-reports, even though they were anonymous, they may be under-estimates. Nevertheless they probably are valid as indicators of trends in drug use, and they certainly suggest that drug use among Ontario adolescents is alive and growing.

The foregoing list of drugs includes many of those that may be used or abused by adolescents, but it is not exhaustive. Others include codeine preparations (codeine is contained in some cough syrups and analgesic preparations); compound tablets containing various mixtures of analgesics, sedatives, antihistamines and/or caffeine; the anti-emetic diphenhydramine (Gravol); and other psychoactive preparations. Those mentioned are the main ones used by adolescents in contemporary Western society. In other parts of the world different drugs may be abused. For example in Southern Africa one of the three most-used drugs is methaqualone (Mandrax) (the other two are alcohol and cannabis) (Parry *et al.*, 2002). But the use or abuse of methaqualone is virtually unknown in Western countries.

The patchy and varied reports on prevalence are summarized by Mirza (2002, pages 333–334).

Comorbidity

Often young people who use drugs also have other psychiatric disorders. These include conduct disorders, depression and adjustment disorders. Suicidal ideation and acts are also frequent accompaniments of substance use.

Management

Adolescent drug abusers rarely seek help from psychiatrists or other mental health workers on their own account. When they do present for help—usually at a special treatment facility for young people with alcohol and drug problems—it is more often under pressure from family, the juvenile court system, social workers, school staff or occasionally employers. Few adolescent addicts have yet suffered enough of the adverse consequences of their addiction to see it as a problem they need to address.

For those who do ask for help, an approach including individual and/or group therapy, appropriate treatment of any comorbid conditions, work with the family, and the provision of educational material for both young person and family is often used. There is much support for the use of family-based treatments for adolescent drug-abuse problems. Rowe and Liddle (2003) consider them 'the most effective approaches', and Robbins and colleagues (2002) report on the successful use of 'brief strategic family therapy'.

Medication has little part to play, but Mirza (2002) discusses what small role it may have, as well as reviewing concisely the neurobiology and other aspects of adolescent substance use. 'Twelve-step' programs such as Alcoholics Anonymous and Narcotics Anonymous can be powerful tools for the addict seeking recovery who is willing to commit wholeheartedly to what these programs recommend. But these programs seem to be of less value to adolescents, perhaps because few have yet reached that state of desperation required to provide the motivation needed.

Disorders that may first develop in adolescence

These include the following:

— Anxiety disorders, which may arise as responses to the stresses of the adolescent period
— Obsessive-compulsive, conversion and dissociative disorders, which also may arise *de novo* during adolescence
— Social phobias and agoraphobia, which may put in their first appearance in the context of difficulty adjusting to the demands of adolescence
— Dysthymia and depression
— Anorexia nervosa, which commonly has its onset during adolescence (see Chapter 17)

(3) Adult-type disorders arising in adolescence

Many of the psychiatric disorders of adult life may put in an appearance before adulthood is reached. Both schizophrenia (Chapter 13) and the major affective disorders (Chapter 11) become more common as adolescence proceeds. This is also the period during which many personality disorders (Chapter 16) make their first, tentative appearance, though diagnosis should be delayed until the clinical picture is clear.

Suicidal behaviour in adolescence

Suicide is rare before puberty, but its incidence increases as the teenage years succeed one another. By the late teens suicide has become a major cause of death. Moreover its incidence has been increasing in many societies over recent decades. The management of suicidal adolescents is therefore an important part of the work of psychiatrists and other mental health professionals who work with this age group.

Although depression is the major risk factor predisposing to suicidal behaviour, there is evidence that individuals with certain personality disorders are also at increased risk. Links and colleagues (2003) review the evidence concerning the risk of suicide and self-harm, and also of violence, in young people with antisocial personality disorder, borderline personality disorder and narcissistic personality disorder. All may be at higher than average risk, whether or not there is accompanying depression.

There is evidence that neurobiological factors may predispose individuals to suicidal behaviour and that assessment of the risk of suicide should include:

— Inquiry for a family and personal history of suicidal behaviour
— A 'clinical assessment of sensitivity to psychosocial stressors and problem-solving capacities' (van Heeringen, 2003)

The term *suicidal behaviour* is sometimes applied to behaviours ranging from the infliction of superficial cuts on the arms to the taking of a massive drug overdose in a situation in which the subject is not likely to be found until well after death.

The term *parasuicide* is sometimes used for self-injurious behaviour that is not life-threatening. While these are sometimes referred to as *suicide attempts*, most of those carrying them out have objectives other than to kill themselves, though there are borderline cases in which the motivation is mixed. They are often cries for help by adolescents suffering distress and wishing to draw attention to their plight. They should not be ignored, but they are not true attempts at suicide. On the other hand, many other suicide attempts are real; the young person truly wants to kill himself or herself, and failure to do so may result from the subject being discovered in the attempt by chance, or because he or she has second thoughts after taking an overdose and seeks help before death ensues.

More adolescent boys than girls commit suicide, ratios of over 4 to 1 being reported in the 15 to 19 age range. On the other hand, attempted suicide, or parasuicide, is more common among adolescent girls.

Assessment of suicide risk

The psychiatric examination of an adolescent should always include an assessment of suicidal risk. It is best to delay this until rapport is well established. The first stage is to explore for *suicidal ideation*. I do this by asking questions such as the following:

— Have you ever felt that life is not worth living?
— Have you ever wished you were dead?

If either of these is answered in the affirmative, I go on to ask questions such as:

— When did you first feel life was not worth living?
— Do you feel that way now, or if you don't when did you last feel that way?
— When was the first time you wished you were dead?
— How often have you felt that way?
— Do you feel that way now?
— (If the subject does not feel that way now) When did you last feel that way?

The above questions address suicidal ideation. The following ones address suicidal intent.

— Have you considered harming yourself in some way?
— (If yes) What have you thought about doing to harm yourself?

— Do you have plans for killing yourself now?
— (If yes) What are you planning to do?
— When might you do it?

Supplementary questions will often be needed after the young person answers some of the above questions. Next I seek information about any previous suicide attempts.

— Have you ever tried to physically hurt or kill yourself?
— (If yes) How many times have you done that?
— When was the last time? What happened?

If there have been previous attempts, I explore these in as much detail as possible:

— What happened to prevent the attempts from being successful?
— How strong was the subject's desire to die?
— Was the young person taken to hospital?
— If so, what treatment was provided?
— Was the young person admitted to hospital and, if so, for how long?

My experience is that most adolescents answer questions such as the above openly and as accurately as they can. Nevertheless some either exaggerate or underplay the severity of their past attempts at suicide. Collateral information from parents, other family members and other people involved in the young person's life should therefore be obtained whenever possible. It is helpful also to know the reaction of parents and others to the suicide attempt. At the same time the parents can be asked whether there is any family history of suicide.

Some other points about suicidal risk are:

— The greater the degree of the depression that is present in seriously suicidal subjects, the greater is the risk of further attempts.

— Suicide is more likely the less communication there is with other people.

— The isolated depressed person is very much at risk, especially when communication channels have recently broken down.

— When there have been previous suicide attempts, the risk may be greater than when that is not the case.

— A long history of self-destructive behaviour is serious and suggests that an in-depth psychiatric investigation, and probably treatment, are needed.

— An important issue is how far suicide attempts, and also parasuicide, have been intended as a means of communication. If they have been, were the communications heeded by those to whom they were addressed—even if indirectly—and has action been taken? If there has been little response to what are basically cries for help, the risk of recurrence may be high.

—Most serious of all is a history of determined attempts at suicide, carried out in isolation, and accompanied by a strong wish to die.

Treatment approaches

Discussion of the treatment of the disorders mentioned in this chapter is to be found in the relevant chapters of this book, but there are some general points about the treatment of adolescents that merit mention here.

—Many adolescents come reluctantly for treatment and at the behest of others, so they are not strongly motivated. Some deny that they have a serious problem or one they cannot solve on their own.

—In view of the above, more time may need to be devoted to the establishment of rapport than with other patients.

—It is essential to discuss with the young person the goals of treatment and how the measures proposed are expected to achieve them. It is not sufficient to get the parents' agreement without involving the young person. More than one interview with the young person may be needed to achieve agreement on the goals of therapy. Without enlisting the co-operation of the adolescent, and agreeing to some goals, success is unlikely. Treating unmotivated adolescents is a thankless task that I do not recommend.

—Without the active, and ideally enthusiastic, co-operation, of the young person compliance with the treatment plan is unlikely. Treatment initiated on the basis of the parents' goals, or those of the young person's social worker or probation officer, or a family court or youth judge, is usually unsuccessful unless the young person subscribes to the plan and its goals.

—Whenever possible, treatment should be carried out while the young person remains in his or her usual environment. In the past, troubled young people have been placed in residential institutions, sometimes for a period of years, but this was seldom successful. Those placed in such institutions might learn to live in a state of reasonable adjustment in that setting (though many did not), but this was not often generalized to life in the community.

—Adolescents who have suffered severe and prolonged deprivation earlier in their lives, especially if this has been combined with physical and/or sexual abuse, usually have difficulty entering into trusting relationships and are a difficult group to treat. Helping them requires long-term commitment and willingness to tolerate much testing behaviour. A telling account of the treatment of an adolescent girl with such difficulties is that by Rossman (1985).

Outcome

It is not possible to generalize on the outcome of psychiatric disorders in adolescence. Some are short-term reactions to the challenges of this period of life. Others represent the early stages of chronic conditions such as schizophrenia. Conduct, oppositional defiant and anxiety disorders often resolve over time. Attention-deficit hyperactivity disorders may also resolve and, when they do not, many subjects learn to adjust to their handicap and find work that is compatible with it. Autistic disorders are chronic conditions that continue substantially unchanged in most cases, but many subjects with Asperger's syndrome learn to live with their condition and find work they can do. The course of the various categories of anxiety disorders is varied.

Chapter 20

Psychiatric Disorders in Mentally Retarded Children

Mental retardation is defined on the basis of both social and intellectual functioning. It is not sufficient to use either criterion alone. If social functioning were to be used as the sole criterion, those with intelligence in or near the average range might be regarded as retarded if their social skills were impaired for other reasons. If assessed intelligence were to be the sole criterion, some of those whose intelligence is well below average, but who nevertheless function satisfactorily in society, might be stigmatized, admitted to institutions, or otherwise deprived of opportunities of which they could make use.

Dividing children into those who are mentally retarded and those who are not has disadvantages. Although arbitrary divisions are made, as in the categories of the degrees of mental retardation listed in ICD-10 and DSM-IV-TR, in reality there is a continuity of functioning and needs from those of intellectually and socially bright children, through those of average ability, to those who are seriously intellectually and socially handicapped. Applying labels indicating individuals' degree of retardation may sometimes be necessary so that they can obtain needed financial assistance, or special educational help, but this is an administrative issue, not a clinical one.

The psychiatric services for mentally retarded should be part of the mainstream of child psychiatry. In the past, and in some parts of the world even today, care for the mentally retarded was provided separately in hospitals and institutions, often large ones, specifically for the retarded. These were often far from the homes and families of the children, and they were administered separately from other child psychiatry services—when these existed. In the years since the Second World War there has been steady progress in integrating services for mentally retarded children with other child psychiatry services.

Prevalence of psychiatric disorders in the mentally retarded

It has long been known that there is a high incidence of psychiatric disorders in mentally retarded children. In the Isle of Wight study (Rutter *et al.,* 1970) it was found that 'intellectually retarded' children (defined as those with IQs on the Wechsler Intelligence Scale for Children that were two or more standard deviations below the mean for the population) had psychiatric disorders three to four times more frequently than did children in the general population. Among severely retarded children not attending school, psychiatric disorder was found in 50%, compared with

Table 20.1   Symptoms reported in 10- and 11-year-old girls (Isle of Wight survey)

	IQ 120 or more (%)	IQ 79 or less (%)
Poor concentration		
Parents' report	2.6	26.4
Teacher's report	9.1	62.3
Fighting		
Parents' report	1.3	9.9
Teacher's report	2.6	11.0

about 6.6% in the general child population of the age studied. Psychoses and the 'hyperkinetic syndrome' were proportionally more common than in children of higher intelligence.

Not only are specific psychiatric disorders more common in children of lower intelligence, but so also are a variety of types of deviant behaviour. Table 20.1 illustrates this, using data from the Isle of Wight findings.

Corbett (1979), in a study in south-east London, found that there were 140 children aged under 15 with IQs below 50, in a population of 175,000. Of these, 43% showed evidence of behavioural disturbance. Common problems were psychoses (17%), stereotypies and pica (10%) and adjustment disorders (6%); conduct, emotional and hyperkinetic disorders were each present in 4% of these children.

Clinical associations and causes of mental retardation

Some of the causes of mental retardation have been mentioned in Chapters 2 and 11. Genetic factors, physical diseases of the brain, brain injury, and environmental factors can all contribute. The high prevalence of psychiatric disorders in individuals of very low intelligence is probably due mainly to the brain damage that is usually present in these cases. The relationship is not however a simple one, and other factors may be involved. The following points are relevant in considering the associations of mental retardation:

(1) There is a relationship between IQ and deviant behaviour in children of normal intelligence as well as in the mentally retarded, intellectually brighter children showing less deviant behaviour. This may be partly because greater intellectual capacity makes social adaptation easier.

(2) Organic brain damage is more common in children of lower intelligence than in those with IQs in the average range, and it is virtually universal in those with IQs below 50. Many brain-damaged children suffer from epilepsy, which itself is associated with an increased incidence of psychiatric disorder. Behaviour may improve following *hemispherectomy*, the surgical removal of the cerebral cortex on one side; this is a procedure that is sometimes carried out when the cerebral cortex on one side is seriously damaged, as in some cases of infantile hemiplegia. Improved behaviour may also follow the surgical removal of an epileptogenic focus from the brain, espe-

cially if the focus is in one of the temporal lobes. All these observations point to brain damage as a factor that sometimes contributes to the development of behaviour problems.

(3) Social factors such as depriving, hostile and rejecting parental attitudes may adversely affect both intellectual development and emotional stability. The lack of a warm, nurturing and affirming family environment in which to grow up can have consequences that are even more devastating for mentally slower children than for those with greater cognitive skills. Rejecting attitudes of other people, including children, may also have adverse effects.

(4) The slower development of retarded children results in their language and other skills comparing unfavourably with those of their peers. These differences, and their slower acquisition of motor skills, and later achievement of bowel and bladder continence, are other factors that may predispose them to the development of psychiatric disorder.

(5) Educational failure is associated with psychiatric disorder. Children whose cognitive skills are progressing more slowly than those of their peers may fail at school, at least in comparison with the progress of others. This can be a factor that makes the development of psychiatric disorder more likely. Much depends on the quality of the education provided and how well it is adapted to the needs of each retarded child.

(6) Institutionalization can adversely affect both intellectual development and emotional growth. The damaging effects on children of life in large, impersonal institutions have long been known (Spitz, 1946; King *et al.*, 1971), yet in some parts of the world orphans, abandoned children and sometimes those regarded as retarded are still placed in such settings. Following the fall of some of the Communist regimes in Eastern Europe, notably that in Romania, many of us were appalled to discover the terrible conditions in which some institutionalized children had been living (Smyke *et al.*, 2002).

(7) There is little evidence that emotional disorders themselves adversely affect intellectual functioning, though they may impair children's cooperation in psychological testing. High levels of anxiety may affect children's performance in school, even though their cognitive skills remain undiminished.

Types of mental retardation

Mental retardation may be divided into two broad categories:

(1) Sociocultural retardation
(2) Retardation due to specific genetic or other physical causes, such as severe brain damage

Sociocultural retardation

In many of the more mildly retarded children, no evidence is found of any underlying medical or neurological disorder. In such children some combination of sociocultural deprivation and polygenic inheritance is probably responsible. Naturally the innate, genetically determined intellectual potential of some children falls at the lower end of the normal range, and when such children also lack proper cognitive stimulation and suffer general sociocultural deprivation a mild degree of mental retardation may result. This may only become apparent when the child starts school and proves to be a slow learner. Such children may not have been regarded, in their families, as having any particular problems.

Retardation due to specific genetic or other physical causes

Down's syndrome or trisomy 21

Individuals with this disorder have additional chromosomal material, usually three, rather than the usual two, chromosome 21s, though sometimes the additional chromosome material is attached to another chromosome, so that the total chromosome number is normal. About 1 in every 700 children born has this condition, and it is more common in children born to older parents, especially older mothers. It is present in about 1 in every 100 children born to mothers aged over 40.

Children with Down's syndrome are usually recognizable at birth. They have the following principal physical features:

— Marked epicanthic folds (vertical folds of skin over the inner angle of the eyes)
— Inwardly slanting eyes
— Small heads
— Short necks
— Small, low-set ears
— Inwardly curving fifth fingers

Moderate to severe mental retardation is present in nearly all cases, though chromosomal mosaics (individuals in whom some cells contain normal chromosomes and others show trisomy 21) sometimes have near-normal intelligence. About 40% of Down's individuals have congenital heart abnormalities, and there is a high incidence of other congenital defects.

The verbal skills of Down's syndrome children are more impaired than their nonverbal ones, and few achieve reading skills better than those of an eight-year-old. They exhibit behaviour problems more often than children of normal intelligence but apparently less often than other children of comparable intelligence.

The fragile X syndrome

This is probably the most common of the specific conditions causing mental retardation.

The Lesch-Nyhan syndrome

This is an inborn error of purine metabolism characterized by severe mental retardation, self-mutilation, aggressive behaviour, increased muscle tone, other neurological abnormalities and renal failure.

The Prader-Willi syndrome
This is characterized by mental retardation, obesity, underdevelopment of the gonads and various behaviour problems, notably insatiable appetite. These children gorge themselves and often steal food from wherever they can get it. Some of them also exhibit pica.

Other genetic disorders
There are many other, mostly very rare, specific disorders, usually with a genetic basis, that can cause mental retardation of various degrees.

Cerebral palsy and other conditions in which there is brain damage
These may be accompanied by mental retardation, though this is not invariably the case. The combination of a severe physical handicap with limited intellectual skills presents a special challenge to those caring for and educating such children. How well they are cared for and the skill with which they are educated are important influences on how they develop.

Clinical management

The management of retarded children requires a thorough assessment of each child's needs. Assessment and the clinical management that follows are best carried out by multidisciplinary teams. These are usually made up as follows:

— *Educational psychologists.* Their main function is the assessment of the skills and potential of these children, and the provision of recommendations on how best to approach their education and general management.

— *Specialist teachers.* Teachers trained specifically for this work should ideally undertake the education of these children. Special personality characteristics and a dedication to this work are required.

— *Social workers.* The role of the social worker is both to assess the stability, strengths and weaknesses of these children's families, and to assist these families in caring for and bringing up their children.

— *Psychiatrists.* The psychiatric contribution may be both with the management of the emotional and behavioural problems these children often have, and with assessing the need for, and monitoring the response to, any pharmacological treatments that may be indicated.

— *Professionals of other disciplines.* The expertise of paediatricians, family physicians, neurologists, occupational therapists, nurses, and speech and language therapists may all be helpful and should ideally be available to the team.

Among the factors that need to be taken into account in developing the management plan for each child are the following:

— The medical, biological and developmental status of the child
— The stability of the family and its capacity to provide needed cognitive stimulation and to promote the child's self-esteem
— The educational status and needs of the child
— Any emotional and/or behavioural problems the child presents

In many developed countries centres have been established for the early detection, assessment and remediation of developmental delays and problems. Teams made up of professionals from various disciplines, as mentioned above, usually staff these centres. A careful appraisal of each child's developmental and learning status and problems, perceptual deficits, emotional status, behavioural characteristics and social background leads to a plan of action to be taken by one, or often more, members of the team.

What may be needed will vary from institutional care with round-the-clock supervision for the profoundly retarded, to attendance in a regular school program with some extra help being provided for the most mildly retarded. The team should monitor progress, and the management plan should be updated regularly.

Treatment approaches

The treatment of the emotional and behavioural problems of mentally retarded children follows the same general lines as the treatment of such disorders in other children, but some special considerations apply. Any of the following may be of benefit.

Behaviour therapy

This is widely used in the treatment of the behavioural problems of mentally retarded children (Yule & Carr, 1980; Crnic & Reid, 1989). Learning theory applies as much to the behaviour of mentally retarded children as it does to that of other children. Retarded children tend to learn more slowly, however, so more behavioural trials may be needed to achieve the desired results. Behaviour therapy program can promote toilet training; the extinction of behaviour such as temper tantrums, rocking and head banging; the development of motor, speech and language skills; and other changes in behaviour.

Other individual therapies

Action-oriented, rather than talking, therapies are particularly suitable for use with retarded children. These include role playing; the prescription of tasks and rituals that may have metaphorical significance; and play therapy in its various forms.

Family therapy

Many of the problems of retarded children and adolescents are intimately grounded in their family systems. Even a well-functioning family may have difficulty caring for a retarded child with behaviour problems, and if there are other problems in the functioning of the family the difficulties they experience may be so much the greater. Family therapy methods are as applicable to the families of retarded children as they are to other families. Retarded family members of any age often participate enthusiastically in the various actions and other special techniques that may be used in family therapy (see Barker, 1998, Chapter 11).

Medication

The indications for the use of psychotropic drugs in retarded children are similar to those for other disturbed children, as discussed in Chapter 22. Epilepsy, if present, should first be controlled by the use of anticonvulsant drugs. Hyperactivity and problems of attention may respond to methylphenidate or amphetamine compounds. If these are ineffective, clonidine may help; its sedative effects can also be of value in children who have problems sleeping at night. In jurisdictions where it is available, such as the United Kingdom, melatonin in doses up to 12 mg may also be helpful for children with serious problems sleeping at night.

The selective serotonin uptake inhibitors (SSRIs) can be helpful both for retarded children who are depressed and for those with anxiety symptoms.

Antipsychotic drugs, especially the newer or 'atypical' ones such as risperidone and olanzapine may be helpful in controlling irrational and aggressive behaviour.

Further information about these and other drugs that may be useful in retarded, as well as non-retarded, children are to be found in Chapter 22.

Day treatment and residential care

Unless the family setting is quite unsuitable, it is best for retarded children to remain at home with their families. If this proves to be an intolerable burden for a family, attendance at a day-treatment centre may provide relief so that the family can keep their child at home.

Residential care is necessary for some children, particularly the most profoundly retarded, such as those who are doubly incontinent and are incapable of the basics of self-care.

Some other points about management

Those who deal with intellectually handicapped children need to steer a middle course between asking too much of them and asking too little. Facing such children with tasks that are beyond them can be emotionally damaging. It may lead to needless anxiety, even despair, and to a lowering of self-esteem. On the other hand, asking too little, as may happen in a large institution, may mean that the child's potential is not realized.

Continuity of care is important. Retarded children tend to find change particularly difficult, so a long-term commitment from those who undertake their care should be required.

Outcome

Clinical experience suggests that psychiatric disorders in retarded children respond to treatment in much the same way as similar disorders in other children do—provided the treatment takes into account the cognitive and social handicaps of the children. It is necessary to distinguish the symptoms and behaviours due to the superimposed psychiatric disorders from those due to these children's delayed cognitive and social development.

The development of retarded children, like that of other children, depends greatly on the general care and the cognitive and other stimulation they receive. Given good care, stable family settings to grow up in, and suitable treatment of any superimposed psychiatric problems, most mildly retarded children make satisfactory adjustments in society. Their intellectual and other limitations do complicate their care, management and education, and place constraints on the ultimate outcomes that may be expected. But sometimes the biggest limiting factor is that imposed by parents and others—even the children themselves—who may take an unduly gloomy view of what these children can achieve.

Chapter 21

Child Abuse and Neglect

Child abuse is not a psychiatric disorder, but abuse and neglect contribute to the problems of many of the children referred to child psychiatrists. All who work with troubled children need to be alert for evidence that abuse or neglect, in any of their forms, has played a part, or may currently be playing a part, in causing their problems.

Background

Child abuse and neglect are not new phenomena. Lynch (1985) points out that they are referred to in literature dating as far back as the second century AD. The London Society for the Prevention of Cruelty to Children dealt with 762 cases in the three years following its founding in 1884. These comprised assaults (333), starvations (81), dangerous neglect (130), desertions (30), cruel exposure to excite sympathy (70), 'other wrongs' (116) and deaths (25). The society took 132 cases, many 'almost incredible', to court, and there were 120 convictions. At the same time Charles Dickens was using the medium of the novel to describe graphically the plight of many children in Victorian days.

For many years there was little communication or understanding between those interested in and dealing with abusive situations in the community (such as voluntary and statutory child welfare agencies and writers like Dickens) and the medical and allied professions. The former saw abuse and neglect as serious social problems, while the latter overlooked their medical and psychological consequences. It is possible that a contributing factor, at least in the case of sexual abuse, was Freud's conclusion—not based on valid research—that the past sexual abuses reported by some of his patients were fantasies rather than historical facts.

Then in 1946 Caffey, a radiologist, described cases of multiple fractures of the long bones of children, in association with subdural haematomas (bleeding under the dural membrane surrounding the brain). He suggested that the fractures were due to inflicted trauma, and it has since been confirmed that physically abused children often show radiological evidence of old fractures.

Kempe and colleagues (1962) coined the term *battered child syndrome.* This seemed to capture the imagination of the medical and related professions. It led to increased interest in, and recognition of, what came to be known as *non-accidental injury* (Scott, 1977). Nowadays the simpler term *child abuse* is generally preferred. This covers not only physical abuse but also sexual and emotional abuse. To that must be added *neg-lect*, which is essentially abuse by default.

Child abuse, in its many and various forms, is important to child psychiatrists for two main reasons:

— It is often a major contributory factor in the disorders of the children we are asked to assess and help.
— Many of the parents of children referred to us have themselves been abused as children and/or adolescents, and this can adversely affect the care they are able to give their children.

Incidence

There are wide variations in the reported incidence of child abuse and neglect. This is no doubt due in part to real differences in the incidence in different populations, but the variations are also due to different definitions of what constitutes abuse and to the use of different methods of ascertainment. In some parts of the world children whose ages are not yet in double figures are systematically exploited in sweatshops, where they toil for long hours for little reward. Others—some not even yet in their teens—are abducted, or sold by their parents, to work as prostitutes in brothels. Yet others are forced to become boy soldiers before they have even reached adolescence.

Unfortunately such exploitation of children is not confined to the 'third world'. Consider this Canadian newspaper report:

'Judge Peter Leveque said it was clear from the sickening testimony he heard that the 16-year-old girl was as much a victim of this child prostitution ring as were the 12-year-old and two 13-year-old girls she controlled.

But Leveque said the 16-year-old's tough plight in life doesn't excuse her from the torment she inflicted on the three girls when they were raped by an Asian gang or forced to have sex with dozens of other customers.' (*Calgary Herald*, 1993)

Incidentally the cavalier attitudes of society and its legal fraternity to cases such as the above are reflected in the fact that, at the time the above report was published, the 26-year-old man alleged to be the brains behind the child prostitution ring had been freed on bail and, not too surprisingly, had failed to appear in court on the required day.

Cases such as the above, though unfortunately not rare, are but a small part of the child-abuse and neglect spectrum. Much abuse, and most neglect, occurs within the family. Moreover, even when the abuse does not occur in the family, the children abused may have suffered a lack of proper care within their families.

In the United States, studies of children aged 3 to 17 have found rates of physical abuse between 19 and 36 per thousand. In Canada, the Ontario Health Supplement (MacMillan *et al.*, 1997) used a self-report instrument to inquire about a history of childhood experiences of physical and sexual abuse among almost 10,000 Ontario residents aged 15 years and older. The percentages of those reporting a history of abuse were:

Physical abuse: 31.2% of the males and 21.1% of the females.
'Severe' physical abuse: 10.7% of males and 9.2% of females.
Sexual abuse: 4.3% of the males and 12.8% of the females.
'Severe' sexual abuse: 3.9% of males and 11.1% of females.

Emotional abuse and neglect were not covered in this survey. They are more difficult to investigate because they refer to processes occurring over time, whereas physical and sexual abuse refer to specific events.

Causes

The causes of child abuse and neglect are complex. Schmidt and Eldridge (1986, page 269) put it well:

'Child maltreatment is a multiply-determined phenomenon that does not lend itself to definitive explanations. The parent, the child, the circumstances, and the environment all contribute to the occurrence of maltreatment.'

MacMillan (2000, page 704) summarizes the 'risk indicators' that have been found to be associated with abuse. For *physical abuse* these are:

(a) Child factor:
    Male sex
(b) Parental factors:
    Young maternal age
    Single-parent status
    History of childhood experience of physical abuse
    Spousal violence
    Unplanned pregnancy or negative attitude toward pregnancy
    History of substance abuse
    Social isolation or lack of social support
(c) Social factors:
    Low socioeconomic status
    Large family size

For *sexual abuse* known 'risk indictors' are:

(a) Child factor:
    Female sex
(b) Parental factors:
    Living in a family without a natural parent

Poor relationship between parents
Presence of a stepfather
Poor child-parent relations

Strictly speaking, the above are *correlates* of abuse, not necessarily *causes*. Nevertheless their presence should alert us to the possibility of abuse and, if several of them are present, to the probability of it.

Adults who abuse children are often found to have serious personality problems. They may lack normal impulse control. In their role as parents they may have difficulty showing love in affectionate, caring ways. Abuse may occur when the perpetrator is under the influence of alcohol or other drugs, which can further impair impulse control.

Abusive and neglectful parents often have problems in other areas of their lives. Their social and vocational skills may be poor or their intelligence below average, and they may have difficulty with the instrumental tasks of daily living. When faced with stressful circumstances the limit of their frustration tolerance may be reached, so that they get angry with and may abuse their children. This does not mean that parents with good incomes and jobs, and middle-class respectability, never abuse their children. Quite the contrary, abuse occurs in all sectors of society, though it seems to be more common in the less well functioning families.

Abuse and neglect by parents sometimes occurs against a background of treatable psychiatric illness, such as depression or schizophrenia. Careful assessment of the mental states of abusing parents is therefore important.

Other associations of abuse and neglect

Clinical experience suggests that a variety of other situations may be associated with, or contribute to the likelihood, of abuse. These include:

— 'Difficult' temperament in the child or a clash of temperaments between parent and child
— Poor self-image in the child, who feels worthy of no better treatment than that which is meted out
— A repetitive pattern in which the attention-needing child learns that the only way to get attention is by behaving provocatively, and thus arousing the parent's anger, despite the risk of this being expressed by violence
— Problems of emotional attachment between parent(s) and child, often going back to early infancy
— Institutional care, whether in correctional, educational or other settings—for example the residential schools to which many native Canadian children were, over many decades, sent and where they were often repeatedly abused physically, sexually and emotionally
— War, insurrection and civil unrest, all of which may cause children to suffer grievously (see Garbarino *et al.*, 1991).

As each successive edition of the book is written the current focus may be a little different, but the suffering of the children remains horrendous; as this edition is being prepared, places where children are suffering abuse and neglect include Angola, Liberia, Palestine and Iraq.

Abuse may be an intergenerational pattern of behaviour. Oliver and Buchanan (1979) describe an extended family network in which there was an established pattern of abuse. Starting with a mentally retarded young woman and the six men she successively lived with, these authors studied her children and their descendents. In all, 40 members of the family, and their spouses or partners, were investigated. This revealed a tragic saga, transmitted from generation to generation, of physical neglect, assaults on the children with hammers and knives, incest, prostitution (sometimes taught to the children by their parents), burns causing persistent poker marks, bites, beatings, and hair pulling. Although families such as this are mercifully relatively uncommon, they do exist, and many others differ only in the degree and extent of the abuse their children suffer.

Clinical considerations

Only a few families come asking for help because they are abusing or neglecting their children. Many parents bring physically abused children to hospital emergency departments with stories, which may be detailed and creative but are untrue and often implausible and inconsistent, that their child's injuries were incurred accidentally. Careful examination, including x-rays, may reveal evidence of previous injury.

Suspected child abuse may be reported to child welfare agencies by neighbours, relatives, day-care staff, teachers, hospital staff or members of the general public. It may come to light during routine medical examinations. Among the injuries that may result from abuse are bruising of any degree of severity, fractures, injury to internal organs, internal bleeding, intracranial haemorrhage and brain damage, and loss of vision due to damage to the eye. Physical abuse may or may not be associated with neglect or emotional abuse.

There is no specific clinical picture that is unique to abused children, but the following features are often encountered in such children:

— Difficulty enjoying themselves
— Hypervigilance
— Oppositional behaviour
— Various other forms of antisocial behaviour
— Withdrawal
— Compulsive behaviour
— Pseudo-adult manner
— Low self-esteem
— Learning problems
— Fear of parents (or anxiety when an abusing parent is expected to come home)
— 'Reversed caring' (for example anxiously looking out to meet their parents' needs)

Sexual abuse

Sexual abuse may occur in the absence of other forms of abuse or neglect, and it may continue for long periods undetected. Girls are abused more often than boys. The abuse may consist of anything from fondling of the child's breasts or genitals to vaginal or anal intercourse. Another form of sexual abuse is the sexual exploitation of children in pornographic movies, videotapes and photographs.

The abuser is often someone known to the child, frequently a family member. Parents, step-parents, other relatives and foster parents may be responsible. The incest taboo, which operates in many families, seems often to be less strong in reconstituted families; this may lead to stepfather-stepdaughter incest.

Sexual abuse by someone outside the family tends to be reported sooner than intrafamilial abuse.

Apart from signs of physical injury in the genital area, or the diagnosis of sexually acquired disease, sexual abuse may be suspected if the child shows one or more of the following:

— Sexually seductive behaviour
— Sexual knowledge inappropriate for his or her age
— Severe psychosomatic symptoms, especially non-epileptic seizures
— Severe acting-out behaviour, especially running away
— Sexually precocious behaviour
— Self-injurious or self-destructive behaviour in the absence of other apparent stress
— Pregnancy in the early teen years, especially if the father is not named

Emotional abuse

Many children's emotional and other psychological needs are not adequately met in the families. How severe a family's failure to meet its children's needs must be to justify the use of the term *emotional abuse* is an arbitrary judgement, although extreme cases are easily identified.

Laws have been enacted in many jurisdictions defining emotional abuse. These aim to provide a legal basis for intervention in cases in which there is no obvious physical abuse or neglect, but there is gross failure to meet the children's emotional and psychological needs. An example of such legislation is to be found in the *Child Welfare Act of the Canadian Province of Alberta* (Government of Alberta, 1984). This uses the term *emotional injury* rather than *emotional abuse*. It states that a child is emotionally injured:

(i) if there is substantial and observable impairment of the child's mental or emotional functioning that is evidenced by a mental or behavioural disorder, including anxiety, depression, withdrawal, aggression or delayed development, and (ii) there are reasonable and probable grounds to believe that the emotional injury is the result of

(a) rejection,
(b) deprivation of affective or cognitive stimulation,

(c) exposure to domestic violence or severe domestic disharmony,
(d) inappropriate criticism, threats, humiliation, accusations or expectations of or towards the child, or
(e) the mental or emotional condition of the guardian of the child or chronic alcohol or drug abuse by anyone living in the same residence as the child.

These criteria are broad and subject to a wide range of interpretations, and some might consider them overinclusive.

Garbarino and colleagues (1986) use the term *psychologically battered child* and define four forms of 'psychically destructive' behaviour:

— *Rejecting:* the adult refuses to acknowledge the child's worth and the legitimacy of the child's needs.
— *Isolating:* the child is cut off by the adult from normal social experiences, prevented from forming friendships and made to believe the world is capricious and hostile.
— *Ignoring:* the adult deprives the child of needed stimulation and fails to respond in suitable ways, stifling emotional growth and intellectual development.
— *Corrupting:* the child is 'mis-socialized', being stimulated to engage in destructive antisocial behaviour and reinforced in such deviant behaviour.

Garbarino and his co-authors (1986) provide examples of ways in which the above types of behaviour by adults may affect children at different stages of development.

In most instances of emotional abuse the child's growth and physical condition are within normal limits, but there are problems of psychological development and of emotional and behavioural adjustment. These may include poor self-esteem, unresolved anger and almost any of the psychiatric syndromes described elsewhere in this book, the main exceptions being those predominantly of organic origin. Conduct disorders, chronic anxiety disorders and academic failure are common consequences, and as the children grow older some come to meet the criteria for personality disorders.

Many parents who fail to meet their children's emotional needs have themselves experienced poor parenting as children. Covitz (1986) describes emotional abuse as the 'family curse', handed down from generation to generation. He points out that it is what parents are and do, rather than what they tell their children, that is important. He also describes three 'abusive styles of parenting'—'the inadequate parent', 'the devouring parent' and 'the tyrannical parent'—and suggests various ways to break the intergenerational cycle of abuse.

The role of psychiatrists

The task of investigating suspected child abuse and neglect usually falls to the staff of the local child welfare (sometimes called 'child protection') service. This service is also responsible for the care and treatment of children who are found to have been subject to abuse or neglect.

Psychiatrists may be involved in any, or all, of the following ways:

— Reporting suspected child abuse or neglect. In most jurisdictions the law requires that anyone with reasonable grounds to suspect that a child is being abused or neglected must inform the relevant authorities (the child welfare or child protection service, or the police). Evidence of abuse and/or neglect sometimes emerges when children referred to child psychiatrists are assessed.

— Carrying out psychiatric assessments of children who have been abused and/or neglected, usually at the request of the child welfare service, and making recommendations for their management and treatment.

— Providing psychiatric assessments of parents and others who have abused and/or neglected children, in order to offer guidance to child welfare workers on any treatment such persons need and, sometimes, on the degree of risk of further abuse or neglect. General adult psychiatrists may provide this service but it may also be carried out by child psychiatrists in conjunction with their assessment of the children involved.

— Providing psychiatric treatment for abused children and/or their families when this is indicated.

— Providing consultation/liaison services to child welfare departments. Many children and families have both psychiatric and social problems, and these are often inextricably mixed. Close co-operation between the staffs of the child psychiatry and child welfare services is therefore important. Regular contact to discuss program issues and to ensure that there is the close communication and a good working relationship between the services is much to be desired.

Paediatricians, family physicians or gynaecologists, rather than psychiatrists, usually carry out the physical examination of children who may have been abused.

Some points about managing abusive and neglectful families

Child abuse and neglect, especially in their severe forms, can be distressing for professionals who encounter them. They may experience emotions such as anger and disgust. It can be hard to remain objective and non-judgemental when faced with parents or others who have gravely injured or sexually abused a child. Nevertheless it is unhelpful for us to express the anger or outrage we may feel. To do so militates against forming effective therapeutic relationships.

Professional staff trained and experienced in this area should carry out the investigation of cases of possible child abuse. Child psychiatrists and other mental health professionals who come across such cases should not attempt to determine whether abuse has occurred; that is the role of the experts from the child welfare services and/or the police. Asking questions, even if they are not leading ones, about possible abuse may make the task of those who have to investigate such cases unnecessarily difficult. They prefer to initiate their investigations themselves. It is best if those they are interviewing have not previously been asked similar questions.

Many approaches to the *prevention* of child abuse have been proposed, but the effectiveness of many of them has not been established by rigorous studies. One that has been shown, in randomized controlled trials, to be effective is a nurse home visitation program provided to first-time mothers who are predominantly single, under 19 years of age and of low socio-economic status. It has been shown that it can prevent both child abuse and neglect (Olds *et al.,* 1986, 1994; Kitzman *et al.,* 1997; MacMillan, 2000).

Outcome

General statements cannot be made about the outcome of child abuse. Many factors affect this, including the nature, severity and duration of the abuse; the personality strengths and previous adjustment of the abused individual; the stability of the abused child's family and its ability to provide needed support to the child or adolescent; and the treatment subsequently provided to the abused individual. A single sexual assault on a previously well-adjusted adolescent from a stable, supportive family is likely to have far fewer consequences than the abduction by force of a pre-adolescent who is forced to become a boy soldier and kill members of the enemy in an African country.

A variety of physical consequences may result from child abuse (Barker, 1993c). These include permanent mental retardation, blindness, cerebral palsy and other physical injuries. The psychological consequences are harder to define, but a poor self-image, personality and behaviour problems, a relative lack of ambition, difficulty making friends, and delayed development in various areas of functioning are among those that have been reported. In the case of intrafamilial physical or sexual abuse it can be hard to separate the effects of the other family problems that are often found to exist. Indeed Elmer (1986) found, in a comparative study of three groups of infants, two of them abused, that the effects of socio-economic status were more marked than those of abuse.

Neglect, especially when it involves serious nutritional deprivation in the first two years of life, can adversely affect brain growth and lead to delayed intellectual development. Lack of cognitive stimulation and a paucity of social experiences can also lead to delayed psychological development.

Chapter 22

Treatment Approaches

Rational treatment for child psychiatric disorders is only possible once there has been a careful assessment of child and family. The diagnostic formulation that results from this is the basis of the treatment plan. Any one, or any combination, of the following measures may be needed:

— Individual psychotherapy for the child
— Therapy or counselling for the parents
— Group therapy for child and/or parents
— Behaviour therapy
— Pharmacotherapy
— Hypnotherapy
— Daypatient treatment
— Inpatient treatment
— Placement in an alternative family setting
— Educational measures
— Speech therapy
— Other environmental change, such as placement in the care of a child welfare service

This list is not exhaustive. Children with particular handicaps—for example motor coordination problems—may need other forms of help. Because most child psychiatric disorders have multiple causes, we often need to use more than one treatment.

Treatment goals

The treatment plan should have specific, well-defined goals. There should be at least broad agreement between therapist(s) and client(s) on what the situation will be when treatment has come to a successful conclusion. When children, especially younger ones, are the focus of treatment, the treatment plan will be worked out mainly between parents and therapists; older children and adolescents should be actively involved in the planning.

I find the concept of an *outcome frame* helpful. This is a description, in positive terms, of how things will be after treatment has been successfully completed. Rather than saying that a child's temper tantrums will have ceased, it is better to describe how that child will behave in situations in which tantrums used to occur.

At times a subject's psychiatric state may make it difficult for that person to participate actively in treatment planning. Depressed individuals may feel that their situation is hopeless, that nothing that might be done will do any good. But even some such people are able to admit that they would like help if it were available.

Individual psychotherapy

The essence of individual psychotherapy is the use of the relationship between therapist and client to promote change in the subject's mental or emotional state or behaviour. Any interaction between child (or adult patient) and therapist has the potential to be therapeutic, although sometimes such interactions can be counter-therapeutic.

There are many schools of psychotherapy (Zeig & Munion, 1990) and much variation in their approaches. The following are some general principles:

(1) Accept your child patients as they are. Whether a child is anxious, depressed, hostile or disinterested, disapproving or judgemental attitudes are likely to worsen the situation. Accepting children as they present does not imply approval of what they say or what they do or have done. Indeed child and therapist are often able to agree on aspects of the child's behaviour, feelings or attitudes that need to change.

(2) Remember that children rarely come for treatment of their own accord. Others who are worried or concerned about them, or perhaps angry with them, usually bring them. Some arrive with the expectation that they will meet someone who will be critical or disapproving, as their parents may have been. Some parents, though nowadays mercifully few, have presented their child's visit to the psychiatrist as a punishment, or they have told them to expect a 'good talking to'. Gaining the confidence of such children can be hard and take a long time.

(3) Don't plunge straight into a discussion of the presenting problems or symptoms, unless the child brings them up.

(4) Concentrate at first on gaining an understanding of the child's feelings and viewpoint. This is a necessary if free communication is to develop between you and the child. Children need to come to see their therapist as being concerned about them and wanting to help them. This will not necessarily prevent the expression of hostile or other negative feelings towards their therapists. Indeed it may facilitate this when such feelings need to be expressed. The experience of giving vent to angry feelings, or revealing 'bad' things about oneself, and not being rejected, lectured, blamed or criticized, can itself be therapeutic.

(5) Remember that, while free expression of feelings is to be encouraged, limits must be set. Physically hurting the therapist, dangerous activities like playing with live electrical fittings, or damaging the fabric of the room and its furnishings and equipment cannot be allowed. It is a good idea to outline the limits of permissible behaviour at the start of treatment. Limits should be set on the basis of 'I can't allow

you to do that', with an explanation of why the behaviour is unacceptable, while accepting the child's desire to engage in the activity in question.

(6) Set out the limits of confidentiality. I usually tell children that everything that passes between us is confidential with two main exceptions. One is that I am obliged by law to report any suspicions I may have that a child is being, or has recently been, abused or neglected. The other is when I learn of something as serious as a child's plan or intention to commit suicide or engage in a major criminal activity. I tell my child patients that in such situations I may feel it necessary to tell the parents or whoever else is caring for the child what I have learned.

What may psychotherapy achieve?

The aims of treatment should have been set out in the diagnostic formulation. The formulation may specify the role individual psychotherapy will play. This can be anything from offering support to a child facing an acute stress to intensive psycho-analytical therapy aiming to explore the child's unconscious life in the context of the relationship between child and therapist.

Psychoanalysis is a highly specialized treatment, requiring long training and often extending over many months or years. For this reason, and because therapists trained in psychoanalysis are few and are unavailable in many communities, it is rarely used. It is however of considerable theoretical interest.

Although the techniques used in psychotherapy with children vary with the theoretical orientation of the therapist, common to all forms are:

— The development of a working relationship with the child
— An appraisal of the feelings and ideas the child expresses in the context of the relationship
— The use of the relationship to help resolve the child's problems

The simplest form of help is accepting the child's feelings. We all tend to feel better after speaking with an accepting person about matters that are sources of anxiety, anger or shame. Children are no exception, and improvement in a child's emotional state sometimes follows a single interview, even one intended to be primarily diagnostic. For certain children it is a new experience to be given the full attention of an accepting, noncritical adult.

In many cases, children need more than having their feelings heard and being offered support. There needs to be an ongoing process of emotional interchange between child and therapist. In the context of the relationship that develops, the child's problems and conflicts can be examined and worked through. This involves helping children understand the issues underlying their symptoms, not just intellectually but at a deeper emotional level. The relationship between therapist and child is used as the context—or perhaps *metaphor* would be a better term—for the resolution of repressed conflicts and other material that may be responsible for the child's symptoms. This is the essence of the approach of such therapists as Allen (1942), Maclay (1970) and Adams (1982).

In *What is Psychotherapy?* (Zeig & Munion, 1990), 81 therapists of different schools describe their varied approaches and offer their definitions of psychotherapy. The subject is thus not a simple one. 'Psychotherapy' means different things to different therapists.

One process that many forms of psychotherapy seem to have in common is that of *reframing*—or changing the perceived meaning of something (Barker, 1994). It may be a symptom, a repetitive behaviour pattern, or a belief system that is reframed.

Positive connotation is the reframing of the intention behind a behaviour. Thus the behaviour of an abusive parent might be reframed as an attempt to discipline a child who is engaging in antisocial behaviour. The intent—to improve the child's behaviour—is laudable, and therapy may then become a search for a better, non-abusive way of achieving this.

Developmental reframing is the relabelling of a behaviour as belonging to an earlier life stage out of which the child or adolescent has not yet grown. So a teenage boy who is having temper outbursts may be said to be immature rather than 'bad'. 'There's nothing really wrong with him, he's just a bit slow growing up' or similar phrasing may be used. Sometimes having their behaviour labelled as young for their years has a salutary effect on teenagers who may previously have seen their aggressive outbursts as 'macho'.

Many other *strategic* therapy techniques are available. Some of these have been developed by family therapists, but most are equally useful in work with individuals. These include the use of metaphor; paradoxical injunctions; rituals and tasks; declaring therapeutic impotence; prescribing interminable therapy; humour; externalising problems; and stories. These, and other strategic approaches, are discussed in Chapters 11 and 12 of *Basic Family Therapy* (Barker, 1998).

The work of Milton Erickson (Haley, 1973; Rosen, 1982; O'Hanlon & Hexum, 1990), a singularly creative psychotherapist, is replete with examples of innovative strategic methods.

Therapy and counselling with parents

It is seldom sufficient to provide treatment for a child and to leave the parents or other caregivers uninvolved. Parents are enormously important in children's lives. The environment they offer their children and what they do in response to problems their children develop are crucial factors in determining the outcome of treatment.

What help may parents need? At the very least they are likely to need counselling concerning the nature of their child's disorder and an explanation of how they can assist in the treatment effort. This is often referred to as *casework*. This process aims to help parents understand how their child's problems have arisen, and what is contributing to their continuation. It is important not to assign blame to the parents. Many of them feel more than enough guilt about having a 'problem' child, and the caseworker must avoid increasing their feelings of guilt. The emphasis should therefore be on what the parents can now do to help. Kraemer (1987) described the caseworker as 'educator, adviser, supporter, manager and, sometimes, psychotherapist.'

Maintaining the caseworker relationship throughout the period of the child's treatment can also avert the danger that the parents will get, or will feel, left out. This is an ever-present risk, especially when treatment extends over a long period or when it involves the child's admission to a residential treatment setting.

Parent management training (PMT) is a more formalized approach to assisting parents in dealing therapeutically with their children. Parents are trained in the application of the principles of learning theory to their interactions with their children. Kazdin (1997) explains how the key 'ingredients' may be represented by the letters A, B and C. A stands for *antecedents*, B for *behaviours* and C for *consequences*.

The 'antecedents' are events that precede behaviours. They can be structured to promote changes in the behaviours that follow. Examples are verbal and physical aides or 'prompts', instructions and modelling.

The 'behaviours' are the positive, 'prosocial' (as opposed to antisocial) behaviours that are to be developed. Even when the objective is to eliminate behaviours (for example fighting, stealing or disobedience) the emphasis is on developing prosocial or 'positive' behaviours that are incompatible with the undesired behaviours, or reduce the likelihood of them occurring.

The 'consequences' are the range of events that may follow behaviour. The aim is to promote desired behaviour by positive reinforcement, which is often social (attention or praise) but may include material rewards or 'points' that can be exchanged for small items or privileges. Mild punishment may also be used (for example, brief 'time-outs', loss of tokens or privileges), but positive reinforcement is preferred.

There is more to PMT than just telling parents what to do. It usually involves a major change in the ways the parents have been dealing with their child. Learning the new methods takes time and usually has to be done in stages, with frequent input being offered the parents over a period of weeks or months. Simple behaviours are tackled first, progression to more complex ones only occurring when simple ones have been achieved. Kazdin (1997) provides a more comprehensive account of PMT. He suggests that programs for mildly oppositional young children may be completed in six to eight weeks, and those for 'clinically referred youths with conduct disorder' may last from 12 to 25 weeks. PMT may be combined with other treatment, and this may lead to a reduction in the time required.

Family therapy

The emotional and behavioural problems of many children arise in the context of a dysfunctional family system. Even if they have not arisen in such a context, the family system may be working to perpetuate the problems, or it may stand in the way of their resolution. Those treating children with psychiatric problems should therefore have training and skills in family therapy, or they should have ready access to colleagues who have such skills.

Some families are grossly and obviously dysfunctional, being unable to provide many of the basic necessities—such as proper food, shelter, clothing and medical care—for their children. In other families the instrumental care of their children is good, but there are other, often less immediately apparent, problems in the family that adversely affect their children. These may include communication problems; emotional over-involvement or under-involvement with a child or children; ineffective, inappropriate or inconsistent behavioural control methods; and role problems, such as when children are 'scapegoated' or when parents, often unwittingly and with good intentions, abrogate their responsibility to provide social training and overindulge their offspring.

Further information on family therapy is to be found in the companion volume *Basic Family Therapy* (Barker, 1998).

Group therapy

Both parents and children may be treated in groups. Members of appropriately selected groups can help each other through their interactions and by the modelling they provide for each other. The active, outgoing child can be a model for the withdrawn, inhibited one, and *vice versa.*

Many theoretical approaches have been used as the basis for group work with children—as they have with individual therapy. One that has some empirical support is *group cognitive behaviour therapy* (GCBT), which has been shown in randomized clinical trials to be effective in childhood anxiety disorders (Menolowitz *et al.* 1989; Silverman & Berman, 2001; Silverman *et al.*, 1999).

Parent groups can sometimes achieve many of the aims of individual casework. They may also be more cost-effective. The focus of the group is usually on the children's problems and their management, with an emphasis on finding solutions rather than on apportioning blame or elucidating causes. The group leader may offer input and ideas, but an important part of the process is the interaction between the parents as they engage in problem-solving discussions. The parents bring their experience of dealing with their children's problems, whether they have been successful or unsuccessful. They can compare what they have all done and may obtain new ideas about how to help their children. Such groups also provide mutual support for their members. It is often helpful for parents to learn that they are not alone in their difficulties.

Behaviour therapy

Behaviour therapy is based on the principles of learning theory. Behaviour therapists are not concerned with the supposed meaning of symptoms, nor with promoting insight into the psychodynamics that may underlie them. They believe that problem behaviours are learned and can be eliminated, or replaced by desired behaviours, through the provision of new learning experiences. The treatment is often located in the child's regular environment—home, school or treatment centre—rather than in a clinic or therapist's office.

Before treatment can be started a careful assessment is necessary. One of the things this should address is whether behavioural problems are due to *skill deficits* or to *performance deficits*. A skill deficit refers to something the subject is unable to do—for example to tie shoelaces. A performance deficit exists when a child is able to tie shoelaces but refuses to do so. Obviously these two types of problem need different approaches.

In the early days of behaviour therapy, the emphasis was on motor functions, but nowadays behaviour therapists define behaviour to include also emotional responses, cognitive processes and physiological functions.

The main behaviour therapy techniques are operant and respondent conditioning; modelling; and cognitive therapy.

Operant and respondent conditioning aim to alter the circumstances following (in operant conditioning) or preceding (in respondent conditioning) the behaviours concerned. An example of the latter is Pavlov's famous work with dogs. Pavlov taught dogs to salivate at the sound of a bell by pairing this with the provision of food. In due course the dogs salivated even when food was not provided.

An example of the use of *respondent conditioning* is *systematic desensitisation*. In treating phobias, the subject is first taught relaxation—the reduction of muscle tension throughout the body. The phobic object is then presented in mild form, or the subject may simply be asked to imagine it. Then the phobic object is presented with increasing intensity, small monochrome pictures of it being succeeded by larger and closer ones, then coloured ones and so on. The rate of increase in the intensity of the stimulus is such that the subject is able to maintain a state of relaxation. This procedure can be of value in treating phobias of dogs, snakes and other animals, water and other objects. It may also be effective in phobias of specific situations, for example heights, closed spaces, open spaces, and travelling on buses or aeroplanes.

Operant conditioning is the planned changing of behaviours by manipulation of the consequences perceived as controlling them. If a person touches something hot and suffers a painful burn, that person will stop touching that object. If a girl gets a smile or a hug when she helps her mother with a household task, this is likely to increase the amount of help she gives her mother—that is if smiles and hugs are reinforcing for her.

The above are examples of *reinforcement*. There is no limit to the number of possible reinforcers. They may be material ones such as foods the subject likes, or social ones such as smiles, attention and praise. In some situations, *token economy* systems are useful. The children acquire tokens for certain specific behaviours and, in some systems, lose them for others. The tokens are redeemable later for rewards such as money, toys, or privileges such as watching television or playing videogames. Such programs may be used in the home, in school and in residential and day-treatment settings.

Operant methods have been used to treat many children's problems including aggressive behaviours, obsessive-compulsive symptoms, anorexia nervosa, tics, speech and language disorders, and enuresis. They have also been used to promote attendance at school and develop social skills.

Modelling is the process whereby the subject observes a behaviour, or series of behaviours, of another person and imitates those behaviours. Normally developing children learn much from observing the behaviour of parents, other family members, and peers and adults with whom they have contact. The best way to teach people things is often to demonstrate the procedure you want them to learn. Parents do not always realize how powerfully their behaviour—even their language—influences their children. Telling children they should not smoke is reasonable, but it is likely to be less effective than quitting smoking.

Cognitive behaviour therapy (CBT), sometimes called just *cognitive therapy,* is based on three premises:

(1) Cognitive activity affects behaviour
(2) Cognitive activity may be monitored and altered
(3) Desired behaviour change may occur as a result of cognitive change (Dobson, 1988)

There is good empirical evidence for the effectiveness of CBT in a wide range of disorders. Negative or maladaptive belief systems are believed to play a part in many anxiety disorders (Prins, 2001), depressive disorders, and conduct and other behaviour disorders (see Kazdin, 2001, pages 420–421). How often they are the primary cause of such disorders is less clear; biological and social factors often contribute, but the promotion of cognitive change can be an effective treatment whatever other factors may be involved.

Patterson and colleagues (1976, 1982, 1993) have pioneered the development of learning-theory-based treatments for children with severe behaviour problems. They have observed high levels of *coercive behaviour* in these families, each member trying to get other members to do as he or she wants them to do by the use of some form of aggressive behaviour. One person makes an aggressive attack (it may just be verbal) on another, who retaliates with behaviour designed to terminate the attack. Whenever coercive (that is, aggressive) behaviour succeeds in terminating another's coercive attack, that behaviour is reinforced, so that over time the severity of each behaviour increases. Patterson's research has shown that careful behavioural analysis, followed by appropriate interventions can reverse such processes.

Pharmacotherapy

Psychoactive drugs have an established place in the treatment of child and adolescent psychiatric disorders. They are usually but one component of a comprehensive treatment plan that takes into account all relevant family and other factors that have an impact on the child's condition.

Drugs for children with attention-deficit hyperactivity disorders (ADHD)

While not all children with the *hyperkinetic disorders* of ICD-10 and the *attention-deficit hyperactivity disorders* of DSM-IV-TR require medication, this is often useful as a part of the treatment plan. Many of these children, whether their main symptom is hyperactivity or short attention span, benefit—sometimes dramatically—from the administration of stimulant drugs.

Popper (2002) dates the beginning of child and adolescent psychopharmacology to 1937, when Bradley (1937) reported the seemingly paradoxical improvement of the behaviour of some, mostly preadolescent, children in a residential facility when they were given amphetamine, a stimulant drug. Dexamphetamine has continued to be used to this day, though currently another stimulant—methylphenidate—is used more extensively.

There is sound evidence from many controlled studies that stimulant drugs are effective in treating the main symptoms of ADHD—overactivity, impulsivity, poor concentration and distractibility—as well as other symptoms that are often associated with these three: failure to remain on task, poor academic progress, difficult relationships with other children, and defiant and aggressive behaviour.

Both methylphenidate and dexamphetamine are short-acting drugs—the former more so than the latter. Consequently they have to be given frequently. Response to methylphenidate usually starts in 30 to 45 minutes and is at its peak one to three hours after the drug is taken. After four hours the effect has largely worn off. While the need to give the drug at frequent intervals can present difficulties, the short half-life has advantages. It means that doses can be timed so that their maximum effects occur when most needed. Some children need the medication only on school days or when faced with homework that requires a period of prolonged concentration.

Long-acting preparations of methylphenidate are available. That marketed in the United Kingdom goes by the proprietary name Concerta XZ; in Canada the proprietary preparation is Ritalin-SR; and in the United States Ritalin LA is available in 20-, 30- and 40-milligram capsules. These are intended to have sustained effects lasting 8 to 12 hours, but children's responses to them vary. Long-acting preparations of dexamphetamine are not currently available.

The side effects of methylphenidate and dexamphetamine can be troubling. Both these drugs cause significant appetite suppression in a minority of cases. If this is severe and prolonged it may lead to delayed growth. Those children whose appetites are affected should preferably be given their doses after meals, and they should be encouraged to eat much nutritious food in the evening, after the effects of the drug have worn off. The height and weight of children on these drugs should be checked regularly to ensure that physical growth is proceeding normally. It is advisable also to check the blood pressure from time to time as these drugs occasionally cause this to be elevated.

Other side effects that may occur include problems getting off to sleep at night, headaches and abdominal pain or discomfort. The headaches and abdominal pain often resolve once the child has been on the medication for a while. Sleep disturbance is most likely if the last dose in given late in the day. Parents can often tell when the medication effects have worn off and should be advised to time the last dose of the day so that its effects have worn off by their child's bedtime.

Pemoline, another stimulant drug, has a longer half-life than methylphenidate and is not so quick to act. Twice-daily dosage is recommended. My practice is usu-

Table 22.1 Some drugs used in the treatment of attention-deficit/hyperactivity disorder

Drugs	Dose	Main side effects
Methylphenidate	2.5–10 milligrams (mg) up to 3 times daily, possibly higher in adolescents	Reduced appetite, growth failure, sleeplessness, abdominal pain, irritability, headaches, excitability
Dexamphetamine sulfate	0.25–0.5 mg/kg per 24 hours	Similar to methylphenidate
Pemoline	0.5–2.0 mg/kg per 24 hours	Similar to above

This table does not provide full prescribing information.

ally to use methylphenidate first; if the response is inadequate or side effects are troublesome, I switch to dexamphetamine and, if necessary, then to pemoline.

Other drugs that have been shown, in clinical trials, to be effective in ADHD include various tricyclic antidepressants, clonidine, carbamazepine and possibly propranolol. None of these appears to be as effective as the stimulants. They should be reserved for use when stimulants have been unsuccessful. Spencer and colleagues (2002) review these and other drugs that have been suggested as possibly effective in ADHD.

Table 22.1 lists the recommended doses and the more common side effects of the principal drugs used in these conditions.

Drugs for children with affective disorders

Although the tricyclic antidepressants (TCAs) have in the past been recommended for the treatment of child and adolescent depression, the evidence for their efficacy is scant (see Ryan, 2002). Moreover they are prone to cause troublesome side effects and are dangerous in overdose. The selective serotonin reuptake inhibitors (SSRIs) are to be preferred. There is more support for their use from clinical trials, they have a better side-effect profile and they are less dangerous in overdose.

It is unclear which of the SSRIs should be the first choice in the treatment of childhood or adolescent depression. The experience of the clinician with the various available drugs may be a relevant factor. Fluoxetine, sertraline, fluvoxamine and citalopram may all be effective. Response to these drugs is slow. It may be two to four weeks before there is any lessening of symptoms, and full response may take two to three months or occasionally longer. SSRIs are metabolized in the liver and because hepatic function is more rapid in young people the doses they require approach those given to adults.

If the response to SSRIs is poor, other antidepressants that may be used are venlafaxine and buproprion.

Table 22.2 lists the antidepressants most commonly used with children and adolescents, with their doses and principal side effects. Further information is to be found in Ryan (2002).

The treatment of mania in children and adolescents follows the same lines as in adults. For acute attacks of mania, antipsychotics such as chlorpromazine, haloperi-

Table 22.2 Some antidepressant drugs for children and adolescents

Drugs	Dose	Main side effects
Selective serotonin reuptake inhibitors (SSRIs)		
Citalopram	(up to 30 mg in adolescents)	
Fluoxetine	10–20 mg daily, occasionally up to 30 mg	Sedation, abdominal pain or discomfort, headaches, palpitations
Fluvoxamine	25–50 mg daily	
Sertraline	25–50 mg daily	
Other antidepressants		
Buproprion	up to 150 mg per day, under specialist supervision	Dry mouth, gastrointestinal symptoms, insomnia, poor concentration, agitation
Venlafaxine	37.5–75 mg daily under specialist supervision	Dry mouth, nausea, constipation, insomnia, drowsiness

Many other antidepressants are available. These have been developed for adult patients, and most have not received regulatory approval for use with children. Some may be of benefit for children, but data are lacking. They should be used only under specialist supervision.

This table is not intended to be used as a substitute for the full prescribing instructions.

dol and olanzapine may be prescribed. Lithium carbonate may also be effective, but it takes a week or more for therapeutic blood levels to be attained. In the meantime an antipsychotic may be given and then gradually withdrawn as lithium levels approach the therapeutic range.

For the prophylaxis of bipolar disorders or recurrent mania, lithium, carbamazepine and valproic acid may be effective. Blood levels of these compounds should be checked regularly. Lithium levels should be maintained between 0.8 and 2.2 milliequivalents per litre. The therapeutic window for lithium is narrow, levels too low being ineffective and levels too high causing side effects; the latter include tremor, anorexia, nausea, abdominal discomfort, thirst, polyuria, fatigue, weakness and goitre.

Drugs for children and adolescents with anxiety disorders

Medication has a limited role in the treatment of child and adolescent anxiety disorders. It should not be considered until child and family have been assessed thoroughly, since these disorders are often associated with problems in the family, school or wider social environment. Administering medication without addressing such problems is unlikely to be successful.

Benzodiazepine drugs such as chlordiazepoxide, alprazolam and clonazepam can help alleviate anxiety symptoms in the short term but should not be used for long-term therapy. Alprazolam, a short-acting drug, can be valuable in the very short-term treatment of acute anxiety, especially that related to acute stressors that are likely to be time limited. Clonazepam, an intermediate-acting drug, may be useful in the short-term treatment of adolescent panic disorder.

The long-term use of benzodiazepines may lead to dependence, and problems can arise if their use is discontinued too abruptly. A main side effect is drowsiness; disinhibition and irritability have also been observed.

Selective serotonin reuptake inhibitors (SSRIs) (see the foregoing section on treatment of depression) currently have an accepted place in the treatment of child and adolescent anxiety disorders. They appear to be of value in selective mutism, panic disorder, obsessive-compulsive disorder (OCD) (Alderman *et al.*, 1998) and probably generalised anxiety disorder (GAD). Their side effects, when they occur, are generally mild, though—rarely—extra-pyramidal side effects have been reported with paroxetine, fluoxetine and sertraline. Long-term use is safe; indeed these drugs usually need to be administered for several weeks before the full therapeutic response occurs.

Table 22.3 summarizes indications, dosage and side effects of these drugs.

The *tricyclic antidepressants* (TCAs) have a limited role in these disorders. However clomipramine has been shown to be effective in OCD. Garland (2002) suggests that TCAs may be used for anxious children with sleep disturbances, panic or separation who have not tolerated SSRIs.

Table 22.3   Some drugs for children and adolescents with anxiety disorders

Drugs	Dose	Main side effects
For short-term use		
Benzodiazepines		
Alprazolam (short acting)	250 micrograms up to 3 times daily	Drowsiness, lethargy, dependence, increased aggressiveness, withdrawal symptoms, confusion
Clonazepam (medium-acting)	0.5–3.0 mg daily	
Diazepam	1–5 mg once or twice daily	
For longer-term use if required		
Selective serotonin reuptake inhibitors (SSRIs)		
Citalopram (may be effective for panic attacks)	10–20 mg daily (up to 30 mg in adolescents)	Sedation, abdominal pain or discomfort, headaches, palpitations
Fluoxetine	10–20 mg daily, occasionally up to 30 mg	
Sertraline	25–50 mg daily, occasionally 100 mg	
(Sertraline and fluoxetine may be of special value in obsessive-compulsive disorders.)		
For obsessive-compulsive disorders		
Clomipramine	10–25 mg daily up to 50 mg daily in adolescents	Sedation, dry mouth, cardiac problems: ECG changes, arrhythmias, heart block, postural hypotension

This is not a complete list of drugs that may be used for anxiety disorders, and it should not be used as a substitute for the full prescribing instructions.

Other drugs that may be used for these children include buspirone, propranolol and clonidine. There is reason to believe that clonidine may help alleviate the symptoms of post-traumatic stress disorder.

Drugs for children and adolescents with schizophrenia

The pharmacological treatment of childhood and adult schizophrenia follows the same general lines as the treatment of this disorder in adults. The antipsychotic medications, or *neuroleptics*, that were introduced in the 1950s were a major advance in the treatment of schizophrenia. Chlorpromazine was the first of these. It was followed by thioridazine, loxapine, fluphenazine and haloperidol, among others. However they are prone to cause side effects, some of them serious, and they are less effective in treating the 'negative' symptoms of these disorders than the 'positive' symptoms (see Chapter 13).

Recent years have seen the introduction of second generation or *atypical* neuroleptics. These tend to cause fewer side effects and are sometimes more effective in the treatment of 'negative' symptoms. They may also benefit the 'positive' symptoms when these have been resistant to treatment with the *typical* neuroleptics. These newer compounds include clozapine, risperidone, olanzapine and quetiapine. None of these drugs is free of side effects however. Clozapine, though an effective neuroleptic, may cause agranulocytosis (reduction in the white blood cells), which may be fatal.

Table 22.4 lists some of the drugs currently available for the treatment of schizophrenia in children. They should be only used by, or in consultation with, a specialist with expertise in this area.

Table 22.4   Some drugs for children and adolescents with schizophrenia

Drugs	Dose	Main side effects
Examples of conventional antipsychotics		
Chlorpromazine	25–75 mg per day up to age 12; higher doses may be needed for adolescents	Sedation, tremor, restlessness, tardive dyskinesia, sedation, convulsions, headaches
Haloperidol	25–50 micrograms/kg initially, up to a daily maximum of 10 mg	Dystonic reactions, other side effects as above
Examples of atypical antipsychotics		
Risperidone	0.5 mg twice daily, increasing to 4 mg daily	Weight gain, dizziness, insomnia, drowsiness, nausea, vomiting
Olanzapine	Should be used only under specialist supervision	As for risperidone
Quetiapine	As for olanzapine	As for risperidone

Many other antipsychotics are available, but their safety and efficacy for use in children and adolescents are not established. They should be used only under specialist supervision.

The atypical antipsychotics are often preferred to the conventional ones because of their better side-effect profile.

This table is not intended to provide complete prescribing instructions. Many side effects in addition to those mentioned above may be experienced.

Drugs for other child and adolescent disorders

Haloperidol and clonidine are often effective in the treatment of tics and Tourette's syndrome. However, sulpiride may be drug of first choice for tic control. Drug treatment may also have a role in the symptomatic treatment of aggressive behaviour, pervasive developmental disorders and eating disorders.

Hypnosis and hypnotherapy

Hypnosis is not widely used in the treatment of child psychiatric disorders, but it probably has a place. The state of trance, which is the essence of hypnosis, is a commonplace one. We all focus our attention on particular things from time to time—a daydream or a story with which we get deeply engrossed, for example. As we do so we are often in a state of light trance—a state not fundamentally different from that induced by the clinical hypnotherapist. In trance our awareness of certain things is heightened and that of others is decreased. Things on which our attention is not focussed are ignored, even though we may be distantly aware of them. Many of us have had the experience of driving somewhere but having no memory of the journey on arrival at our destination. This is an example of an everyday trance.

Children tend to be good hypnotic subjects. Brown and Fromm (1986) point out that children usually spend much of their time in a world of imagery. The hypnotherapist may use this characteristic to advantage.

The following are among the uses hypnotherapy may have in treating children with psychiatric disorders:

(1) It may help troubled children gain access to emotional and other mental states that are more conducive to adaptive behaviour.

(2) It may promote access to material that is not currently available at a conscious level. Such *repressed* or *state-dependent* material may be responsible for anxiety, phobic or other symptoms. In the trance state such material may become available so that it can be dealt with in psychotherapy.

(3) It may enable children to obtain access to resources of which they have been unaware. We have seen how important it is for children to grow up with a good sense of self-esteem. Many children (and adults too) are consciously unaware of many of their strengths and capabilities, and they have repressed the memory of their past achievements. In trance they can become aware of these, which may help them acquire a better sense of self-esteem and increased confidence in themselves.

(4) It facilitates mind-body communication (Rossi, 1986a). This may lead to better healing of wounds and burns (Edwards and van der Spuy, 1985), and reduction of nausea and of bleeding.

(5) It can help control anxiety, often through some of the processes mentioned in uses 1, 2 and 3 above.

(6) It can assist in pain control.

(7) It can help diminish or abolish abnormal repetitive behaviours.

(8) It may be a helpful adjunct in the treatment of a variety of disorders, including learning difficulties, temper tantrums, hair pulling, prolonged thumb sucking, phobias (for example of needles, animals and school), shyness, and drug abuse. The quality of the scientific evidence for the effectiveness of hypnosis in many conditions varies, and much depends on the skill of the therapist.

In none of the above conditions is hypnosis a panacea, and inducing trance itself is of little therapeutic value beyond—usually—facilitating a state of relaxation. Moreover it is seldom sufficient simply to offer suggestions that symptoms will improve. Furthermore the susceptibility of individuals to hypnosis varies.

Further information on this subject is to be found in *Hypnosis and Hypnotherapy with Children* (Olness and Kohen, 1996).

Day treatment

Most child and adolescent psychiatric disorders can be successfully treated in outpatient or office settings. When this is ineffective and there are major problems in dealing with the child or adolescent in such settings, attendance at a daypatient unit may be indicated. In such units the patients spend substantial parts of their waking hours in a therapeutic milieu where they can receive a range of treatments, as well as help with the educational problems many of them have.

Most daypatient programs operate five days a week, usually from 8 or 9 a.m. until 4 or 5 p.m., though their hours vary. These units usually have an educational component and tend to be organized around the school day, with active involvement of the families. Some programs offer half-day attendance for younger children, and in some there is the option of having children attend less often than five days a week. Staffing may be more consistent in day programs than in residential ones. In the latter the staff have to cover all 24 hours and weekends, unless it is a five-day program. In day programs the working hours of the staff usually approximate to the hours the children attend.

While day treatment relieves parents and other family members of some of the strain of caring for their disturbed children, it ensures continuing contact between child and family. Loss of such contact is one of the risks of inpatient treatment and residential care.

Day treatment may be of particular value when a child's problems are selectively manifest at school, adjustment at home being relatively satisfactory. Day treatment may not be suitable for the following:

— Children who are dangerous to themselves or others
— Children whose parents or other care providers are themselves seriously disturbed, dangerous and/or abusive
— Children with a physical illness or handicap that necessitates round-the-clock care

Day treatment may be of short or long duration. It may extend from a week or two to many months, occasionally even longer. Many of these programs operate in association with both inpatient and outpatient services. Day attendance may then be just one phase in a treatment program that includes periods of inpatient and outpatient therapy.

Inpatient and residential treatment

Inpatient treatment usually refers to treatment in a hospital unit for disturbed children or adolescents, and *residential treatment* to that provided in other specialized centres. The former tend to be shorter-term units than the latter, though there are exceptions; indeed the distinction between the two types of units in not always clear-cut.

Treatment away from home and family, especially for long periods, should be avoided whenever possible. The empowering of parents to meet their children's needs, as can often be achieved during outpatient or day-patient therapy, is much to be preferred to removing children to other settings in which professionals take over children's care. Active involvement of families is almost always to be desired, even if children are in a residential setting. Visits home are helpful and should occur as often as practicable.

Inpatient units can have assessment and treatment functions. They can help with *assessment* when the diagnosis is in doubt, especially in complex and severe disorders, and also when it is unclear to what extent a child's symptoms are being maintained as a result of the home or, in some instances, the school and/or wider social environment.

Admission for *treatment* may be indicated because:

— The child's behaviour is so disturbed that management elsewhere is impractical, as with some children with severe conduct disorders, especially those complicated by severe hyperactivity and impulsive behaviour, and some with severely autistic or psychotic behaviour.

— There is a serious risk of suicide or harm to others.

— The child's environment is very unfavourable and efforts to improve it have failed.

— The child suffers from severe anorexia, less intrusive treatments have failed, and there is a risk of a fatal outcome.

Most inpatient units admit children and adolescents for fairly short periods, as part of a larger, ongoing treatment plan. These units are staffed by multidisciplinary teams made up from the disciplines of psychiatry, psychology, nursing, social work, child care, and occupational, recreational and speech therapy. Any of the treatments discussed in the previous sections of this chapter may be employed. There is usually an educational component to the program, and there may be one or more child psychotherapists. In many cases family therapy is an important part of the treatment plan.

Educational measures

Many children and adolescents with psychiatric problems have concomitant educational problems. For example, delay in developing reading skills is common in children with conduct disorders. In these cases, educational help needs to be part of the management plan. A careful assessment by an educational psychologist is useful in determining what help is required. This may consist of remedial teaching, changes in the educational methods being used, transfer to a more suitable school or class, or some combination of these measures.

In many jurisdictions there are special classes, or even day or residential schools, dedicated to the education of children with psychiatric, behavioural and educational problems. These usually have small classes, staffed by specially trained teachers, with a low staff:child ratio. Great Britain has a long and proud history of the provision of 'residential schools for maladjusted children.' The early development of this movement was chronicled by Bridgland (1971). *The Management of Behaviour in Schools* (Varma, 1993) addresses the problems of managing behaviourally disturbed children in schools.

Speech and language therapy

Speech and language disorders are often associated with psychiatric disorders in children. Treatment plans therefore frequently need to include treatment of such disorders. Speech therapists, sometimes known as speech pathologists, assess children's speech and language development, and either themselves provide, or assist teachers, parents and others in providing, needed remedial help.

Removal from parental care

Sometimes disturbed children are found to be living in severely dysfunctional families in which their basic emotional, even their physical, needs are not being met. They may have experienced, or still be experiencing, physical, sexual or emotional abuse, or they may be subject to neglect. They may face any combination of these problems. When such situations come to light, the immediate priority is to assure the safety of the child. Then efforts must be made to enable the parents to care adequately for their child. This may not be successful. Some parents seem to lack the motivation to make the necessary changes. They may have problems such as the chronic abuse of alcohol and/or other drugs; they may themselves have serious mental health problems; sometimes the marital relationship is grossly unstable or abusive.

When efforts to help such families fail, removing their child or children may be necessary. Removal may be to a foster home or a 'group home' (the usual North American term) or 'children's home' (the U.K. term). Group and children's homes may be run by professional child-care staff working shifts, or by couples (sometimes individuals) assisted by additional paid staff. Residential care may be short term or long term. It usually involves the statutory social service authorities taking custody of the child, either temporarily or permanently. Some children who are in permanent social service care may in due course be placed for adoption in carefully selected families.

Psychiatrists and other mental health professionals have much to contribute to the decision-making processes that are necessary in the management of children in care. These issues are comprehensively reviewed in *The Least Detrimental Alternative: A Systematic Guide to Case Planning and Decision Making for Children in Care* (Steinhauer, 1991).

Child psychiatric consultation and liaison

There are, and probably always will be, more disturbed children in the community than can be assessed and treated by the available numbers of psychiatrists and other child mental health professionals. Psychiatrists can however do much to help such children and their families by providing consultation to those caring for the many children and adolescents who cannot receive direct service. Psychiatrists may offer guidance to the staffs of group homes, schools and other institutions about how the needs of the children in their care may best be met. Their skills are thus spread more widely, if somewhat less thickly, over a wide range of young people.

Psychiatric liaison, as opposed to consultation, work addresses not the needs of particular children, or even of groups of children, but those of the agencies, schools, other institutions and caregivers dealing with disturbed children. It is concerned with such matters as program development, improvement of the milieu in residential and other settings, and the fostering of the skills of the staff. Psychiatric liaison work can play an important role in the prevention of psychiatric disorders.

Chapter 23

Prevention

It is better to prevent disorders rather than waiting until they occur and then attempting to treat them. The three main categories of preventive measures are:

— *Primary prevention.* This consists of measures applied to a population not currently suffering from the disorder(s) concerned. They are designed to reduce, or ideally eliminate, the disorders in the population. Immunizing healthy subjects against infectious diseases is an example of primary prevention.

— *Secondary prevention.* This aims at early diagnosis and case finding, followed by intervention to bring the disorder under control as quickly as possible.

— *Tertiary prevention.* This aims to limit the effects of established disorders, preventing them from getting worse and supporting afflicted individuals and/or their families.

The distinction between some forms of what is often regarded as primary prevention, such as the 'indicated' measures mentioned below, and secondary prevention, is not always clear. For practical purposes, however it is not really important.

Definitions

(1) *Epidemiology.* This is the study of the incidence, prevalence and distribution of disorders in populations. It is a basic tool of primary prevention, which requires baseline information about the prevalence of the disorders concerned in the population. It can also help identify risk factors.

(2) *Risk factors.* These are circumstances that make the development of a disorder more likely.

(3) *Incidence.* This is the number of new cases occurring in a population over a specified period.

(4) *Duration.* This is the length of time a disorder persists, from the time of onset until recovery or death.

(5) *Prevalence.* This is a measure of the number of cases of a disorder present at a given time in a specified population. It is a function of the two independent variables—incidence and duration.

(6) *Intervening variables.* In the present context, these are the factors that determine whether individuals at risk develop the disorder in question. Risk factors never lead to the disorder in 100% of those at risk. In any epidemic, some individuals will escape the disease. Primary prevention aims to alter the environment so that more

individuals escape, as well as improving the status of individuals so that they are less likely to develop disorders.

Primary prevention

Primary prevention attacks risk factors. These include the following:

(1) *Genetic factors.* The role of genetic factors was outlined in Chapter 2. Our knowledge of the genetic background of many disorders is increasing by leaps and bounds. This is opening up the prospect that we may be able to prevent many disorders in which genetic factors play a part, be it a small one or a big one. Sometimes parents choose to have a pregnancy terminated if it has been established that the fetus has a serious genetic abnormality.

(2) *Pregnancy risk factors.* These include the health and nutritional state of the mother, the use of alcohol and drugs during the pregnancy, and specific disorders such as toxaemia (a condition in which there is fluid retention and raised blood pressure), and infections such as rubella, syphilis, toxoplasmosis and AIDS. Medication is available that can greatly reduce the chance of HIV transmission from mother to fetus. The importance of good antenatal care can scarcely be overemphasized.

(3) *Birth trauma.* Good obstetric care reduces the risk of brain damage during birth.

(4) *Prematurity and neonatal difficulties.* These may lead to brain damage, and prolonged periods in hospital during the first year can lead to problems in the development of emotional attachment between parents and child.

(5) *Accidents in and outside the home.* These have the potential to cause neurological and other injuries. These may, in turn, lead to developmental and psychiatric problems.

(6) *Poisons.* Lead has been largely removed from children's environment in most of the developed world, but lead poisoning is a danger that children in other parts of the world still face. Second-hand smoke can adversely affect children's development, and the importance of protecting them from this is increasingly being realized.

(7) *Physical illness.* Illnesses, especially those affecting the central nervous system, may place children at risk of developing psychiatric disorders (Barker, 1993a). The risks are greater for children who are repeatedly admitted to hospital.

(8) *Deprivation, ill-treatment and neglect.* These are frequently encountered risk factors. Cultural deprivation, poor nutrition and lack of medical care can all result in failure of development and poor progress in school. Children who come to school hungry and poorly clothed, and who are not encouraged by their families and given help with their homework when they need it, are at a big disadvantage. Such children tend to live in chaotic families and those in which there is serious disharmony and disruption (Barker, 1993b). Child abuse and neglect are potent causes of psychiatric disorder. They are discussed in Chapter 21.

(9) *Parental illness.* This is an especially serious risk factor when both parents suffer from mental illness, and when their illnesses are prolonged.

(10) *Early school failure.* This is often associated with specific learning disorders, hyperkinesis and neurological problems.

(11) *'Difficult' temperament.* See discussion of temperament in Chapter 2.

(12) *The experience of being, or having been in the care of a child welfare agency.*

(13) *Living in a disorganized community, especially when there is a high crime rate, widespread drug use and/or a lack of services for young people.*

(14) *Peer group factors.* These include associating with delinquent peers and those with antisocial attitudes.

(15) *School factors.* The culture and quality of children's school environments are important influences (Rutter, 1980). Poor school organization and morale are risk factors for the children in the school; so is the availability or use of alcohol and drugs within the school.

(16) *Large family size.*

(17) *Father absence.*

(18) *Poverty.*

Protective factors

These are the converse of risk factors. They reduce the likelihood of disorders appearing. A list of protective factors could simply consist of the opposite of each of the above risk factors. Thus children in stable, well-functioning, two-parent families living in upscale neighbourhoods in which there is little crime, and where there are good services for young people, have many protective factors on their side. This is even more so if they are intellectually well endowed, with no learning difficulties, and they attend well-organized schools in which there is a culture that promotes learning and prosocial attitudes. Other protective factors include female gender, because girls seem to be less susceptible to psychosocial stress in childhood than boys, and favourable temperamental characteristics.

There are however some specific factors that may be protective for children who face various risk factors. These include:

(1) *Isolated nature of stresses the child faces.* Even chronic stresses, if isolated, may cause less damage than multiple stresses, each of which tend to potentiate the adverse results of the others.

(2) *Coping skills.* Children can acquire the skills to cope with various stressful circumstances. For example, if they are used to brief, happy separation experiences such as short stays with relatives or friends, they usually cope better with admission to hospital.

(3) *A good relationship with one parent.* This helps protect against the adverse effects that may result when a child grows up in a discordant, unhappy home. A good, long-term relationship with another adult, who need not be a family member, has also been shown to be protective.

(4) *Success and/or good experiences outside the home.* Good schooling, for example, or success in sports, can help mitigate the effects of a bad home environment.

(5) *Improved family circumstances.* Later years spent in a harmonious family setting seem to lessen the effects of earlier adverse experiences.

Variations in vulnerability

It has long been recognized that children vary in their vulnerability to psychosocial and other stresses. This should not surprise us. In an influenza epidemic, not every one exposed to the virus develops the disease. Lung cancer does not develop in every heavy cigarette smoker. Similarly, not every child exposed—even to multiple risk factors—develops a psychiatric disorder.

The study of factors that lead to reduced vulnerability is not easy, and resilience is not a unitary characteristic (Luthar, 1993), but a classic longitudinal study of children carried out on the Hawaiian island of Kauai gave us some pointers. The authors pointed out that:

> 'From an epidemiological point of view, these children were at high risk, since they were born and reared in poverty, exposed to high rates of prematurity and perinatal stress, and reared by mothers with little formal education.' (Werner & Smith, 1982, page 153)

The children were followed from birth into adult life, with less than a 10% drop-out rate. Some triumphed strikingly over adversity, becoming competent and autonomous young adults. These resilient children:

— Had few serious illnesses in their first two decades and they recovered quickly from those they had
— Were perceived to be *very active* and *socially responsive* as infants
— Showed advanced self-help skills and adequate sensori-motor and language development in the second year of life
— Had adequate problem-solving and communication skills and age-appropriate perceptual and motor development in middle childhood
— Had a more internal locus of control, a better self-concept, and a more nurturant, responsible, achievement-oriented attitude towards life as late adolescents than their less successful peers

The above list describes resilience/invulnerability rather than explaining it or elucidating its causes.

The environmental factors that were found to be associated with resilience and stress resistance may be more helpful in understanding this phenomenon:

— The age of the parent of the opposite sex (younger mothers for resilient boys and older fathers for resilient girls)
— Four or fewer children in the family
— A spacing of more than two years between a child and the next-born sibling
— The presence and number of 'alternate care-takers' (father, grandparents, older siblings) available to the mother within the household; the amount of attention given to the child by the primary care-taker(s) in infancy

— The availability of a sibling as care-taker or confidant in childhood; the cumulative number of chronic stressful life events experienced in childhood and adolescence

Other factors that emerged were the mother's workload, the cohesiveness of the family, and whether there was an informal multigenerational network of kin and friends in adolescence.

'The physical robustness of the resilient children, their activity level, and their social responsiveness were recognized by the caregivers and elicited a great deal of attention. There was little prolonged separation of the infants from their mothers and no prolonged bond disruption during the first year of life. The strong attachment that resulted appears to have been a secure base for the development of self-help skills and autonomy noted among these children in their second year of life.

Though many of their mothers worked for extended periods and were major contributors to family subsistence, the children had support from alternate caretakers, such as grandmothers or older sisters, to whom they became attached.' (Werner & Smith, 1982, pages 155–156)

Primary prevention methods

These may be of three types: universal, selective or indicated:

— A *universal* preventive intervention is applied to an entire, defined population.

— A *selective* intervention is applied to individuals who are at greater risk of developing a disorder than the general population—usually because of environmental factors such as some of those listed previously.

— An *indicated* intervention is one applied to asymptomatic individuals who, because of known genetic or other predisposing factors, are believed to be at risk of developing a disorder.

Universal preventive measures include many of the public health and educational programs that societies and their governments implement—with varying degrees of success—with the aim of promoting children's healthy emotional and social development. Examples are good, freely available antenatal care; high-quality perinatal and neonatal services; the elimination—or at least amelioration—of poverty in families with children; well-funded and organized schools; and the elimination of hazards (for example lead) in the environment. They include promoting child safety in cars and other interventions, such as education about the risks of 'street' drug use. However such measures have wider aims than simply the prevention of psychiatric disorders in children. Poverty in families not only increases the risk of the children developing psychiatric disorders but also has other adverse effects. It is considered by many to be a blight on society, something that should not, for ethical reasons, exist in a compassionate society.

Selective interventions may be applied to subgroups of populations, such as those living in deprived, inner-city areas where incomes are low and crime and drug use rates are high. Head Start programs were established in the United States in the mid-1960s. By the mid-1980s there were 9400 of these serving some 500,000 children, supported by federal government funding of $1 billion (Parker *et al.*, 1987). The Head Start centres aimed to provide intensive cognitive and emotional stimulation for preschool children and their families. Although they resulted in spurts in children's development, the long-term results were modest at best. One study suggested that the mothers derived benefit, experiencing fewer psychological symptoms, increased feelings of mastery and more satisfaction with life (Parker *et al.*, 1987).

LeMarquand and his colleagues (2001) reviewed the available reports of research studies that aimed to test the effectiveness of interventions designed to reduce the prevalence of conduct disorders. They found only 20 published studies that met their 'minimal methodical requirements'. Eight of these were of the 'selective' variety. Among the interventions there was a head start-type program, several using parent training and education, counselling and the provision of help with nutrition, health and safety, consultation with teachers and work with families.

Indicated interventions were the subject of 10 of the reports reviewed by LeMarquand and colleagues (2001). The children included in these programs were showing aggressive behaviour, high absenteeism from school, poor peer relationship skills, negative peer interactions and low IQs. They tended to come from families of low socio-economic status. Interventions included counselling, parent training, casework with the families, education focussing on the acquisition of language skills, consultation with teachers, behavioural shaping, improving communication, and compensatory and enrichment activities, among other things.

LeMarquand *et al.* discuss which preventive experiments were effective and which were not. Preschool interventions that focussed on improving cognitive skills yielded positive results; so too did home visits offering the parents assistance in improving their parenting skills. But it is clear that much more research in this area is needed.

Klingman (2001) discusses the prevention of anxiety disorders, taking post-traumatic stress disorder as a model.

High-risk programs are a category of indicated programs. They aim to prevent the appearance of disorders in children belonging to groups at high risk. These include children subject to any number of the risk factors listed above. Generally speaking, the more risk factors there are the greater is the chance of disorders developing. Many programs have been developed for such children. Cadman and colleagues (1987) reviewed programs designed to reduce the incidence of emotional, behavioural and family problems in children with chronic medical illnesses. The late Paul Steinhauer (1984, 1991) was a tireless advocate for children in the care of child welfare services, a group at high risk. He suggested ways of preventing *drift* (the all-too-common process whereby children taken into care languish in 'temporary' placements for extended periods), minimizing emergency placements, and providing effective placements for the children and their families.

Prevention Programs for Youth (Stowell, 1998) presents a concise survey of approaches to prevention. The first two chapters deal with, respectively, program evaluation and the 'theory and practice' of preventive work. The meat of the book is to be found in Chapter 3, which provides concise descriptions of a wide range of prevention programs.

Among the problems targeted by the programs mentioned are strengthening various categories of families; helping girls avoid such risky behaviour as drug use and sexual activity; promoting 'responsible sexuality' in Grade 9 students; preventing the spread of HIV and AIDS in adolescent runaways and in adolescents detained in jail; reducing truancy and school drop-outs; and reducing criminal and other violent behaviour and school-based violence. There are several programs designed to help young people resist or avoid becoming involved in illicit drug use. There are also suicide prevention and life skills programs, and 'the 7 generation prevention project' for Native American children—a program that aims to reduce the incidence of fetal alcohol syndrome.

Following the brief description of each program, the evidence (or lack of it) for the program's effectiveness is summarized.

The final two chapters discuss how to write effective proposals and reports, and sources from which funding for prevention programs may be obtained. The book confines itself to prevention programs from the United states, but many of the ideas presented will be of value in other countries. It concludes with an extensive list of agencies and organizations that may be of help to those wishing to develop preventive programs. For the most part, the programs described come in the category of primary prevention.

Secondary prevention

Secondary prevention is closely related to *early childhood intervention.* It aims to 'influence the development and learning of children from birth to five years who have a developmental disability/delay, or who are at risk due to biological or environmental factors (McCollum, 2002; Baker & Feinfield, 2003).

Baker and Feinfield (2003) review recently published accounts of early intervention programs and their results. Among the 'at risk' groups for whom intervention programs have been reported are:

— Low birth weight children
— Disturbances in parent-child interactions due to maternal affective disorders and other mental health problems
— Children with developmental disabilities and delay
— Children with autism
— Children living in poverty

Home visitation by nurses is mentioned in Chapter 21 as an effective method for the prevention of child abuse. It can also have many other benefits. Olds (2002) has shown that a regular program of prenatal and early childhood visits by nurses to the homes of low-income single mothers can be of real benefit to these mothers and their children. The benefits even extend to less antisocial behaviour in the children at age 15.

Baker and Feinfield (2003) review current work in this area. The *Handbook of Early Childhood Intervention,* 2nd edition (Shonkoff & Meisels, 2000) is a source of further information.

Tertiary prevention

This consists of work done with established disorders to limit their progress and effects. It involves the prompt and energetic use of the treatment methods outlined elsewhere in this book at the earliest possible stage once disorders are present. For example, the prompt treatment of attention-deficit hyperactivity disorders, the symptoms of which develop early in childhood, can pay dividends. Clinical experience is that the longer treatment is delayed the more serious the consequences usually are. These may include failure in school, reluctance or refusal to attend school, a variety of behaviour problems, and even family breakdown.

Delayed or inadequate treatment of most other child psychiatric disorders can have similarly unfortunate results.

Conclusion

In many ways prevention has been the Cinderella of child psychiatry. Many more books, journal articles and research projects are devoted to clinical aspects of child psychiatric disorders than are devoted to their prevention. The money spent on prevention in most, probably all, jurisdictions is minuscule compared to that spent on treatment. This no doubt is a result of social and political pressures rather than logic. Yet the individual, or even the group, treatment of established disorders by highly paid professionals is enormously expensive and probably not the best use of available funds. There are good reasons to believe that money spent on prevention leads to better results in the long term. It is money well spent—better spent than much of the money currently devoted to treatment services.

References

Achenbach, T.M. & Edelbrock, C.S. (1983). *Manual for Child Behaviour Checklist and Revised Child Behaviour Profile*. Burlington: Department of Psychiatry, University of Vermont.

Adams, P.L. (1982). *A Primer of Child Psychotherapy*, 2nd edn. Boston: Little Brown.

Adlaf, E.M., Paglia, A., Ivis, F.J. & Ialomiteanu, A. (2000). 'Highlights from the 1999 Ontario Student Drug Use Survey'. *Canadian Medical Association Journal*, **162**, 1677–1680.

Ainsworth, M.D.S., Blehar, M.C., Waters, E. & Wall, S. (1978). *Patterns of Adjustment: A Psychological Study of Strange Situations*. Hillsdale, NJ: Lawrence Erlbaum.

Akiskal, H.S. & Weller, E.B. (1989). 'Mood disorders and suicide in children and adolescents'. In: *Comprehensive Textbook of Psychiatry*, 5th edn., eds. H.I. Kaplan & B.J. Sadock. Baltimore: Williams & Wilkins, pages 1981–1996.

Albertini, R.S. & Phillips, K.A. (1999). 'Thirty-three cases of body dysmorphic disorders in children and adolescents'. *Journal of the American Academy of Child & Adolescent Psychiatry*, **38**, 453–459.

Alderman, J., Wolkow, R., Chung, M. & Johnston, H.F. (1998). 'Sertraline treatment of children and adolescents with obsessive-compulsive disorder or depression: pharmacokinetics, tolerability, and efficacy'. *Journal of the American Academy of Child & Adolescent Psychiatry*, **37**, 386–394.

Allen, F.H. (1942). *Psychotherapy with Children*. New York: Norton.

Allen, J.P. (1999). 'Attachment in adolescence.' In: *Handbook of Attachment*, eds. J. Cassidy & P.R. Shaver. London: Guilford, pages 319–335.

Alsobrook, J.P. & Pauls, D.L. (2002). 'A factor analysis of tics in Gilles de la Tourette's syndrome'. *American Journal of Psychiatry*, **159**, 291–296.

American Academy of Child & Adolescent Psychiatry (2001). 'Practice parameter for the assessment and treatment of children and adolescents with schizophrenia'. *Journal of the American Academy of Child & Adolescent Psychiatry*, **40**(7) (Suppl.), 4S–23S.

American Psychiatric Association (1994). *Diagnostic and Statistical Manual of Mental Disorders*, 4th edn. (*DSM-IV*). Washington, DC: APA.

American Psychiatric Association (2000). *Diagnostic and Statistical Manual of Mental Disorders*, 4th edn., text revision (DSM-IV-TR). Washington, DC: APA.

Anders, T., Goodlin-Jones, B. & Sadeh, A. (2000). 'Sleep disorders'. In: *Handbook of Infant Mental Health*, 2nd edn., eds. C.H. Zeanah Jr. New York: Guilford, pages 326–338.

Angold, A. & Costello, E.J. (2001) 'The epidemiology of disorders of conduct: nosological issues and comorbidity'. In: *Conduct Disorders in Childhood and Adolescence*, eds. J. Hill & B. Maughan. Cambridge University Press, pages 126–168.

Anthony, E.J. (1957). 'An experimental approach to the psychopathology of childhood: encopresis'. *British Journal of Medical Psychology*, **30**, 146–147.

Anthony, J.C. (2001). 'The promise of psychiatric enviromics'. *British Journal of Psychiatry*, (Suppl. 40), s8–s11.

Anthony, J.C., Eaton, W.W. & Henderson, A.S. (1995). 'Looking to the future in psychiatric epidemiology'. *Epidemiologic Reviews*, **17**, 240–242.

Asher, S.R., Parkhurst, J.T., Hymel, S. & Williams, G.A. (1990). 'Peer rejection and loneliness in childhood'. In: *Peer Rejection in Childhood*, eds. S.R. Asher & J.D. Coie. Cambridge University Press, pages 253–273.

Asperger, H. (1944). 'Die "Autischen Psychopathen" im Kindesalter' [Autistic psychopathy in childhood]. *Archiv für Psychiatrie und Nervenkrankheiten*, **117**, 76–136.

Bailey, A., Phillips, W. & Rutter, M. (1996). 'Autism: towards an integration of clinical, genetic, neuropsychological, and neurobiological perspectives'. *Journal of Child Psychology and Psychiatry*, **37**, 89–126.

Baker, B.L. & Feindfield, K.A. (2003). 'Early intervention'. *Current Opinion in Psychiatry*, **16**, 503–509.

Bandler, R. & Grinder, J. (1979). *Frogs into Princes*. Palo Alto, CA: Science and Behaviour.

Barker, P. (1984). 'Recognition and treatment of anxiety in children by means of psychiatric interview'. In: *Anxiety in Children*, ed. V.P. Varma. London: Croom Helm, pages 35–55.

Barker, P. (1990). *Clinical Interviews with Children and Adolescents*. New York: Norton.

Barker, P. (1993a) 'The effects of physical illness'. In: *How and Why Children Fail*, ed. V. Varma. London: Jessica Kingsley, pages 77–89.

Barker, P. (1993b). 'The child from the chaotic family'. In: *How and Why Children Fail*, ed. V.P. Varma. London: Jessica Kingsley, pages 103–113.

Barker, P. (1993c). 'The effects of child abuse'. In: *How and Why Children Fail*, ed. V.P. Varma. London: Jessica Kingsley, pages 90–102.

Barker, P. (1994). 'Reframing: The Essence of Psychotherapy'. In: *Ericksonian Methods: The Essence of the Story*, ed. J.K. Zeig. New York: Brunner/Mazel, pages 211–223.

Barker, P. (1998). *Basic Family Therapy*, 4th edn. Oxford: Blackwell.

Barton, M.L. & Robins, D. (2000). In: *Handbook of Infant Mental Health*, 2nd edn., ed. C.H. Zeanah Jr. New York: Guilford, pages 311–325.

Battle, J. (1994). *Promoting Self-esteem, Achievement and Well-being*. Edmonton, Canada: James Battle & Associates.

Bender, L. & Schilder, P. (1940). 'Impulsions: a specific disorder of the behaviour of children'. *Archives of Neurology and Psychiatry*, **44**, 990–1008.

Benninga, M.A. & Taminiau, J.A.J.M. (2001). 'Diagnosis and treatment efficacy of functional non-retentive fecal soiling in childhood'. *Journal of Pediatric Gastroenterology & Nutrition*, **32** (Suppl.), S42–S43.

Benoit, D. (1993). 'Failure to thrive and feeding disorders'. In: *Handbook of Infant Mental Health*, ed. C.H. Zeanah Jr. New York: Guilford, pages 317–331.

Benoit, D. (2000). 'Feeding disorders, failure to thrive and obesity'. In: *Handbook of Infant Mental Health*, 2nd edn., ed. C.H. Zeanah Jr. New York: Guilford, pages 339–352.

Bergman, R.L., Piacenti, J. & McCracken, J.T. (2002). 'Prevalence and description of selective mutism in a school-based sample'. *Journal of the American Academy of Child & Adolescent Psychiatry*, **41**, 938–946.

Berney, T.P. (2000). 'Autism: an evolving concept'. *British Journal of Psychiatry*, **176**, 20–25.

Bernstein, G.A. & Garfinkel, B.D. (1986). 'School phobia: the effective overlap of affective and anxiety disorders'. *Journal of the American Academy of Child Psychiatry*, **25**, 235–241.

Birmaher, B., Brent, D.A. & Benson, R.S. (1998). 'Summary of the practice parameters for the assessment and treatment of children and adolescents with depressive disorders'. *Journal of the American Academy of Child & Adolescent Psychiatry*, **37**, 1234–1238.

Birmaher, B., Brent, D.A., Kolko, D., Baugher, M., Bridge, J., Holder, D., Iyengar, S. & Ulloa, R.E. (2000). 'Clinical outcome after short-term psychotherapy for adolescents with major depressive disorders'. *Archives of General Psychiatry*, **57**, 29–36.

Blacher, J., Kraemer, B. & Schalow, M. (2003). 'Asperger syndrome and high functioning autism: research concerns and emerging foci'. *Current Opinion in Psychiatry*, **16**, 535–542.

Blank, S., Zadik, Z., Katz, I., Mahazri, Y., Toker, I. & Barak, I. (2002). 'The emergence of treatment of anorexia and bulimia nervosa: a comprehensive and practical model'. *International Journal of Adolescent Medicine & Health*, **14**, 257–260.

Boachie, A., Goldfield, G.S. & Spettigue, W. (2003). 'Olanzapine use as an adjunctive treatment for hospitalized children with anorexia nervosa: case reports'. *International Journal of Eating Disorders*, **33**, 98–103.

Boer, F. & Lindhout, I. (2001) 'Family and genetic influences: is anxiety "all in the family"'? In: *Anxiety Disorders in Children and Adolescents*, eds. W.K. Silverman & P.D.A. Treffers. Cambridge University Press, pages 235–254.

Bowlby, J. (1969). *Attachment*. London: Hogarth; New York: Basic.

Bowlby, J. (1979). *The Making and Breaking of Affectional Bonds*. London: Tavistock.

Boyle, M.H. & Offord, D.R. (1986). 'Smoking, drinking and the use of illicit drugs among adolescent in Ontario'. *Canadian Medical Association Journal*, **135**, 1113–1121.

Boyle, M.H., Offord, D.R, Hofman, H.G., Catlin, G.P., Byles, J.A., Cadman, D.T., Crawford, J.W., Links, P.S., Rae-Grant, N.I. & Szatmari, P. (1987). 'Ontario Child Health Study: methodology.' *Archives of General Psychiatry*, **44**, 826–831.

Brandenburg, N.A., Friedman, R.M. & Silver, S.E. (1990). 'The epidemiology of child psychiatric disorders: prevalence findings from recent studies'. *Journal of the American Academy of Child & Adolescent Psychiatry*, **29**, 76–83.

Bradley, C. (1937). 'The behaviour of children receiving Benzedrine'. *American Journal of Psychiatry*, **11**, 577–585.

Brennan, P.A., Mednick, S.A. & Jacobsen, B. (1995). 'Assessing the role of genetics in crime using adoption cohorts'. In: *Genetic of Criminal and Antisocial Behaviour* (Ciba Foundation Symposium 194), eds. G.R. Bock & J.A. Goode. Chichester: John Wiley & Sons, pages 115–128.

Bridgland, M. (1971). *Pioneer Work with Maladjusted Children*. London: Crosby Lockwood Staples.

Brown, B.D. & Fromm, E. (1986). *Hypnosis and Hypnotherapy*. Hillsdale, NJ: Lawrence Erlbaum.

Brown, B. & Lloyd, H. (1975). 'A controlled study of children not speaking in school'. *Journal of the Association of Workers for Maladjusted Children*, **3**, 49–63.

Butler, R.J., Holland, P. & Robinson, J. (2001). 'Examination of the structured withdrawal program to prevent relapse of nocturnal enuresis'. *Journal of Urology*, **166**, 2463–2466.

Cadman, D., Rosenbaum, P. & Pettinghill, P. (1987). 'Prevention of emotional, behavioural, and family problems of children with chronic medical illness'. *Journal of Preventive Psychiatry*, **3**, 147–165.

Caffey, J. (1946). 'Multiple fractures in the long bones of infants suffering from chronic subdural haematoma'. *American Journal of Roentgenology*, **56**, 163–173.

Calgary Herald (1993). Article by Bob Beaty, 27 November 1993, page A1.

Caplan, R., Guthrie, D., Fish, B., Tanguay, P.E. & David-Lando, G. (1989). 'The Kiddie Formal Thought Disorder Rating (K-FTDS): clinical assessment, reliability and validity'. *Journal of the American Academy of Child & Adolescent Psychiatry*, **28**, 208–216

Caplan, R., Guthrie, D. & Foy, J.G. (1992). 'Communication deficits and formal thought disorder in schizophrenic children'. *Journal of the American Academy of Child & Adolescent Psychiatry*, **31**, 151–159.

Caplan, R., Guthrie, D., Tang, B., Komo, S. & Asarnow, R.F. (2000). 'Thought disorder in childhood schizophrenia: replication and update of concept'. *Journal of the American Academy of Child & Adolescent Psychiatry*, **39**, 771–778.

Carlson, G.A. (1990). 'Child and adolescent mania: diagnostic considerations'. *Journal of Child Psychology & Psychiatry*, **31**, 331–341.

Carter, E.A. & McGoldrick, M. (1989). *The Changing Family Life Cycle: A Framework for Family Therapy*. New York: Gardner.

Casey, J.E. & Rourke, B.P. (1992). 'Disorders of somatosensory perception in children'. In: *Handbook of Neuropsychology*, Vol. 6: *Child Neuropsychology*. Amsterdam: Elsevier, pages 477–494.

Casey, J.E., Rourke, B.P. & Picard, E.M. (1991). 'Syndrome of nonverbal learning disabilities: age differences in neuropsychological, academic, and socioemotional functioning'. *Development & Psychopathology*, **3**, 329–345.

Casey, P., Dowrick, C & Wilkinson, G. (2001). 'Adjustment disorders: fault line in the psychiatric glossary'. *British Journal of Psychiatry*, **179**, 479–481.

Cass, H., Owen, L., Wisbech, A., Weekes, L., Slonims, V., Wsigram, T. & Charman, T. (2003). 'Findings from a multidisciplinary clinical case series of females with Rett syndrome'. *Developmental Medicine & Child Neurology*, **45**, 325–337.

Cheng, A.T.A. & Lee, C.S. (2000). 'Suicide in Asia and the Far East'. In: *The International Handbook of Suicide and Attempted Suicide*, eds. K. Hawton & C. van Heeringen. Chichester: John Wiley & Sons, pages 29–48.

Chess, S. & Thomas, A. (1984). *Origin and Evolution of Behaviour Disorders from Infancy to Early Adult Life*. New York: Brunner/Mazel.

Clarke, D.M & McKenzie, D.P. (1994). 'A caution on the use of cut-points applied to screening instruments or diagnostic criteria'. *Journal of Psychiatric Research*, **28**, 185–188.

Clore, R.R. & Hibel, J. (1993). 'The parasomnias of childhood'. *Journal of Pediatric Health Care*, **7**, 12–16.

Cohen, P., Cohen, J. & Brook, J. (1993a). 'An epidemiological study of disorders in late childhood and adolescence: II. Persistence of disorder'. *Journal of Child Psychology & Psychiatry*, **34**, 869–877.

Cohen, P., Cohen, J., Kasen, S., Velez, C.N, Hartmark, C., Johnson, J., Rojas, M., Brook, J. & Streuning, E.L. (1993b). 'An epidemiological study of disorders in late childhood and adolescence: I. Age and gender specific prevalence.' *Journal of Child Psychology & Psychiatry*, **34**, 851–867.

Conture, A.G. (1990) *Stuttering*, 2nd edn. Englewood Cliffs, NJ: Prentice Hall.

Corbett, J.A. (1979). 'Psychiatric morbidity and mental retardation'. In: *Psychiatric Illness and Mental Handicap*, eds. F.E. James & R.P. Smith. London: Gaskell, pages 11–25.

Costello, E.J. & Angold, A. (2001) 'Bad behaviour: an historical perspective on disorders of conduct'. In: *Conduct Disorders in Childhood and Adolescence*, eds. J. Hill & B. Maughan. Cambridge University Press, pages 1–31.

Covitz, J. (1986). *Emotional Child Abuse*. Boston: Sigo.

Crnic, K.A. & Reid, M. (1989). 'Mental retardation'. In: *Treatment of Childhood Disorders*, eds. E.J. Mash & E.A. Barkley. New York: Guilford, pages 247–285.

Cunningham, C.E. (1999). 'In the wake of the MTA: charting a new course for the study and treatment of children with attention-deficit hyperactivity disorder'. *Canadian Journal of Psychiatry*, **44**, 1000–1006.

Daalsgard, S., Mortensen, P.B., Frydenberg, M. & Thomsen, P.H. (2002). 'Conduct problems, gender and adult psychiatric outcome of children with attention-deficit hyperactivity disorder'. *British Journal of Psychiatry*, **181**, 416–421.

Dale, R.C. & Heyman, I. (2002). 'Post-streptococcal autoimmune psychiatric and movement disorders in children'. *British Journal of Psychiatry*, **181**, 188–190.

Dauvilliers, Y., Mayer, G., Lecendreux, M., Neidhart, E., Peraita-Adrados, R., Sonka, K., Billiard, M. & Tafti, M. (2002). 'Kleine-Levin syndrome: an autoimmune hypothesis based on clinical and genetic analysis'. *Neurology*, **59**, 1739–1745.

DiLeo, J.H. (1983). *Interpreting Children's Drawings*. New York: Brunner/Mazel.

Dilts, R., Grinder, J., Bandler, R., Bandler, L.C. & DeLozier, J. (1980). *Neurolinguistic Programming*, Vol. 1. Cupertino, CA: Meta.

Dixon, S.D. & Stein, M.T. (1992). *Encounters with Children*. St. Louis: Mosby Year Book.

Dobson, K.S. (ed.) (1988). *Handbook of Cognitive-Behavioural Therapies*. New York: Guilford.

Dummit, E.S., III, Klein, R.G., Tancer, N.K., Asche, B., Martin, J. & Fairbanks, J.A. (1997). 'Systematic assessment of 50 children with selective mutism'. *Journal of the American Academy of Child & Adolescent Psychiatry*, **36**, 653–660.

Duvall, E.M. & Miller, B.C. (1985). *Marriage and Family Development*, 6th edn. New York: Harper & Row.

Edwards, S.D & van der Spuy, H.I.J. (1985). 'Hypnotherapy as a treatment for enuresis'. *Journal of Child Psychology & Psychiatry*, **26**, 161–170.

Eggers, C. & Bunk, D. (1997). 'The long-term course of childhood-onset schizophrenia: a 42-year follow-up'. *Schizophrenia Bulletin*, **23**, 105–117.

Elmer, E. (1986). 'Outcome of residential treatment for abused and high-risk infants'. *Child Abuse & Neglect*, **10**, 351–360.

Epps, K & Hollin, C.R. (2000) 'Understanding and treating adolescent firesetters'. In: *Violent Children and Adolescents: Asking the Question Why*, ed. G. Boswell. London: Whurr, pages 36–55.

Erikson, E. H. (1965). *Childhood and Society*. London: Penguin.

Erikson, E. H. (1968). *Identity and the Life Cycle*. London: Faber.

Erickson, M.H., Hershman, S. & Secter, I.I. (1961). *The Practical Application of Medical and Dental Hypnosis*. Chicago: Seminars on Hypnosis.

Ferguson, B.C. (1986). 'Kleine-Levin syndrome: a case report'. *Journal of Child Psychology & Psychiatry*, **27**, 275–278.

Field, A.P. & Davey, G.C.L. (2001). 'Conditioning models of childhood anxiety'. In: *Anxiety Disorders in Children and Adolescents'*, eds. W.K. Silverman & P.D.A. Treffers. Cambridge University Press, pages 187–211.

Fisher, G.C. & Mitchell, I. (1992). 'Munchausen's syndrome by proxy (factitious illness by proxy)'. *Current Opinion in Psychiatry*, **5**, 224–227.

Fisman, S. (2002). 'Pervasive development disorder'. In: *Practical Child & Adolescent Psychopharmacology*, ed. S. Kutcher. Cambridge University Press, pages 265–304.

Flavell, J. H. (1963). *The Developmental Psychology of Jean Piaget*. Princeton: van Norstrand.

Fombonne, E. (1998). 'Suicidal behaviour in vulnerable adolescents: time trends and their correlates'. *British Journal of Psychiatry*, **173**, 154–159.

Fombonne, E. (1999). 'The epidemiology of autism: a review'. *Psychological Medicine*, **29**, 769–786.

Fombonne, E. (2002). 'Prevalence of childhood disintegrative disorder'. *Autism*, **6**, 149–157.

Fombonne, E., Wostear, G., Cooper, V, Harrington, R. & Rutter, M. (2001a). 'The Maudsley long-term follow-up of child and adolescent depression. 1. Psychiatric outcomes in adulthood'. *British Journal of Psychiatry*, **179**, 210–217.

Fombonne, E., Wostear, G., Cooper, V, Harrington, R. & Rutter, M. (2001b). 'The Maudsley long-term follow-up of child and adolescent depression. 2. Suicidality, criminality and social dysfunction in adulthood'. *British Journal of Psychiatry*, **179**, 218–223.

Fossen, A., Knibbs, J., Bryant-Waugh, R. & Lask, B. (1987). 'Early onset anorexia nervosa'. *Archives of Disease in Childhood*, **62**, 114–118.

Freud, A. (1966). *Normality and Pathology in Childhood*. New York: International Universities Press; London: Hogarth.

Gabel, S. & Hsu L.K.G. (1986). 'Routine laboratory tests in adolescent inpatients'. *Journal of the American Academy of Child and Adolescent Psychiatry*, **25**, 113–119.

Gadoth, N., Kesler, A., Vainstein, G., Peled, R. & Lavie, P. (2001). 'Clinical and polysomnographic characteristics of 34 patients with Kleine-Levin syndrome'. *Journal of Sleep Research*, **10**, 337–341

Gadow, K.D. & Weiss, M. (2001). 'Attention-deficit hyperactivity disorder in adults: beyond controversy'. *Archives of General Psychiatry*, **58**, 784–785.

Garbarino, J., Guttman, E. & Seeley, J.W. (1986). *The Psychologically Battered Child*. San Francisco: Jossey-Bass.

Garbarino, J., Kostelny, K. & Dubrow, N. (1991). *No Place to Be a Child: Growing Up in a War Zone.* Lexington, MA: Lexington.

Garfinkel, P.E. & Garner, D.M. (1982). *Anorexia Nervosa: A Multidimensional Perspective*. New York: Brunner/Mazel.

Garland, E.J. (2002). 'Anxiety disorders'. In: *Practical Child and Adolescent Psychopharmacology*, ed. S. Kutcher. Cambridge University Press, pages 187–229

Garner, D.M. & Garfinkel, P.E. (1980). 'Sociocultural factors in the development of anorexia'. *Psychological Medicine*, **10**, 647–656.

Geller, D.A., Hoog, S.L., Heiligenstein, J.H., Ricardi, R.K., Tamura, R., Kluszynski, S., Jacobson, J.G. & the Fluoxetine Pediatric OCD Study Team. (2001). 'Fluoxetine treatment for obsessive-compulsive disorder in children and adolescents: a placebo-controlled clinical trial'. *Journal of the American Academy of Child & Adolescent Psychiatry*, **40**, 773–779.

Glazener, C.M. & Evans, J.H. (2002). Desmopressin for nocturnal enuresis in children'. *Cochrane Database of Systematic Reviews*, **3**, CD002112.

Gordon, N. (1999). 'Episodic dyscontrol syndrome'. *Developmental Medicine & Child Neurology*, **41**, 786–788.

Government of Alberta (1984). *Child Welfare Act*. Edmonton, Canada: Queen's Printer.

Graham, P.J. (1985). 'Psychosomatic relationships'. In: *Child and Adolescent Psychiatry: Modern Approaches*, 2nd edn., eds. M. Rutter & L. Hersov. Oxford: Blackwell, pages 599–613.

Group for the Advancement of Psychiatry (1968). *Normal Adolescence: Its Dynamics and Impact.* New York: GAP; London: Crosby Lockwood Staples.

Haley, J. (1973). Uncommon Therapy: The Psychiatric Techniques of Milton H. Erickson, M.D. New York: Norton.

Halmi, K.A. (2002). 'Eating disorders in females: genetics, pathophysiology, and treatment'. *Journal of Pediatric Endocrinology & Metabolism*, **15** (Suppl. 5), 1379–1386.

Hanna, G.L., Piacentini, J., Cantwell, D.P., Fischer, D.J., Himle, J.A. & Van Etten, M. (2002). 'Obsessive-compulsive disorder with and without tics in a clinical sample of children and adolescents'. *Depression & Anxiety*, **16**, 59–63.

Hassanyeh, F. & Davidson, K. (1980). 'Bipolar affective psychosis with onset before age 16 years: report of 10 cases'. *British Journal of Psychiatry*, **137**, 530–537.

Herbert, J. & Martinez, M. (2001) 'Neural mechanisms underlying aggressive behaviour'. In: *Conduct Disorders in Childhood and Adolescence*, eds. J. Hill & B. Maugham. Cambridge University Press, pages 67–102.

Heinssen, R.K., Liberman, R.P. & Kopelowicz, A. (2000). 'Psychosocial skills training for schizophrenia: lessons from the laboratory'. *Schizophrenia Bulletin*, **26**, 21–46.

Hirshberg, L.M. (1993). 'Clinical interviews with infants and their families'. In: *Handbook of Infant Mental Health*, ed. C.H. Zeanah. New York: Guilford, pages 173–190.

Horowitz, K., Gorfinkle, K., Lewis, O, & Phillips, K.A. (2002). 'Body dysmorphic disorder in an adolescent girl'. *Journal of the American Academy of Child & Adolescent Psychiatry*, **41**, 1503–1509.

Howlin, P. (2000). 'Outcome in adult life for more able individuals with autism or Asperger syndrome'. *Autism*, **4**, 63–83.

Kanner, L. (1943). 'Autistic disturbance of affective contact'. *Nervous Child*, **2**, 217–250.

Kanner, L. (1944). 'Early infantile autism'. *Journal of Pediatrics*, **35**, 211–217.

Katrz, J.D. & Ropper, A.H. (2002). 'Familial Kleine-Levin syndrome': two siblings with unusually long hypersomnic spells'. *Archives of Neurology*, **59**, 1959–1961.

Kaufman, G., Raphael, L. & Espeland, P. (1999). *Stick Up for Yourself*. Minneapolis, MN: Free Spirit.

Kazdin, A.E. (1997). 'Parent management training: evidence, outcomes, and issues'. *Journal of the American Academy of Child & Adolescent Psychiatry*, **36**, 1349–1356.

Kazdin, A.E. (2001) 'Treatment of conduct disorders'. In: *Conduct Disorders in Childhood & Adolescence*, eds. J. Hill & B. Maugham. Cambridge University Press, pages 408–446.

Kempe, C.H., Silverman, F.N., Steele, B.F., Droegemueller, W. & Silver, H.K. (1962). 'The battered child syndrome'. *Journal of the American Medical Association*, **191**, 17–23.

Kendall, P.C. (1990). *The Coping Cat Workbook*. Merion Station, PA: Temple University.

Kendall, P.C. (1994). 'Treating anxiety disorders in children: results of a randomized clinical trial'. *Journal of Consulting Clinical Psychology*, **62**, 100–110.

Kendall, P.C., Flannery-Schroeder, E., Panichelli-Mindel, S.M., Southam-Gerow, M., Henin, A. & Warman, M. (1997). 'Therapy for youths with anxiety disorders: a second randomized clinical trial'. *Journal of Consulting & Clinical Psychology*, **65**, 366–380.

Kendall, P.C. & Southam-Gerow, M.A. (1996). 'Long-term follow-up of a cognitive behavioral therapy for anxiety disorders'. *Journal of Consulting & Clinical Psychology*, **64**, 724–730

Kendler, K.S. (1993). 'Twin studies of psychiatric illness: current status and future directions'. *Archives of General Psychiatry*, **50**, 905–915.

Kendler, K.S., Neale, M.C., Kessler, R.C., Heath, A.C. & Eaves, L.J. (1992). 'Generalized anxiety disorder in women: a population-based twin study'. *Archives of General Psychiatry*, **49**, 267–272.

King, R.D., Raynes, N.V. & Tizard, J. (1971). *Patterns of Residential Care*. London: Routledge & Kegan Paul.

Kitzman, H., Olds, D.L., Henderson, C.R., Jr., Haanks, C., Cole R., Tatelbaum, R., McConnochie, K.M., Sidora, K., Luckey, D.W., Shaver, D., Engelhardt, K., James, D. & Barbard, K. (1997). 'Effect of prenatal and infancy home visitation by nurses on pregnancy outcomes, childhood injuries, and repeated childbearing'. *Journal of the American Medical Association*, **278**, 644–652.

Klein, M. (1948). *Contributions to Psychoanalysis 1921–1945*. London: Hogarth.

Klin, A., Volkmar, F.R. & Sparrow, S.S. (2000). *Asperger Syndrome*. New York: Guilford.

Klingman, A. (2001). 'Prevention of anxiety disorders: the case of post-traumatic stress disorder'. In: *Anxiety Disorders in Children and Adolescents*, eds. W.K. Silverman & P.D.A. Treffers. Cambridge University Press, pages 368–391.

Kolko, D.J. & Kasdin, A.E. (1991). 'Motives of childhood firesetters: firesetting characteristics and psychological correlates'. *Journal of Child Psychology & Psychiatry*, **32**, 535–550.

Kolvin, I. & Fundudis, T. (1981). 'Electively mute children: psychological development and background factors'. *Journal of Child Psychology & Psychiatry*, **22**, 219–232.

Korndorfer, S.R., Lucas, A.R., Suman, V.J., Crowson, C.S., Krahn, L.E. & Melton, L.J., III (2003). 'Long-term survival of patients with anorexia nervosa: a population-base study in Rochester, Minn.' *Mayo Clinic Proceedings*, **78**, 278–284.

Kotler, L.A., Devlin, M.J. & Walsh, B.T. (2002). 'Eating disorders and related disturbances'. In: *Practical Child & Adolescent Psychopharmacology*, ed. S. Kutcher. Cambridge University Press, pages 410–430.

Kraemer, S. (1987). 'Working with parents: casework or psychotherapy?' *Journal of Child Psychology & Psychiatry*, **28**, 207–213.

Kristensen, H. & Torgersen, S. (2001). 'MCMI-II personality traits and symptom traits in parents of children with selective mutism: a case-control study'. *Journal of Abnormal Psychology*, **110**, 648–652.

Kumpulainen, K., Rasanen, E. & Henttonem, I. (1999). 'Children involved in bullying: psychological disturbance and the persistence of the involvement'. *Child Abuse & Neglect*, **23**, 1253–1262.

Kumra, S., Shaw, M., Merka, P. & Nakayama, E. (2001). 'Childhood-onset schizophrenia: research update'. *Canadian Journal of Psychiatry*, **46**, 923–930.

Kusumaker, V., Lazier, L., MacMaster, F.P. & Santor, D. (2002). 'Bipolar mood disorder: diagnosis, etiology and treatment'. In: *Practical Child and Adolescent Psychopharmacology*, ed. S. Kutcher. Cambridge University Press, pages 106–133.

Kwok, H.W.M. (2003). 'Psychopharmacology in autism spectrum disorders'. *Current Opinion in Psychiatry*, **16**, 529–534.

La Greca, A.M. (2001). 'Friends or foes? Peer influences on anxiety among children and adolescents'. In: *Anxiety Disorders in Children & Adolescents*, eds. W.K. Silverman & P.D.A. Treffers. Cambridge University Press, pages 159–186.

Leckman, J.F. & Cohen, D.J. (1994). 'Tic disorders'. In: *Child and Adolescent Psychiatry: Modern Approaches*, 3rd edn., eds. M. Rutter, E. Taylor & L. Hersov. Oxford: Blackwell, pages 455–466.

Leff, J.P. & Vaughn, C. (1985). *Expressed Emotion in Families*. New York: Guilford.

LeMarquand, D., Tremblay, R.E. & Bukowski, W.M. (2001). 'The prevention of conduct disorder: a review of successful and unsuccessful experiments'. In: *Conduct Disorders in Childhood and Adolescence*, eds. J. Hill & B. Maugham. Cambridge University Press, pages 449–477.

Leonard, H.L. & Swedo, S.E. (2001). 'Paediatric autoimmune psychiatric disorders associated with streptococcal infection (PANDAS)'. *International Journal of Neuropsychopharmacology*, **4**, 191–198.

Lewinshon, P.M., Allen, N.B., Seeley, J.R. & Gotlib, I.H. (1999). 'First onset versus recurrence of depression: differential processes of psychosocial risk'. *Journal of Abnormal Psychology*, **198**, 483–489.

Lewinshon, P.M., Klein, D.N. & Seeley, J.R. (1995). 'Bipolar disorder in community sample of older adolescents: prevalence, phenomenology, comorbidity and course'. *Journal of the American Academy of Child & Adolescent Psychiatry*, **34**, 454–463.

Liebowitz, M.R., Turner, S.M., Piacentini, J., Beidel, D.C., Clarvit, S.R., Davies, S.O., Graae, F., Jaffer, M., Lin, S., Sallee, F.R., Schmidt, A.B. & Simpson, H.B. (2002). 'Fluoxetine in children and adolescents with OCD: a placebo-controlled trial'. *Journal of the American Academy of Child & Adolescent Psychiatry*, **41**, 1431–1438.

Lindenfield, G. (2000). *Confident Children*. London: Thorsens.

Links, P.S., Gould, B. & Ratnayake, R. (2003). 'Assessing suicidal youth with antisocial, borderline, or narcissistic personality'. *Canadian Journal of Psychiatry*, **48**, 289–291.

Lock, J. (2002). 'Treating adolescents with eating disorders in the family context: empirical and theoretical considerations'. *Child & Adolescent Psychiatric Clinics of North America*, **11**, 331–342.

Loening-Baucke, V. (2002). 'Encopresis'. *Current Opinion in Pediatrics*, **14**, 570–575.

Luby, J.L. (2000). 'Depression'. In: *Handbook of Infant Mental Health*, 2nd edn., ed. C.H. Zeanah Jr. New York: Guilford, pages 382–396.

Luthar, S.S. (1993). 'Methodological and conceptual issues in research in childhood resilience'. *Journal of Child Psychology & Psychiatry*, **34**, 441–453.

Lynam, D.R. & Henry, B. (2001). 'The role of neurological deficits in conduct disorders'. In: *Conduct Disorders in Childhood and Adolescence*, eds. J. Hill & B. Maugham. Cambridge University Press, pages 235–263.

Lynch, M.A. (1985). 'Child abuse before Kempe: an historical literature review'. *Child Abuse & Neglect*, **9**, 7–15.

Maclay, D. (1970). *Treatment for Children in Child Guidance*. New York: Science House.

MacMillan, H.L. (2000). 'Child maltreatment: what we know in the year 2000'. *Canadian Journal of Psychiatry*, **45**, 702–709.

MacMillan, H.L., Fleming, J.E., Trocme, N., Boyle, M.H., Wong, M., Beardslee, W.R. & Offord, D.E. (1997). 'Prevalence of child physical and sexual abuse in the community: results from the Ontario Health Supplement'. *Journal of the American Medical Association*, **278**, 131–135.

Main, M. & Solomon, J. (1990). 'Procedures for identifying infants as disorganized/disoriented during the Ainsworth Strange Situation'. In: *Attachment in the Preschool Years*, eds. M.T. Greenberg, D. Cicchetti & E.M. Cummings. Chicago: Chicago University Press, pages 121–160.

Malchiodi, C.A (1998). *Understanding Children's Drawings*. New York: Guilford.

Malhotra, S. & Gupta, N. (2002). 'Childhood disintegrative disorder: re-examination of the current concept'. *European Child & Adolescent Psychiatry*, **11**, 108–114.

March, J. & Wells, K. (2002). 'Combining medication and psychotherapy'. In: *Pediatric Psychopharmacology: Principles and Practice*, eds. J.F. Leckman, A. Martin, L. Scahill & D.S. Charney. London: Oxford University Press, pages 426–443.

Manassis, K. (2001). 'Child-parent relations: attachment and anxiety disorders'. In: *Anxiety Disorders in Children and Adolescents*, eds. W.K. Silverman & P.D.A. Treffers. Cambridge University Press, pages 255–272.

Manassis, K., Mendlowitz, S.L., Scapillato, D., Avery, D., Fiksenbaum, M.A., Friere, M., Monga, S. & Owens. M. (2002). 'Group and individual cognitive-behavioral therapy for childhood anxiety disorders: a randomized trial'. *Journal of the American Academy of Child & Adolescent Psychiatry*, **41**, 1423–1430.

Marriage, K. (2002). 'Schizophrenia and related psychoses'. In: *Practical Child and Adolescent Psychopharmacology*, ed. S. Kutcher. Cambridge University Press, pages 134–158.

Martin, H., Scourfield, J. & McGuffin, P. (2002). 'Observer effects and habitability of childhood attention-deficit hyperactivity disorder'. *British Journal of Psychiatry*, **180**, 260–265.

Masi, G., Toni, C., Perugi, G., Mucci, M., Millepiedi, S. & Akiskal, H.S. (2001). 'Anxiety disorders in children and adolescents with bipolar disorder'. *Canadian Journal of Psychiatry*, **46**, 797–802.

Maughan, M. & Rutter, M. (2001). 'Antisocial children grown up'. In: *Conduct Disorders in Childhood and Adolescence*, eds. J. Hill & B. Maughan. Cambridge University Press, pages 507–552.

McCollum, J.A. (2002). 'Influencing the development of young children with disabilities: current themes in early intervention'. *Child & Adolescent Mental Health*, **7**, 4–9.

McElroy, S.L. (1999). 'Recognition and treatment of DSM-IV intermittent explosive disorder'. *Journal of Clinical Psychiatry*, **60** (Suppl. 15), 12–16.

Mendlowitz, S., Manassis, K., Bradley, S., Scapillato, D., Mietzitis, S. & Shaw, B. (1989). 'Cognitive behavioral group treatments in childhood anxiety disorders: the role of parental involvement'. *Journal of the American Academy of Child & Adolescent Psychiatry*, **38**, 1223–1229.

Mirza, K.A.H. (2002). 'Adolescent substance use disorder'. In: *Practical Child and Adolescent Psychopharmacology*, ed. S. Kutcher. Cambridge University Press, pages 328–381.

Moffat, T.E. & Silva, P.A. (1988). 'Self-reported delinquency, neuropsychological deficit, and history of attention deficit disorder'. *Journal of Abnormal Child Psychology*, **16**, 553–569.

Moog, U., Smeets, E.E., van Roozendaal, K.E., Schoenmakers, S., Herbergs, J., Schoonbrood-Lenssen, A.M & Schrander-Stumpel, C.T. (2003). 'Neurodevelopmental disorders in males related to the gene causing Rett syndrome in females (MECP2)'. *European Journal of Paediatric Neurology*, **7**, 5–12.

MTA Cooperative Group (1999). 'A 14-months randomized clinical trial of treatment strategies for attention-deficit/hyperactivity disorder'. *Archives of General Psychiatry*, **56**, 1073–1086.

Mundy, P., Sigman, M., Ungerer, J. & Sherman, T. (1986). 'Defining the social deficits in autism'. *Journal of Child Psychology & Psychiatry*, **27**, 657–669.

Mussen, P.H., Huston, A.C. & Kagan, J. (1990). *Child Development and Personality*. New York: Harper Collins.

Neiderhiser, J.M. (2001). 'Understanding the roles of genome and envirome: methods in genetic epidemiology'. *British Journal of Psychiatry*, **148** (Suppl. 40), s12–s17.

Offord, D.R., Boyle, M.H., Szatmari, P., Rae-Grant, N.I., Links, P.S., Cadman, D.T., Byles, J.A., Crawford, J.W., Blum, H.M., Byrne, C., Thomas, H. & Woodward, C.A. (1987). 'Ontario Child Healthy Study: prevalence of disorders and rates of service utilization'. *Archives of General Psychiatry*, **44**, 832–836.

O'Hanlon. W.H. & Hexum, A.L. (1990). *An Uncommon Casebook: The Complete Clinical Work of Milton H. Erickson, M.D.* New York: Norton.

Olds, D. (2002). 'Prenatal and infancy home visiting by nurses: from randomized trial to community replication'. *Preventive Science*, **3**, 153–172.

Olds, D.L., Henderson, C.R., Jr., Chamberlin, R. & Tatelbaum, R. (1986). 'Preventing child abuse and neglect: a randomized trial of home visitation'. *Pediatrics*, **78**, 65–78.

Olds, D.L., Henderson, C.R., Jr. & Kitzman, H. (1994). 'Does pre-natal and infancy home visitation have enduring effects on qualities of parental caregiving and child health at 25 to 50 months of life?' *Pediatrics*, **93**, 89–98.

Oliver, J.E. & Buchanan, A.H. (1979). 'Generations of maltreated children and multiagency care in one kindred'. *British Journal of Psychiatry*, **135**, 289–303.

Olness, K. & Kohen, D.P. (1996). *Hypnosis and Hypnotherapy with Children*, 3rd edn. New York: Guilford.

Ozonoff, S., South, M. & Miller, J.N. (2000). 'DSM-IV-defined Asperger syndrome: cognitive, behavioural and early history differentiation from high-functioning autism'. *Autism*, **4**, 29–46.

Palmer, R.L. (2003). 'Death in anorexia nervosa' [Letter]. *Lancet*, **361**, 1490.

Parker, F.L., Piotrkowski, C.S. & Peay, L. (1987). 'Head start as a social support for mothers'. *American Journal of Orthopsychiatry*, **57**, 220–233.

Parry, C.D., Bhana, A., Pluddemann, A., Myers, B., Siegfried, N., Morojele, N.K., Flisher, A.J. & Kozel, N.J. (2002). 'The South African Community Network on Drug Use (SACENDU): description, findings (1997–99) and policy implications'. *Addiction*, **97**, 969–976.

Patterson, G.R (1976). 'The aggressive child: victim or architect of a coercive system'. In: *Behaviour Modification and Families*, eds. E.J. Mash, L.A. Hamerlynck & L.C. Handy. New York: Brunner/Mazel, pages 267–316.

Patterson, G.R. (1982). *Coercive Family Process*. Eugene, OR: Castalia.

Patterson, G.R. (1996). 'Some characteristics of a developmental theory for early onset delinquency'. In: *Frontiers of Developmental Psychopathology*, eds. M.F. Lenzenweger & J.J. Haugaard. New York: Oxford University Press, pages 81–124.

Patterson, G.R., Dishion, T.J. & Chamberlain, P. (1993). 'Outcomes and methodological issues relating to treatment of antisocial children'. In: *Handbook of Effective Psychotherapy*, ed. T.R. Giles. New York: Plenum, pages 43–87.

Patterson, G.R. & Yoerger, K. (1997). 'A developmental model for late-onset delinquency'. In: *Motivation and Delinquency*, ed. W.D. Osgood. Lincoln: University of Nebraska Press, pages 110–177.

Pearce, J. (1994). *Growth and Development*. London: Thorsens.

Pinkerton, P. (1958).'Psychogenic megacolon in childhood: the implications of bowel negativism'. *Archives of Disease in Childhood*, **33**, 371–380.

Popper, C.W. (2002). 'Child and adolescent psychopharmacology at the turn of the millenium'. In: *Practical Child and Adolescent Psychopharmacology*, ed. S. Kutcher. Cambridge University Press, pages 1–37.

Prins, P.J.M. (2001). 'Affective and cognitive processes and the development and maintenance of anxiety and its disorders'. In: *Anxiety Disorders in Children and Adolescents*, eds. W.K. Silverman & P.D.A. Treffers. Cambridge University Press, pages 23–44.

Puig-Antich, J. (1986). 'Psychobiological markers: effects of age and puberty'. In: *Depression in Young People: Developmental and Clinical Perspectives*, eds. M. Rutter, C.A. Izard & P.B. Read. New York: Guilford.

Rajeev, J., Srinath, S., Reddy, Y.C.J., Shashikiran, M.G., Girimaji, S.C., Seshadri, S.P. & Subbakrishna, D.K. (2003). 'The index manic episode in juvenile-onset bipolar disorder: the pattern of recovery'. *Canadian Journal of Psychiatry*, **48**, 52–55.

Reader's Digest Association (1998). *Merriam Webster's Deluxe Dictionary*. Pleasantville, NY: Reader's Digest, 1998.

Remschmidt, H., Poller, M., Herpertz-Daahlmann, B., Hennighause, K. & Gutenbrunner, C. (2001). 'A follow-up study of 45 patients with elective mutism'. *European Archives of Psychiatry & Clinical Neuroscience*, **251**, 284–296.

Remschmidt, H.E., Schulz, E., Martin, M., Warnke, A & Trott, G.E. (1994). 'Childhood-onset schizophrenia: history of the concept and recent studies'. *Schizophrenia Bulletin*, **20**, 727–745.

Rett, A. (1966). 'Über ein bisher nicht bekanntes Krankheitsbild einer angeborenen Stoffwechselstörung'. *Krankenschwester*, **19**(9), 121–122.

Richman, N. (1985). 'A double-blind drug trial of treatment of sleep disorders: a pilot study'. *Journal of Child Psychology & Psychiatry*, **26**, 591–598.

Richman, N., Douglas, J., Hunt, H., Lansdown, R. & Levere, R. (1985). 'Behavioural methods in the treatment of sleep disorders: a pilot study'. *Journal of Child Psychology & Psychiatry*, **26**, 581–590.

Rigby, K. & Slee, P. (1999). 'Suicidal ideation among adolescent school children, involvement in bully-victim problems and perceived social support'. *Suicide and Life-threatening Behaviour*, **29**, 119–130.

Robbins, M.S, Bachrach, K. & Szapocznik, J. (2002). 'Bridging the gap in adolescent substance abuse treatment: the case of brief strategic family therapy'. *Journal of Substance Abuse Treatment*, **23**, 123–132.

Robinson, A. & de la Chappelle, A. (1977). 'Sex chromosome anomalies'. In: *Principles and Practice of Medical Genetics*, eds. D. Rimoin, J.M. Connor & R.E. Pyeritz. New York: Churchill Livingstone, pages 973–999.

Rosen, S. (ed.) (1982). My Voice Will Go With You: The Teaching Tales of Milton H. Erickson, M.D. New York: Norton.

Rossi, E. (1986a). *The Psychobiology of Mind-Body Healing*. New York: Norton.

Rossi, E. (1986b). 'The state-dependent memory and learning theory of therapeutic hypnosis'. In: *Mind-Body Communication in Hypnosis*, by M.H. Erickson, eds. E.L. Rossi & M.O. Ryan. New York: Irvington, pages 203–248.

Rossman, P.G. (1985). 'The aftermath of abuse and abandonment: a treatment approach for ego disturbance in female adolescence'. *Journal of the American Academy of Child Psychiatry*, **24**, 345–352.

Rourke, B.P. & Tsatsanis, K.D. (2000). 'Nonverbal learning disabilities and Asperger syndrome'. In: *Asperger Syndrome*, eds. A. Klin, F.R. Volkmar & S.S. Sparrow. New York: Guilford, pages 231–253.

Rowe, C.L. & Liddle, H.A. (2003). 'Substance abuse'. *Journal of Marital & Family Therapy*, **29**, 97–120.

Rowland, A.S., Umbach, D.M., Catoe, K.E., Stallone, L., Long, S., Rabiner, D., Naftel, A.J., Panke, D., Faulk, R. & Sandler, D.P. (2001). 'Studying the epidemiology of attention-deficit hyperactivity disorder: screening method and pilot results'. *Canadian Journal of Psychiatry*, **46**, 931–940.

Rumsey, J.M., Rapoport, J.L. & Sceery, W.R. (1985). 'Autistic children as adults'. *Journal of the American Academy of Child & Adolescent Psychiatry*, **24**, 465–473.

Russell, A.T., Bott, L. & Sammons, C. (1989). 'The phenomenology of schizophrenia occurring in childhood'. *Journal of the American Academy of Child & Adolescent Psychiatry*, **28**, 399–407.

Rutter, M. (1980). 'School influences on children's behaviour and development'. *Pediatrics*, **65**, 208–220.

Rutter, M., Cox, A., Tupling, G., Berger, M. & Yule, W. (1975). 'Attainment and adjustment in two geographical areas. I. The prevalence of psychiatric disorder'. *British Journal of Psychiatry*, **126**, 493–501.

Rutter, M., Maughan, N., Mortimore, P. & Ouston, J. (1979). *Fifteen Thousand Hours*. London: Open.

Rutter, M. & Rutter, M. (1993). *Developing Minds*. New York: Basic.

Rutter, M., Tizard, J. & Whitmore, K. (1970). *Education, Health and Behaviour*. London: Longmore.

Ryan, N.D. (2002). 'Depression'. In: *Practical Child and Adolescent Psychopharmacology*, ed. S. Kutcher. Cambridge University Press, pages 91–105.

Salle, F.R. & March, J.S. (2001). 'Neuropsychiatry of paediatric anxiety disorders'. In: *Anxiety disorders in Children and Adolescents*, eds. W.K. Silverman & P.D.A. Treffers. Cambridge University Press, pages 90–125.

Salmon, G., James, A. & Smith, D.M. (1998). 'Bullying in schools: self-reported anxiety, depression and self-esteem in secondary school children'. *British Medical Journal*, **317**, 924–925.

Scahill, L., Leckman, J.F., Schultz, R.T., Katsovich, L. & Peterson, B.S. (2003). 'A placebo-controlled trial of risperidone in Tourette syndrome'. *Neurology*, **60**, 1130–1135.

Schaeffer, J.L. & Ross, R.G. (2002). 'Childhood-onset schizophrenia: premorbid and prodromal diagnostic and treatment histories'. *Journal of the American Academy of Child & Adolescent Psychiatry*, **41**, 538–545.

Scheeringa, M.S., Zeanah, C.H., Myers, L. & Putnam, F.W. (2003). 'New findings on alternative criteria for PTSD in preschool children'. *Journal of the American Academy of Child & Adolescent Psychiatry*, **42**, 561–570.

Schmidt, E. & Eldridge, A. (1986). 'The attachment relationship and child maltreatment'. *Infant Mental Health Journal*, **7**, 264–273.

Schulman, S.L., Stokes, A. & Salzman, P.M. (2001). 'The efficacy and safety of desmopressin in children with primary enuresis'. *Journal of Urology*, **166**, 2427–2431.

Scott, F.J., Baron-Cohen, S., Bolton, P. & Brayne, C. (2002). 'Brief report: Prevalence of autistic spectrum conditions in children aged 5–11 in Cambridgeshire, UK'. *Autism*, **6**, 231–237.

Scott, P.D. (1977). 'Non-accidental injury in children'. *British Journal of Psychiatry*, **131**, 366–380.

Seligman, S. (2000). 'Clinical interviews with families of infants'. In: *Handbook of Infant Mental Health*, 2nd edn., ed. C.H. Zeanah Jr. New York: Guilford, pages 211–221.

Serra, M., Loth, F.L., van Geert, P.L.C., Hurkens, E. & Minderaa, R.B. (2002). Theory of mind in children with 'lesser variants' of autism: a longitudinal study. *Journal of Child Psychology & Psychiatry*, **43**, 885–900.

Shafti, T. (1986). 'The prevalence and use of transitional objects'. *Journal of the American Academy of Child Psychiatry*, **25**, 805–808.

Shaw, D.S., Gilliom, M. & Giovanelli, J. (2000). 'Aggressive behaviour disorders'. In: *Handbook of Infant Mental Health*, 2nd edn., ed. C.H. Zeanah Jr. New York: Guilford, pages 397–411.

Shonkoff, J.P. & Meisels, S.J. (2000). *Handbook of Early Childhood Intervention*, 2nd edn., eds. J.P. Shonkoff & S.J. Meisels. New York: Cambridge University Press.

Silverman, W.K. & Berman, S.L. (2001). 'Psychosocial interventions for anxiety disorders in children'. In: *Anxiety Disorders in Children and Adolescents*, eds. W.K. Silverman & P.D.A. Treffers. Cambridge University Press, pages 313–334.

Silverman, W.K., Kurtines, W.M, Ginsburg, G.S, Weems, C.F., Lumpkin, P.W. & Carmichael, D.H. (1999). 'Treating anxiety disorders in children with group cognitive-behaviour therapy'. *Journal of Consulting & Clinical Psychology*, **67**, 995–1003.

Silverman, W.K. & Treffers, P.D.A. (eds) (2001). *Anxiety Disorders in Children and Adolescents.* Cambridge University Press.

Simonoff, E. (2001). 'Genetic influences on conduct disorder'. In: *Conduct Disorders in Childhood and Adolescence*, eds. J. Hill & B. Maughan. Cambridge University Press, pages 202–234.

Singer, H.S. & Walkup, J.T. (1991). 'Tourette syndrome and other tic disorders: diagnosis, pathophysiology and treatment'. *Medicine*, **70**, 15–32.

Skynner, A.C.R. (1975). *One Flesh: Separate Persons*. London: Constable. [Published in the United States as *Systems of Family and Marital Therapy*. New York: Brunner/Mazel.]

Smyke, A.T., Dumitrescu, A. & Zeanah, C.H. (2002). 'Attachment disturbances in young children. I. The continuum of caretaking casualty'. *Journal of the American Academy of Child & Adolescent Psychiatry*, **41**, 972–982.

Spencer, T., Biederman, J. & Wilens, T. (2002). 'Attention-deficit/hyperactivity disorder'. In: *Practical Child and Adolescent Psychopharmacology*, ed. S. Kutcher. Cambridge University Press, pages 230–264.

Spitz, R.A. (1946). 'Anaclitic depression'. *Psychoanalytic Study of the Child*, **2**, 113–117.

Stanley, L. (1980). 'Treatment of ritualistic behaviour in an eight-year-old boy by response prevention'. *Journal of Child Psychology & Psychiatry*, **21**, 85–90.

Steinhauer, P.D. (1984). 'The management of children admitted to child welfare services in Ontario'. *Canadian Journal of Psychiatry*, **29**, 77–88.

Steinhauer, P.D. (1991). *The Least Detrimental Alternative: A Systematic Guide to Case Planning and Decision Making for Children in Care*. Toronto: University of Toronto Press.

Steinhausen, H.C. & Adamek, R. (1997). 'The family history of children with elective mutism'. *European Child & Adolescent Psychiatry*, **6**, 107–111.

Stock, S.L., Werry, J.S. & Berman, S.L. (2001). 'Pharmacological treatment of paediatric anxiety'. In: *Anxiety Disorders in Children & Adolescents*, eds. W.K. Silverman & P.D.A. Treffers. Cambridge University Press, pages 335–367

Stowell, K. (ed.) (1998). *Prevention Programs for Youth: A Guide to Outcomes Evaluation, Best Practices, and Successful Funding*. Providence, RI: Manisses Communications Group.

Striegel-Moore, R.H., Seeley, J.R. & Lewinsohn, P.M. (2003). 'Psychosocial adjustment in young adulthood of women who experienced an eating disorder during adolescence'. *Journal of the American Academy of Child & Adolescent Psychiatry*, **42**, 587–593.

Sullivan, P.M & Knutson, J.F. (2000). 'The prevalence of disabilities and maltreatment among runaway children'. *Child Abuse & Neglect*, **24**, 1275–1288.

Sund, A.M. & Wichstrøm, L. (2002). 'Insecure attachment as a risk factor for future depressive symptoms in early adolescence.' *Journal of the American Academy of Child & Adolescent Psychiatry*, **41**, 1478–1485.

Swedo, S.E. (2001). 'Genetics of childhood disorder. XXXIII. Autoimmunity, Part 6: Poststreptococcal autoimmunity'. *Journal of the American Academy of Child & Adolescent Psychiatry* **40**, 1479–1482.

Swirsky-Sacchetti, T. & Margolis, C.G. (1986). 'The effect of a comprehensive self-hypnosis training program on the use of factor VIII in severe haemophilia'. *International Journal of Clinical & Experimental Hypnosis*, **34**, 71–83.

Tantum, D. (2000). 'Adolescence and adulthood in individuals with Asperger syndrome'. In: *Asperger Syndrome*, eds. A. Klin, F.R. Volkmar & S.S. Sparrow. New York: Guilford, pages 367–399.

Terr, L. (1988). 'What happens to early memories of trauma? A study of twenty children under age five at the time of documented traumatic events'. *Journal of the American Academy of Child & Adolescent Psychiatry*, **27**, 96–104.

Thapar, A., Hervis, A. & McGuffin, P. (1995). 'Childhood hyperactivity scores are highly heritable and show sibling competition effects: twin study evidence'. *Behavior Genetics*, **25**, 537–544.

Thapar, A., Holmes., Poulton, K. & Harrington, R. (1999). 'Genetic basis of attention deficit and hyperactivity'. *British Journal of Psychiatry*, **174**, 105–111.

Thomas, A. & Chess, S. (1977). *Temperament and Development*. New York: Brunner/Mazel.

Thompson, T.R. (1987). 'Childhood and adolescent suicide in Manitoba: a demographic study'. *Canadian Journal of Psychiatry*, **32**, 264–269.

Tyler, K.A. & Caunce, A.M. (2002). 'Perpetrators of early physical and sexual abuse among homeless and runaway adolescents'. *Child Abuse & Neglect*, **26**, 1261–1274.

van Heeringen, K. (2003) 'The neurobiology of suicide and suicidality'. *Canadian Journal of Psychiatry*, **48**, 292–300.

Varma, V.P (ed.) (1993) *Management of Behaviour in Schools*. London: Longman.

Verhulst, F.C. (2001). 'Community and epidemiological aspects of anxiety disorders in children'. In: *Anxiety Disorders in Children and Adolescents*, eds. W.K. Silverman & P.D.A. Treffers. Cambridge University Press, pages 273–292.

Verhulst, J.H.L., Akkerhuis, G.W., Sanders-Woudstra, J.A.R., Timmer, F.C & Donkhorst, I.D. (1985). 'The prevalence of enuresis'. *Journal of Child Psychology & Psychiatry*, **26**, 989–993.

Walkup, J.T. (2002). 'Tic disorders and Tourette's syndrome'. In: *Practical Child and Adolescent Psychopharmacology*, ed. S. Kutcher. Cambridge University Press, pages 382–409.

Weiss, G. & Hechtman, L.T. (1986). *Hyperactive Children Grown Up*. New York: Guilford.

Weller, E.B., Calvert, S.M. & Weller, R.A. (2003). 'Bipolar disorder in children and adolescents: diagnosis and treatment'. *Current Opinion in Psychiatry*, **16**, 383–388.

Werner, E.E. & Smith, R.S. (1982). *Vulnerable but Invincible: A Longitudinal Study of Vulnerable Children and Youth*. New York: McGraw-Hill.

Whitaker, A., Johnson, J., Shaffer, D., Rapoport, J.L., Kalikoe, K., Walsh, B.T., Davies, M., Braiaman, S. & Dolinsky, A. (1990). 'Uncommon troubles in young people'. *Archives of General Psychiatry*, **47**, 487–496.

Whitney, I. & Smith, P.K. (1993). 'A survey of the nature and extent of bullying in junior/middle and secondary schools'. *Educational Research*, **35**, 3–25.

World Health Organization (WHO) (1992a). *International Classification of Diseases and Related Health Problems*, 10th revision. Geneva: WHO.

World Health Organization (WHO) (1992b). *The ICD-10 Classification of Mental and Behavioural Disorders: Clinical Descriptions and Diagnostic Guidelines*. Geneva: WHO.

Wright, H.H., Miller, M.D., Cook, M.A. & Littman, J.T. (1985). 'Early identification and intervention with children who refuse to speak'. *Journal of the American Academy of Child & Adolescent Psychiatry*, **24**, 739–746.

Wynne, L.C. (1981). 'Current concepts about schizophrenia and family relationships'. *Journal of Nervous & Mental Disease*, **116**, 144–158.

Yule, W. & Carr, J. (eds.) (1980). *Behaviour Modification for the Mentally Handicapped*. London: Croom Helm.

Yule, W., Perrin, S. & Smith, P. (2001). 'Traumatic events and post-traumatic stress disorders.' In: *Anxiety Disorders in Children and Adolescents*, eds. W.K. Silverman & P.D.A. Treffers. Cambridge University Press, pages 212–234.

Zeanah, C.H., Jr. (ed.) (2000). *Handbook of Infant Mental Health*, 2nd edn. New York: Guilford.

Zeanah, C.H., Jr. & Boris, N.W. (2000). 'Disturbances and disorder of attachment in early childhood'. In: *Handbook of Infant Mental Health*, 2nd edn., ed. C.H. Zeanah Jr. New York: Guilford, pages 353–368.

Zeanah, C.H., Jr., Larrieu, Heller, S.S. & Valliere, J. (2000). 'Infant-parent relationship assessment'. In: *Handbook of Infant Mental Health*, 2nd edn., ed. C.H. Zeanah Jr. New York: Guilford, pages 222–235.

Zeig, J.K. & Munion, W.M. (eds.) (1990). *What Is Psychotherapy?* San Francisco: Jossey-Bass.

Zero to Three, National Center for Clinical Infant Programs (1994). *Diagnostic Classification: 0-3. Diagnostic classification of mental health and developmental disorders of infancy and early childhood*. Washington, DC: Author.

Zoccolillo, M. (1992). 'Co-occurrence of conduct disorder and its adult outcomes with depressive and anxiety disorders: a review'. *Journal of the American Academy of Child & Adolescent Psychiatry*, **31**, 547–556.

Subject Index

Author Index